Dear Jon –

Enjoy as you start your
journey to History in earnest.

Love,
Mom

YMH3 1990

ACCIDENTAL ENCOUNTERS WITH HISTORY

ACCIDENTAL ENCOUNTERS WITH HISTORY

(and some lessons learned)

Lincoln Palmer Bloomfield

HotHouse
PRESS

Library of Congress Cataloging-in-Publication Data

Bloomfield, Lincoln Palmer, 1920–
    Accidental encounters with history (and some lessons learned) /
by Lincoln Palmer Bloomfield.
        p. cm.
    ISBN 0-9755245-0-X
1. United States — Foreign relations — 1945–1989. 2. United States —
Foreign relations — 1989– 3. United States — Politics and government —
1945–1989. 4. World politics — 20th century. 5. Bloomfield, Lincoln
Palmer, 1920– 6. Historians — United States — Biography. 7. Political sci-
entists — United States — Biography. 8. United States. Dept. of State —
Officials and employees — Biography. 9. National Security Council (U.S.)
— Officials and employees — Biography. 10. Massachusetts Institute of
Technology — Biography. I. Title.
    E744.B595 2005
    327.73'0092--dc22

                                  2005001610

Printed in the United States of America
Book design by DeNee Reiton Skipper

Hot House Press
760 Cushing Highway
Cohasset, MA 02025
www.hothousepress.com

FOR NICHOLAS, ADRIAN, AND NOELLE

PERMISSIONS

An abridged version of the chapter entitled "Bureaucracy II:1953–57 The Genetically-Engineered Secretary of State" first appeared in the *Foreign Service Journal* July–August 2002 and is reprinted here with permission.

The chapter entitled "Playing Games With Foreign Policy" appeared in abridged form in the *Proceedings* of the US Naval Institute in July, 2003, and is reprinted here with permission © US Naval Institute/ www.navalinstitute.org.

I first chronicled the South African episode in the chapter "The Rest of the Map" in the *Christian Science Monitor* (www.csmonitor.com) on June 8, 1984. Material on the India-Pakistan conflict in the chapter entitled "My Moderate Utopia" was in an OpEd article in the *Monitor* on June 13, 2002. Both are drawn from here with permission.

CONTENTS

Preface ix

A Brief Bio-Chronology 1

1 BUREAUCRACY I: 1941–71 5
Dreams — and Nightmares — of Public Service

2 BUREAUCRACY II: 1953–57 26
The Genetically-Engineered Secretary of State

3 BUREAUCRACY III: 1979–80 40
The Atmosphere Gets Rarified

4 BUREAUCRACY IV: 1945–2005 51
The Triangular Foreign Policy Machine

5 COLD WAR SCHOLAR I: 1957–70 59
The Leaning Tower of Ivory

6 COLD WAR SCHOLAR II: 1958–71 73
Playing Games With Foreign Policy

7 THE REAL WORLD I: 1970–89 92
The Soviet Union From Tyranny To Turmoil

8 THE REAL WORLD II: 1976 121
The Middle East: Kings, Bombs, and Touch Football

9 THE REAL WORLD III: 1961–93 140
The Rest of the Map

10 LESSONS I 170
Can Foreign Policy Ever Be Rational?

11 LESSONS II 186
My Moderate Utopia

INDEX 219

Preface

From 1989 to 1992, the publishers of the *Christian Science Monitor* newspaper undertook a noble experiment in high-grade, edifying national television. One of the features of the *Monitor* TV Channel was a daily half-hour program called *Fifty Years Ago Today*. It featured a guy in a sports jacket who sat on a high stool and leafed through the pages of a fifty year-old newspaper. He began by reporting the news—things like "Hitler Attacks Soviet Union," "FDR Meets Churchill at Sea," "India Struggles for Independence," "Miners Threaten Coal Strike," "Bobby Riggs Wins US Tennis Open," "Cary Grant Charms Movie Audiences."

After reading the headlines, which were backed by newsreel clips and occasional "I was there" guests, the sport-coated guy would take off his reading glasses and informally update stories that interested him, such as the ultimate collapse of the Soviet Union, India and Pakistan still battling over Kashmir, how the Atlantic Charter led to the UN, the change to graphite in tennis rackets, and the mixed reactions around today's world to America's pop culture. *Fifty Years Ago Today* won a regional Emmy, and collected a gaggle of faithful fans around the country. Some were aging history buffs; some were students bored by history but attracted to a painless way for retrieving what they had been dodging in school.

I was the guy in the sports jacket. After spending an absurdly over-programmed day shooting the entire week's programs, I would race back to Massachusetts Institute of Technology (MIT) to meet my political science classes and do my research, a schedule bordering on the insane. Alas, this worthy TV venture proved too costly for its churchly sponsors, and the *Monitor* Channel went belly-up. But the experience taught me a lot, including the value of bringing history to life in 3-D, as it were, through a personalized lens.

Hosting Fifty Years Ago Today *on the* Monitor *Channel.*

In an oblique sort of way this book picks up where I left off as host of *Fifty Years Ago Today*. Not literally. But in the sense of recapturing—through the prism of reflections and recollections based on fortuitous exposures to recent history—a feel for the incredible half century that, as Winston Churchill once said of the Balkans, produced more history than it could consume.

I should confess that this book was more fun to write than its more serious scholarly predecessors. It aims to entertain as well as inform and, I hope, is relatively painless to read. It is something of a hybrid—neither a full-bore autobiography, nor a standard history of the second half of the twentieth century. Neither is it a systematic analysis of American foreign policy nor—perish the thought—another textbook on international relations.

So what is it?

In broad terms, it is a semi-serious semi-memoir that recounts the Odyssey of one idealistic American confronted along the way with both golden opportunities and harsh realities—the latter ranging from war and fateful policy choices to disaffected students and aggrieved foreign cultures.

The framework is a linked series of highly personal essays on foreign affairs and the world scene; all drawn from experience, and

illustrated with first-hand recollections based on life in the State Department, the White House staff, the university, and the lecture platform in thirty-five countries.

My professional life might have been easier to write about if it
had unfolded in a linear fashion faithful to calendar and clock. But it
wasn't. Instead it ran along several parallel tracks that kept crossing.
The lessons of wartime service proved applicable to the postwar civilian
bureaucracy. In turn, government service, full-time and part-time,
occasionally blurred with academic life and vice-versa. And being a
full-time professor also meant lecturing, debating, and learning in
other countries.

The end-product is a political memoir constructed of "chunks"
of personalized history that run along those metaphorical tracks.
Since the story I want to tell is not neatly chronological, I hope that
the dates supplied for each chapter will help the reader. For the more
orderly mind, a short "bio-chronology" follows this preface.

What gives the story coherence is my concern for three things:
education, governance, and rationality.

Somewhere along the way, doubtless not at school, I seem to
have developed a fixation on *education,* broadly conceived, including
my own. In early mid-career I did become a professor, which was enormously rewarding. Chapter 5 about MIT, where I taught and ran research
programs for thirty years, offers an impressionistic glimpse of the world's
premier research university in days of calm, and in days of storm in
the riotous '60s and '70s. But the rest of my professional life had a subtext of constant learning, along with trying to educate everyone else.

Thus this book can be read as an account of lessons learned by a mid-
level participant-observer in an improbable variety of settings. A cynic
quipped that education is wasted on the young (and retirement on
the old). That is of course nonsense. But I have to say that, in the non-
teaching roles I have played (government official to consultant to lecturer to TV commentator to writer), I found myself following Thomas
Jefferson's prescription for democracy by nagging audiences to learn
more, and higher-ups to become better educators.

Two other themes run through these pages. The first recurrent
theme, no surprise for a dues-paying political scientist, is a deep

interest in *governance*. That means not only the nature and quality of leadership but, almost as important, the working of *bureaucracies*. Chapter 1 recounts early experiences as a junior bureaucrat in various parts of government including the wartime Navy and the post-war State Department.

Chapter 2 takes a not completely friendly stab at that same State Department under the shadow of both Joe McCarthy and John Foster Dulles, including hitherto unreported Dulles views of McCarthyism and "Massive Retaliation." Chapter 3 picks up the bureaucratic tale at a loftier level, when I returned to government as Director of Global Issues on President Carter's National Security Council Staff.

Concern with governance also means concern with the geometry of *power*: who has it and how is it used? Chapter 4 plays with a little equation I dreamed up to relate modern presidents to their secretaries of state and national security advisers. Other equations of power around the globe are visible in chapters on the former USSR, the Middle East, and other foreign climes.

The second recurrent theme is a life-long quest, mostly Quixotic, for greater *rationality* in foreign policy. Chapter 10 plumbs this issue with some painfully learned pointers for better policy planning. It is near the end of the book because, like the final chapter, it is more of a think-piece than the rest. But the issue of rationality permeates the style of governance everywhere in a world where one culture's definition of rationality is another culture's definition of madness. Poorly understood cultural gulfs certainly undercut efforts to act "rationally" and perhaps in my next incarnation I will be a cultural anthropologist so I can understand better why high-level foreign policymaking sometimes resembles Plato's shadow-watchers in their cave.

To me rational behavior means planning ahead on the basis of good information. In foreign policy and national security decision-making, crisis management invariably drives out serious forward planning. Moreover, even where people are receptive to improving the quality of decisions, good techniques for overcoming the culture-bind are hard to find.

Political gaming is no panacea for that flaw. But if done right, it is the best method I have come across to try to bring order into a decision process that in theory is systematic, but in real life is often chaotic. Chapter 4 is the first authoritative account I know of that details the origins of the technique/art form of political gaming originated at RAND, developed by me at MIT, and spread to classrooms and governments the world over, including games I ran for the Soviets in Moscow, for 28 governments in Vienna, and for the US Joint Chiefs of Staff.

As scholar and practitioner, I have read a lot of secret cables and not so secret books and Op-Ed pieces about dealing with people in foreign cultures. What happens when you try to actually do this in the real world? Three chapters tell stories that illustrate differences in governance, rationality, and power observed in non-US settings. I was never a full-time diplomat, but these encounters represented a kind of part-time diplomacy and certainly taught me a lot about the subject.

Chapter 7 is a time-lapse sequence of snapshots of observed decline and collapse over the final twenty years of the decaying Soviet Union. Chapter 8 is about that other prime Cold War hotspot—the Middle East—where the potential for self-deception emerged in a private audience with the King of Saudi Arabia, and the capacity for violence was underscored with a bombing in Damascus just before I was to lecture the Syrian political establishment.

My overseas education was richly nourished and challenged by lecturing to audiences and meeting with people high and low in thirty-five other countries. Chapter 9 tells of some occasionally serious, sometimes mad attempts to communicate about America in assorted corners of the globe. Some of those encounters put to an acid test my pet theories and preconceptions about governance and power. They certainly highlighted the cultural gulf between American "rationality" and everyone else's version. And it was interesting to compare with on-the-ground reality results of some political games I had run. But I confess that these ten tales were chosen because they seemed to me the most interesting!

The final chapter is different from the rest. It tells no stories, and was the hardest of all to write. It is an essay based on my own beliefs, hopes, fears, and aspirations. It identifies dilemmas that beset America abroad, and suggests some ways to repair flaws in US foreign policy—and in a UN that has become indispensable before it has become effective. All that, I trust, in the spirit of greater rationality, humanity, and common sense realism.

　　To the naked eye, the subject matter of this book appears weighty. But in the process of looking back at some serious matters, the quotient of absurdities in the system has made a moderately light-hearted tone impossible to suppress.

Lincoln Palmer Bloomfield
Cohasset, Massachusetts 2005

A Brief Bio-Chronology

1920	Born in Boston.
1937–41	Harvard College, graduated in 1941.
1941	Internship in US Surplus Marketing Administration, placed in charge of Federal School Lunch and Food Stamp Program for the state of Oregon.
1942–46	US Navy. Served aboard U.S.S. *Ranger* in the Atlantic, various shore duties, in 1945 assigned to Office of Strategic Services (OSS) in India, Burma, and China.
1946–57	US Department of State, various positions in bureau dealing with UN policy, 1956–57 policy planner on UN Affairs.
1948	Married at New Zealand Embassy, Washington DC, to NZ diplomat Irirangi Coates.
1952	Leave of absence on Littauer Fellowship at Harvard University to complete MPA.
1954–55	Leave of absence on Rockefeller Fellowship at Harvard University to complete Ph.D. Awarded Harvard's Chase Prize for thesis, published as *Evolution or Revolution: The United Nations and the Problem of Peaceful Territorial Change* (Harvard University Press, 1958).
1957–63	Center for International Studies, Massachusetts Institute of Technology, as director of United Nations projects. Authored *The United Nations and US Foreign Policy: A New Look at the National Interest* (Little Brown, 1960, revised 1968).
1960–75	Directed MIT Arms Control Project. Developed the RAND/ MIT Polex (Political Game). Directed research projects on Control of Conflict and Soviet Arms Control policy under sponsorship of US Arms Control and Disarmament Agency.

1960–71	Co-Chaired Joint Harvard–MIT Arms Control Seminar with Thomas Schelling.
1961	Edited for the American Assembly *Outer Space: Prospects for Man and Society.* (Praeger, 1961, revised 1968, with editions in Arabic, Japanese, Spanish et al.)
1963–91	Professor of Political Science at MIT.
1964	Visited UN peacekeeping forces in Congo and Gaza Strip under State Department and UN sponsorship, with Rockefeller Foundation grant and co-authored and edited *International Military Forces: Peacekeeping in an Armed and Disarming World.* (Little Brown, revised 1971).
1965–79	Visiting Professor, Graduate Institute of Advanced International Studies, Geneva, Switzerland.
1966	Co-authored *Krushchev and the Arms Race: Soviet Policy Toward Arms Control and Disarmament, 1954–64* (MIT Press).
1969	Co-authored with Amelia Leiss *Controlling Small Wars: A Strategy for the 1970's* (Knopf).
1970	Visited Moscow as first academic guest of Soviet Institute of the USA and Canada.
1970–71	Member, Presidential Commission on the 25th anniversary of the United Nations.
1972–85	Lecturer on foreign policy and international relations in 35 countries under auspices of US State Department and US Information Agency.
1972–89	Participated in seven meetings in Soviet Union, six times under sponsorship of UN Association of USA, once as delegate to UN disarmament conference.
1974	Authored *In Search of American Foreign Policy: The Humane Use of Power* (Oxford University Press).
1975	Visiting Scholar, Rockefeller Foundation, Villa Serbelloni, Bellagio, Italy.
1975–76	Directed State Department-sponsored MIT study on interdependence.
1979–80	Director of Global Issues, National Security Council, White House, Washington, DC.

1980's	Served on Board of Visitors of National Defense University. Appointed by Canadian Government to Board of Directors, Canadian Institute for International Peace and Security. Elected Fellow of World Academy of Art and Science.
1982	Authored *The Foreign Policy Process: A Modern Primer* (Prentice-Hall).
1984	Developed scenario for HBO's Mid-East nuclear crisis drama "Countdown to Looking Glass" which won 1985 ACE Award for Best Dramatic Show on cable television.
1987	Co-edited with Harlan Cleveland *Prospects for Peacemaking: A Citizen's Guide to a Sane Nuclear Strategy* (MIT Press). Edited *The Management of Global Disorder: Prospects for Creative Problem-Solving* (University Press of America).
	Awarded EDUCOM prize for distinguished software in political science for CASCON computerized conflict analysis system developed with Allen Moulton.
1989–92	Hosted daily television program *Fifty Years Ago Today* for *Christian Science Monitor,* carried nationally on super-station WWOR during 1990, and in 1991–92 on the *Monitor* Channel. In 1990 Finalist at International Film and TV Festival, in 1992 awarded an Emmy in 15th Annual New England awards. Named "Best of Boston" by *Boston* Magazine.
1990	Directed workshop on interdependence for 21st Century Trust at Windsor Park, England.
1992–1999	Organized and moderated monthly MIT-sponsored "Seminar on Foreign Policy and Global Issues" in State Department Foreign Service Institute.
1995	Named Distinguished Visiting Lecturer by State Department Foreign Service Institute.
1997	Leadership Award by UN Association of Greater Boston. Authored *Managing International Conflict: From Theory to Policy* (St. Martin's Press) containing CASCON program developed with Allen Moulton.

1 BUREAUCRACY I: 1941–71

Dreams — and Nightmares — of Public Service

Before I settled in as a professor, I had spent the first sixteen years of my professional life as a callow bureaucrat in Oregon, an involuntary junior naval officer, a State Department workaholic, and later as a senior staffer in the National Security Council. I am very aware of the knock on Americans who "feed at the public trough" rather than "meet a payroll." It's sad but true that neither the academic life nor government work involves making a profit. But I cling to the notion that public service is not only respectable, but also high-minded and, at least for me, often rewarding, and invariably instructive.

This chapter tells of early experiences in the federal bureaucracy, each of which was a learning experience, even when I hated what I was doing.

These were the lessons: In college, I learned that public service could be an alternative to becoming a doctor. In the year that followed graduation, I learned that grass root service could mobilize the youthful idealism with which I was burning. In the wartime Navy, I learned how to pursue a diagonal dotted line to cut across a formal organization chart. In eleven years in the State Department, I learned that our government, with a favoring wind at its back in the shape of a supportive public and Congress, can do marvelous things to avoid war, foster peace, and help our neighbors. I also learned the painful lesson, elaborated in the next chapter, that when the negatives start to dominate — as they did in the McCarthy era and the Dulles secretaryship of state—the dream of public service can become a nightmare. During the ill-starred Nixon administration I learned about the tactical uses of presidential commissions. And later in White House service, as told in "The Atmosphere Gets Rarified," I learned how much easier it is to get things done in proximity to the top—and how hazardous that altitude can be to one's equilibrium.

1940–42: JUNIOR BUREAUCRAT

President John F. Kennedy once described public service as a "proud and lively career." I anticipated this by two decades when, as a junior at Harvard College, I chaired its first intercollegiate conference on careers in government and community service. The university's crusty President James Bryant Conant felt strongly that Harvard should not be in the business of "vocational guidance," the early twentieth century American movement pioneered in part by my late father. Over the administration's opposition, the undergraduate Phillips Brooks House Association, dedicated to social service in the community, sponsored the conference. It attracted several hundred students from a variety of colleges, plus a stellar lineup of speakers who were either feeding at the public trough or helping other people to do so.

Until junior year I had been committed to a medical career, inspired by a pair of youthful MDs who exuded high idealism in the service of humankind. (I also enjoyed cutting up frogs in the biology lab.) My medical fantasy turned into a shambles in Harvard's Mallinckrodt Lab, where I broke more glassware than I could afford, and wound up unable to write with chronically bandaged fingers. I also found organic chemistry highly stressful, particularly when in desperation I sought help from the great Professor Louis Fieser, who later invented napalm. His monumental disinterest provided an invaluable lesson for this future professor about how not to behave when a scared sophomore approaches a teacher for help.

There had been earlier signs of my proclivity for political science. I began a habit of clipping and filing the *New York Times* at the age of 12, suggesting a career as a file clerk. I also filled my schoolbooks with detailed drawings of military uniforms, and was excited by a magazine story featuring a dashing young diplomat who wowed the ladies at receptions with his red sash, chest full of medals, and dazzling smile. My transformation to a "Government" major (Harvard College disdained the term "political science") was, thus, entirely logical.

As perhaps the only participant who actually absorbed the message of the careers conference, I began to think about somehow getting a job in the government, seeking advice from a US Supreme Court Justice my father had known. Surprise, surprise, he declared that legal training was a ticket to success in any field of endeavor—a fallacy that might help explain America's obsessive litigiousness. Harvard Law School agreed to serve as my detour to fame and fortune. But I was saved from that fate by a seductive phone call from Washington, and soon en route to San Francisco as an intern in the federal Surplus Marketing Administration (SMA).

The SMA was in the business of disposing of the surplus commodities that were piling up on American farms and dragging down farm prices. The agency was run by a man named Milo Perkins who believed in youth—including youth who couldn't tell the difference between a harvester and a manure-spreader, but who could be trained to look and sound as if they did. At the ripe age of 21, I wound up as acting area supervisor for the state of Oregon, responsible for the federal food stamp plan and school lunch program in that beautiful state.

It was a great lesson, even though—or perhaps because—my ignorance was vast and my arrogance breathtaking. Among other things, I learned that skepticism is inevitable when a youthful federal bureaucrat tries to tell farmers and their wives, assembled in schoolrooms in small Oregon towns, what to do with their crops. I also absorbed the invaluable teaching that things don't happen in a democracy without public support.

The Portland School Board represented the chief hurdle to my success as a budding bureaucrat. Other communities had happily accepted surplus commodities from Department of Agriculture warehouses to provide a nutritious lunch to children, some of whom came to school having had no breakfast, even carrying stones in their lunch bags because the family couldn't afford food. The Portland School Board was dominated by a noted writer of western romance stories who was an equally noted hater of anything emanating from Franklin

Roosevelt's Washington. By the time I entered the scene, the board had already rejected an offer of surplus food for Portland's needy kids.

As I got better at the game, I wound up writing anonymous editorials promoting our program in the *Oregonian,* probably the best paper in the Pacific Northwest, thanks to the encouragement of its editor E. "Ep" Palmer Hoyt, later editor of the *Denver Post.* I also learned to cultivate community organizations like the League of Women Voters, the Grange, the American Legion, and others sympathetic to supplemental school lunches in Portland's schools. However, after I presented the case for the program at the school board's first public meeting on the subject I was told, in effect, "Beat it, kid, you're bothering us."

I picked myself off the canvas and revisited all the support groups. From now on it would be hardball—no more Mr. Nice Guy. The climax came at a second open school board public meeting, this time featuring an overflow audience stacked with supporters from the citizen groups. After being denounced as a "long-haired radical" (I happened to sport a crewcut at the time), I had the pleasure of seeing the now-intimidated school board narrowly but decisively reverse itself.

The denouement for me came during a radio interview soon thereafter. It was conducted by Portland's former congresswoman, a popular lady named Nan Wood Honeyman. Her other guest was a henchman of my right-wing nemesis on the school board. The time was early 1942, a few weeks after Pearl Harbor, and the bad guy insinuated that I was a shameless draft-dodger. My golden moment came when I casually mentioned that I had just been sworn in as an ensign in the United States Naval Reserve and was off on the morrow to save his sorry derrière. (I didn't actually say that, but I like to think my meaning was clear.)

Needless to say, public service is not all so universally high-minded. Within a week of the Pearl Harbor attack, the Surplus Marketing Administration had, without missing a beat, executed a 180-degree turn, altered one initial in its name—SMA to AMA, standing for Agricultural Marketing Administration—and adopted as its slogan "Food will win the war and write the peace." With lightning speed, surplus commodities had metamorphosed into scarce commodities. My own shamelessness ran to being photographed in the state capital building

Junior bureaucrat with Oregon's Governor Sprague.

holding up one end of a banner celebrating our new turf-preserving slogan, with good Republican Governor Sprague holding up the other end. Moral: draft a "sunset law" for government agencies so they will expire when their assigned mission is completed, or else they will live on like an earthworm that has been cut in half.

1942–46: TIME OUT: WORLD WAR II

My naval service at sea, at home, and finally with the Office of Strategic Services (OSS) in India, China, and Burma was all involuntary, but did teach another key lesson about the way organizations work.

In my third year of service I was stuck at Yale University as personnel officer of the V-12 program, which used the campus to train wartime naval officers. It was better, but not by much, than getting seasick on aircraft carriers and subchasers. The executive officer of the unit was a thoroughgoing sadist who, after his earlier retirement, had become a discipline officer at a prep school. He was constantly on my case. The commanding officer, on the other hand, was an agreeable four-striper for whom assignment to Yale was punishment for having been at Pearl Harbor when the Japanese struck. He drank heavily, but somehow played a canny tennis game. His aide would call me in the morning and instruct me to report to the New Haven Lawn Tennis Club at 1500 hours. Captain Gill would be sitting on the veranda finishing a martini, after which we would have a lively game. This further infuriated the Exec, who took vengeance on me by endorsing as "disapproved" all my requests for transfer.

I finally escaped by having a friend in the wartime spy agency OSS cut orders for me that bypassed the whole naval establishment—a classic case of informal, diagonal cross-cutting communication that gets things done by ignoring the neat boxes and vertical lines on official organization charts. The OSS gave me an intensive refresher course in German until, at the last minute, in typical military fashion, they switched my assignment to China.

Final training took place on Catalina Island off Los Angeles, with a crash course in jungle warfare. There I learned how to disembowel a mountain goat as well as how to kill a man with two fingers, neither of which turned out to be applicable to my subsequent careers. However, the curriculum also included a lock-picking course, which came in handy in Nanking, when the lock jammed on the great bronze doors to the tomb of modern China's founder Sun Yat-Sen atop Purple Mountain. I was happy to demonstrate Western superiority by picking the lock for the frustrated guards.

The war ended when I arrived in India in the company of a fellow officer with whom I had started a gin rummy game in New York. Because the brilliant egomaniac commanding the Pacific theater of war, General Douglas MacArthur, somehow got away with refusing to admit OSS officers to "his" theater, we were soon sent to Rangoon. There we investigated a Navy OSS doctor whose crimes were living with a Burmese woman, and making a pair of nylon pajamas out of a parachute he liberated from a downed US C–47. He cured the ear infection we had incurred in Calcutta swimming in the British Officers Club pool, and the three of us became fast friends.

The US Navy commander in India subsequently reprimanded us for making a farce out of what was clearly nonsense to begin with, and suddenly we were on a smallish plane flying to China over the notorious mountain route known as "The Hump." We wound up in

With US allies in Nanking, China.

Shanghai, where we contributed in a minor way to the misinformation sent to Washington that led to the disastrous visit in late 1945 of General George C. Marshall. US intelligence had reported enthusiastically on the burgeoning Chinese "democratic movement," which turned out in the end to consist of about three guys who hadn't yet been liquidated by Chiang Kai-shek's near-fascist Kuomintang .

The Japanese had melted down the radiators in Shanghai's hotels to make munitions, so the only way to keep warm at night was to keep the inner fire stoked with a bottle of Stolichnaya vodka, the ink on whose label was still wet. We used the occasion to write a play that I thought was pretty good. My fellow globe-circling gin-rummy player and co-author, Franklin James Schaffner, went on to win an Academy Award for directing *Patton,* but alas, never saw fit to produce our magnum opus.

Another valuable wartime lesson in detouring around formal organization lines came in late December, 1945, when Frank and I were told we couldn't hang around Shanghai any longer even though

Navy playwrights at work in Shanghai, China.

we had not yet finished our play. We had three options for returning home from which to choose: as naval officers, with the OSS, or via the US Army that supported the OSS in Shanghai. Our first stop was the US flagship anchored offshore. The executive officer told us we would be most welcome to ship home aboard the USS *Whatever*. Of course, he continued, you will stand regular deck watches. This obviously wouldn't work, since we had no intention of standing any more deck watches, and moreover had given all our uniforms except one ragged set of khakis to our room boy in exchange for carting upstairs buckets of hot water to fill our bathtub.

Our next stop was the local OSS office. Among the options on offer, we elected to depart Shanghai on a freighter heading for the US East Coast via the Panama Canal, promising a slow voyage that would enable us to finish our play. Sadly, the freighter struck a mine in the Yangtze estuary and sank before it arrived in Shanghai. Our final stop was the US Army office in downtown Shanghai. Our prospects were pretty bleak there, since legions of army personnel in the China theater were booked to fly home. However, Frank and I were snugly bundled up in our (synthetic) fur-lined navy parkas, while the major was shivering in his short Eisenhower jacket. He asked point-blank if we knew where he could get his hands on a warm parka like ours. We expressed pessimism at the prospect, but promised to make a maximum effort.

The quest was not difficult, since we already had an extra parka in our closet. After a suitable delay, we returned with the parka and promptly received Army orders to fly out of Shanghai on New Year's Eve. Landing in Manila at 3 A.M. on New Year's Day, we found our long johns and parkas obviously unsuitable for the 100-degree Manila heat. Relief on that first post-war New Year's Eve took a long while to materialize, given that most of the airport personnel were understandably drunk. After a cold open-air shower on a nearby hilltop, we had no further logistical problems; our DC-6 puddle-jumped to Kwajalein, Saipan, Johnson Island, and Oahu. The only bad time was when the pilot got lost between Hawaii and San Francisco.

We went through a similar routine in San Francisco in quest of orders that would get us to the East Coast by train so we could finish the play. Fortunately, we got a compartment where we could set up our portable typewriter. Unfortunately for literary creativity, the train contained a good many attractive people celebrating war's end, and somehow the play never got finished.

1946–57: PRESENT AT THE CREATION

My former OSS boss (and later best man) Calvin Nichols had become executive officer of the State Department bureau responsible for US participation in the newly created United Nations. Unaccountably, he wanted me as his deputy. Serving in the State Department had its ups and downs, as recounted in the next chapter. But there was no question about the first few years. I was in spirit with William Wordsworth when he wrote of the early, heady days of the French Revolution: "Bliss it was that dawn to be alive" and, even more to the point, "But to be young was very heaven."

My service began with that extraordinary five-year period of inventiveness and political daring when the basic institutional structures of cooperation such as the UN system, the World Bank and Fund, and NATO were put in place to build a more peaceful, secure, and just world on the ruins of the one that had just cost over 50 million lives and dozens of broken nations. Though I was among the lowliest in the State Department's Bureau of Special Political Affairs, I was intoxicated with the elixir of the times. Like many of my contemporaries, I had come of age in the grim days of the Great Depression with fascism on the march, and wound up in uniform for four years. How could one not thrill at the prospect of a more hopeful future of cooperation instead of war, justice instead of domination, and economic coordination instead of the destructive Hawley-Smoot Tariff Act of 1930 that either bankrupted or made enemies of practically everyone?

In my eleven years in State I did everything from drafting budgets to planning US policies in the United Nations, and I loved most of it. It was the beginning of the modern age of local conflicts and small wars, virtually all of which landed on the agenda of the United Nations Security Council. The United States was what my boss Dean Rusk called the fat boy in the canoe: "When we roll, everyone rolls with us."

With our help, the UN sent out bevies of peace observers and mediators. The marvelous if flawed notion of UN peacekeeping was invented in the middle of the night in late October, 1956, when President Eisenhower forced the British, French, and Israelis to abort their ill-conceived attack on Egypt, which had nationalized the British-French owned and operated Suez Canal. Most of the conflicts of the 1950s grew out of the dismantling of Western Europe's African and Asian colonies, and some turned into "proxy wars" between the nuclear superpowers. These were often shooting wars in which people were killed or wounded. But I have to confess that I enjoyed the excitement and the responsibility, and felt gratifyingly useful and important.

One of the side-benefits of this adventure was exposure to some people who had previously been only headline names to me. Some of the headliners had egos to match their headlines. But a few others shone with the light of genuine modesty. Eleanor Roosevelt, widow of the late President Franklin D. Roosevelt, was the US representative on the United Nations Human Rights Commission. One day she came to visit my boss, Assistant Secretary John Hickerson. I was his staff assistant, meaning that I screened his cables and intelligence reports and, with mounting resentment, did whatever else he wanted. After Mrs. Roosevelt had dealt with the boss she made a point of coming to visit me in my tiny office, which is just one small example of the human qualities that so distinguished her.

This rare brand of modesty among the great was matched by the gentlemanly Christian Herter, who served briefly as secretary of state in the late 1950s. He had just undergone hip surgery, and I can still see him on crutches, painfully making his way down our long corridor to pay his respects to the assistant secretary and his staff, and then repeating the effort throughout the building.

The contrast was striking with Herter's immediate predecessor John Foster Dulles and, at least for a while, Massachusetts Senator Henry Cabot Lodge, Jr. In November, 1952, Lodge had been defeated in a senate race by another Massachusetts politician named John Fitzgerald Kennedy. To assuage Lodge's bruised ego, President-elect Dwight D. Eisenhower named him permanent representative to the United Nations.

A few years earlier, I had laid eyes on that tall and handsome grandson of the senator of the same name, the one who had helped cripple the League of Nations Covenant which President Woodrow Wilson had brought back from Paris in 1919. The occasion was a hearing by the Senate Foreign Relations Committee to which I accompanied my boss. I confess to a kind of puritanical shock at seeing the still-youthful Senator Lodge, his feet sprawled on the Committee table with unabashed self-confidence. When Lodge was ready to be briefed for his new job at the UN, he rejected an office in the State Department building as beneath his dignity. Ike had foolishly promised him cabinet status (setting a precedent that the White House would later regret) and a White House office. Lodge's reputation preceded him, and when I was dispatched to liaise with him in his White House lair, I concluded it was because I was expendable.

My first couple of sessions with Lodge confirmed the impression that he was a bully. I was yelled at a few times, not for my own shortcomings but for those of the bureaucracy in general and the State Department in particular. After one particularly unjust tirade, something inspired me to yell back. From that day forward Cabot Lodge and I were fast friends. When he finally deigned to visit the State Department bureau that would be back-stopping him, the assistant secretary, deputies, and division chiefs crowded the reception room to greet him. When Lodge arrived, he stopped at the door, spotted me in the back of the crowd, elbowed his way through my superiors, and greeted me effusively, either raising my stature in the eyes of my colleagues or, more likely, proving that I had shamefully sucked up to our new permanent representative at the UN in New York.

Alas, the charmed life ended when, in June, 1950, Communist North Korea, cheered on by Moscow and Beijing, invaded South Korea. Although it was not directly a Soviet operation, it took this shock to make it clear that the brave new world we thought we were building was under mortal threat from Joseph Stalin's Soviet Union and its puppets in Eastern Europe and Asia. Apart from a near breakdown from overwork and stress, I and everyone else redoubled our efforts.

But morale in the building began to plummet when John Foster Dulles took over in 1953 and created a dark mood described in the next chapter. The unending litany of international crises continued, and I still worked 12-hour days plus weekends. But it was with a diminished sense of joy. The scorn for government "time-servers" was valid for some then, as it is now. But it had little or no relevance to the people I worked with, or to overworked colleagues a couple of decades later when I returned to full-time government service with the National Security Council.

1970–71: Presidential Commissions and White House Dinners

My personal acquaintance with US presidents has been modest. As a junior officer in the State Department I got to shake the hand of Harry Truman, and when I was a professor, US Ambassador to the UN and future president George H.W. Bush (Bush 41, historically) occasionally invited me in for advice. I later worked full-time for President Jimmy Carter, whom, despite his weaknesses as a leader, I admired greatly for his decency and integrity, as well as for his policy goals I was engaged in furthering. But the memory that stands out is a state dinner where I was a guest of President Richard Milhous Nixon whom, unlike Carter, I did not admire all that much. The Nixon State dinner was a sidebar to another lesson in the bureaucratic canon, namely the phenomenon known as the "presidential commission."

This is what happened. Nixon decided to set up a presidential commission on the occasion of the 25th Anniversary of the United Nations. The commission's ostensible purpose was to study the UN and advise the president on how to resuscitate it from its moribund condition. The subtext, it turned out, was to give the president a frictionless way to change our increasingly counterproductive opposition to a UN seat for mainland China, then in power for over twenty years. My former State Department colleague, now Assistant Secretary of State Sam de Palma called to say that the proposed commission had gotten snarled in White House politics, but that if I agreed to become its executive director "perhaps it wouldn't be just a cosmetic operation." Happy as a clam at MIT, I declined. Later someone called to ask if I would be willing to serve as a member of the commission, and I said sure.

There ensued weeks of muffled thuds as the list of potential members was massaged in the White House political command post, with names added daily and just as quickly expunged. At one point during the stormy gestation period of the commission, I received a letter from Massachusetts Senator Ed Brooke saying how delighted he was to give political clearance for my appointment to something with a name like Defense Logistics Arrangements Advisory Board. I thanked him for his confidence in me, but questioned both the existence of such a board and my qualifications for serving on it. He confessed that it had sounded pretty implausible to him, too.

Months went by. At a lunch with UN Secretary-General U Thant in his dining room overlooking the polluted East River, US Permanent Representative Charlie Yost told me that, considering the growing confusion, he was going to try to kill the Commission if it wasn't set up within a week. But if it were set up, he was counting on me to see that it did "something constructive." Sure. The whole exercise almost came unglued in April, 1970, when Cambodia was invaded, and some potential commission members denounced the president. A call from the White House political staff asked if I was willing to be considered for appointment to the Commission. I replied somewhat testily to the nice lady that we had been all through that. She explained that they wanted to make sure people hadn't become so disaffected by Cambodia that they would embarrass the president by refusing to serve after being appointed.

After some other cryptic telephone calls, I decided to forget the whole thing, until, that is, the mail brought a gorgeously engraved invitation to dine with the president. Black tie was specified. Soon after came a telegram informing me that the presidential commission would be sworn in that afternoon, and please don't breach the news embargo on this important presidential announcement. Important?

On the designated day, in the antique-filled John Quincy Adams Suite on the State Department's eighth floor, forty-odd (with emphasis on the odd) Americans were sworn in. Apart from Senator William J. Fulbright and a couple of other members of Congress, the rest ranged from mid-western tycoons to representatives of the arts (Philadelphia Orchestra conductor Eugene Ormandy) and the entertainment biz (Shirley Temple Black and Art Linkletter). The only actual experts I could detect were my last State Department boss Francis O. Wilcox, and me. And of course the chairman, Henry Cabot Lodge, Jr.

We adjourned to the International Conference Suite, where the members of the commission were suitably arrayed. At my place was a long cardboard tube addressed to the honorable me containing a presidential commission replete with seals and testimonies to my fidelity and integrity. There was also a letter from my old nemesis/friend the chairman, a batch of papers to sign, a set of background documents, and a little box with a souvenir pen. As I played with my party favors, I looked around for Lodge, who was not there. The board chairman of Lehman Brothers read out the list of those Lodge wanted to act as an executive committee headed by Fran Wilcox (who had already made clear that I was expected to "do most of the work" and "come up with most of the ideas"). In his most querulous tone Senator Fulbright made a tasteless intervention about how he thought all he was supposed to do was go to dinner with the president and now he learned that he was supposed to work on a commission. We eventually adjourned in some confusion.

At eight P.M., adorned in my old tuxedo and armed with all the little engraved passes to get me in, I entered the White House through the seldom-used north door, where an usher relieved me of my raincoat. In the main entrance hall the Marine Band, in resplendent red, played selections from operettas. One of the uniformed military aides, aiguillettes of gold braid (what in the Navy we called chicken-guts) descending from his shoulder, strong-armed me to the entrance of the East Room, where the guests were gathering. My presence was announced over a mike, and to my relief I spotted a few friendlies— National Security Adviser Henry Kissinger, UN Representative Charlie Yost, and Undersecretary of State Joe Sisco. As more guests arrived, a squad of butlers passed industrial-strength drinks.

At precisely 8:15, with a great flurry, the Color Guard preceded the president and first lady down the grand staircase. The Marine band broke into "Ruffles and Flourishes"; the head usher announced in portentous tones "Ladies and Gentlemen, the President of the United States of America and Mrs. Nixon"; and the band struck up "Hail to the Chief." Four flag bearers swept into the room, came to a stop, and sidestepped in unison. Between them marched the president and Mrs. Nixon, along with the guest of honor, the diminutive UN Secretary-General U Thant of Burma. The three arrayed themselves by the door, and we lined up to be presented by Bus Mosbacher, the Chief of Protocol (who by press accounts was about to be fired for having botched the visit of French President Pompidou). The president, whom the liberal press, along with his own checker-ed (sic) record, had inclined me to dislike, was very gracious. To my astonishment U Thant seized my hands with both of his and said, "Keep up your important work." Mrs. Nixon, who was taller and prettier than I had realized, shook hands lightly but cordially.

A state dinner in the State Dining Room is impressive, particularly when the gold service has been wheeled out. I had read of the president's fondness for meatloaf, but the menu was in fact quite special, with wines worth remembering (a 1967 Bernkasteler Doktor with the Salmon a la Gelée, a 1962 Chateau La Tour with the Chateaubriand, and a 1962 Dom Perignon with the "Mousse en Surprise United Nations"). My neighbor was New York's Cardinal Cooke, who had rushed into the ceremony just as we broke up. He explained to me that he had been in the sky above Washington for two and a half hours, which seemed appropriate for a prince of the church.

As a dinner companion, the Cardinal came off as folksy, shrewd, political, and good company. He gave an impromptu invocation, which he had the courtesy to make ecumenical (the guest of honor was a Buddhist). Media star Reverend Norman Vincent Peale, who gave the benediction, displayed no such sensitivity. To make conversation, I mentioned to His Eminence that on the plane coming down I had been reading the work of Teilhard de Chardin—a defrocked Jesuit who had wound up on the Index Expurgatorius. To my surprise, he said the de Chardin theme of human and political unity was the only basic truth to be pursued.

The dinner was just getting going when a side door opened to disgorge a red-coated Marine running at top speed while strumming a guitar. He was followed by a running Marine accordion player, followed in turn by fifteen other sprinting Marines armed with violins. They surrounded us, sawing away on their instruments in the fashion of gypsy musicians in a Budapest café.

What we were witnessing was a souped-up Nixon version of the "Strolling Violins" with which presidents impress the natives at state dinners. I couldn't help recalling an early Nixon PR gaffe, when he had ordered the White House guards to be outfitted in a kind of musical comedy get-up complete with high-pointed helmets (the uniforms were soon donated to a college marching band). A few years later, the ascetic President Jimmy Carter downplayed all such ceremony to the point of renaming the Executive Mansion the "Residence," and wearing a cardigan sweater on television to dramatize the energy crisis. But I'm not complaining about the delightful Nixon cuisine and cellar.

When the guests were sated with food and drink, the president rose and spoke briefly about world peace and the UN: Charlie Yost said a few diplomatic words; and Shirley Temple Black told a strange anecdote about encountering the politically radioactive Cuban delegate in the UN ladies room. Finally the legendary black US-UN diplomat Ralph Bunche, now quite blind and ailing, gave a moving tribute to U Thant, typically addressing himself to his boss's qualities and not his own. At the end, U Thant spoke quietly of an intolerant world's need for tolerance and other Buddhist attributes. The president ended the dinner with a toast to the UN. I wished that he had meant it.

Afterwards the president and Mrs. Nixon entertained in the Blue Room, which is much smaller and more informal. The remaining guests stood around knocking back brandy and coffee. I had an urgent errand, and sought out the nearest tuxedoed secret service agent, recognizable as a non-guest from his bulging muscles and hearing aid. He said there was no plumbing on the main floor of the White House and sent me downstairs, where a White House cop led me through a little library into a facility in which there were wash basins and, discreetly placed behind a pair of small closed doors, the porcelain target.

I make a point of this because once, as the only American participant at an otherwise all-British conference at England's elegant Ditchley Park, I was assigned the so-called "Queen's Bedroom," adjoining which was the queen's loo. I readily identified a long tub, complete with a picture window so she (and now I) could lie in the tub and watch sheep safely graze across miles of greensward. But when it came to any other problem, the queen's bathroom displayed only a collection of Hepplewhite and Chippendale style pieces. It was only by disassembling one of the latter that I came upon the desired object. Obviously the president (and, for that matter, the queen) were in the end (so to speak) constructed like everyone else. Another illusion shot.

On reentering the Blue Room, I found the President more or less alone, many guests having departed. State Department types stood around discreetly, but I had the temerity to walk over for a chat with our host. He complained of U Thant's public praise of the Soviet Middle East proposals but not of ours. But he said he didn't care what anyone said so long as it would lead to the guns not being fired. He said the problem wasn't that the Arabs and the Israelis were killing each other, it was the Russians. But, he said, "the Russians now get the message."

Just as I started to enlighten him with some profound policy insights that Henry Kissinger would never have thought of, I realized that the president was looking, not at me, but at Reverend Peale. That author of a thousand religious platitudes magically occupied the spot where I had been standing, and I was obviously conversational toast. Consoling myself that Nixon obviously had a warmer spot for a man with a hotline to Heaven than one with a hotline to anti-Nixon students, I took my leave, with both Nixons still hanging around. Not the protocol I was taught, but the times they were a-changing.

As for the commission itself, following Lodge's private urging, I wound up drafting the recommendation for getting China back into the UN. Lodge didn't back down when Senator Bourke Hickenlooper accused me of everything from treason to matricide. In fact, we had already put to the test the long-standing Washington conviction that China policy was a political third rail. One of our members whose newspaper covered the Ohio heartland of isolation and conservatism had reported back to us that an editorial trial balloon on changing China policy had aroused zero negative comment.

Almost a year after our appointment ceremony, on one of Washington's fabulous May days, we presented our report to the President. While the cameras ground away in the Cabinet Room, Nixon chatted with each member. After asking if we had been paid (of course we had not), he handed each man a set of cufflinks with the presidential seal and each woman an equivalent pin. On this particular close-up, I confirmed that in profile his nose was shaped exactly like that of long-time Soviet Foreign Minister Andrei Gromyko. I also thought he looked particularly cheery for a man whose town had just hosted 200,000 anti-Nixon protesters. My family watched the ceremony spectacle on *CBS News* and was suitably impressed with the cufflinks.

The subtext of our mission had been dealt with, supplying the President with political cover for a decision to end the China-UN stalemate. Lamentably, he ignored our many other proposals to improve the UN system and US participation therein, including some I had cribbed from my own writings. Nevertheless, it was a fascinating exercise, and included a drop-in visit from George H. W. Bush, just defeated for congress in Texas, and named by Nixon to be his Ambassador to the UN as a consolation prize. The future president ("Bush 41") told us that he had "stars in his eyes" when he contemplated his new mission. In later conversations with him in New York, I found him considerably more realistic.

SOME REFLECTIONS ON AMERICANS VERSUS THEIR GOVERNMENT

Popular American attitudes about government, particularly the federal government, follow a roller coaster trajectory. At times of crisis, Americans consider government a good thing, combining patriotic feeling and a sense that their tax money is buying protection. But normally they feel distanced from government and often contemp-

The Lodge Commission gets presidential cufflinks: With President Nixon and Lodge in the Cabinet Room, the White House.

tuous of people who work in Washington. At worst, the old slur "those who can, do, those who can't, teach" acquires a corollary: "those who can't even teach become civil servants." All too often there isn't much encouragement for the best and brightest to aspire to a career in either teaching or government service.

That tends to change in times of crisis. In our own times, the 9/11 terrorist attack on New York and Washington initiated an extraordinary, if temporary, period of enthusiasm for public service. Despite obvious governmental failures in intelligence and security, for a while polls showed the highest percentage in years trusting the feds to do the right thing most of the time. (*New York Times,* November 3, 2001). TV bureau-dramas like *JAG, The West Wing,* and *The Agency* surged in popularity, supplying, according to a *Times* editorial, "on-screen comfort food to a shaken population that needs, *once again,* to believe in the competence and dedication of public officials" (April 7, 2002).

However, history suggests that deep suspicion of government is the more authentic popular stance, even absent the backlash against George W. Bush's war in Iraq. Americans have never been as accepting of public authority as Europeans. Indeed, the US Constitution was designed to keep King George III from ever getting back in America's face. It limited the central government's powers, via the Tenth Amendment, to those expressly delegated. Historian Joseph J. Ellis writes that "the dominant intellectual legacy of the Revolution . . . depicted any energetic expression of governmental authority as an alien force that all responsible citizens ought to repudiate and, if possible, overthrow." (*The Founding Brothers,* New York, Knopf, 2000, p.11)

Moreover, the American political system has a built-in obstacle to efficiency, thanks to the separation of powers between executive and legislative branches. This concept, borrowed from the great French political philosopher Montesquieu, is a brilliant deterrent to tyranny. But, as the constitutional scholar Edwin Corwin once remarked, it makes the Constitution an invitation for President and Congress to struggle for the control of foreign affairs.

Let's face it: some government agencies exhibit bureaucratic rigidity plus a tendency to goof off, particularly at the lower levels, irritating citizens who have to deal with them. The fact that trying to get courteous, efficient help in some department stores is at least as common, doesn't lessen the chronic beef about government. But the American bias against Washington is so deeply grounded that Americans will never be entirely comfortable with the idea of government, short of a crisis that mobilizes the nation.

Chronic distaste for Washington was increased by the behavior of some recent presidents. Lyndon Johnson abused his trust by lying to the public about Vietnam, and Richard Nixon not only lied but used official machinery, including the intelligence services, to undermine his enemies and conceal his own cover-up. In the 1990's Clinton's sexual games in the Oval Office encouraged popular disillusionment, magnified by the switch in the mainstream media, once discreet about private peccadilloes of Presidents Franklin Roosevelt and John Kennedy, to journalistic bottom-feeding. The increasingly intrusive background checks, Congressional exposés, and leaks to the press made people with normal résumés think three times before inviting that kind of exposure. Alienation from government was not all unwitting. President Ronald Reagan shamelessly exploited popular skepticism about Washington by demonizing government itself, and President George W. Bush liked to distance himself from anything inside the Beltway.

At the very fringe, some extra-chromosome types, whether right wing survivalists or left-wing anarchists, want no government at all.

But no government at all is not the same as *limited* government. That concept remains eternally correct, given what we know of dictatorships and tyrannies. But seeking political brownie points by sowing hostility to government and contempt for public service is highly corrosive to the nation's larger purposes.

2 BUREAUCRACY II: 1953–57
The Genetically-Engineered Secretary of State

"That inconsiderate S.O.B." growled a voice somewhere behind me. I couldn't see the malcontent through the crowd. But as I blew on my fingertips to fend off frostbite, it was hard to disagree with his characterization of the new secretary of state. It was only later that I fully appreciated the profundity of his description of the Honorable John Foster Dulles. These recollections aim at fleshing out that rather terse summation.

ECCE HOMO

Washington had never looked more beautiful than on that sparkling January day in 1953, a week after the inauguration of President Dwight D. Eisenhower. The temperature hovered near the 30 degree mark and the sky was azure blue. The memo had summoned everyone in the building to congregate at noon in the parking lot so our new leader could greet us. It probably wouldn't take long, so we didn't bother with overcoats. Shortly before noon, several hundred State Department employees trooped outdoors to give the 51st secretary of state a proper reception.

By now, however, we had been standing in the cold for almost half an hour. Feet were being stamped, arms beaten against chests, lips beginning to match the color of the sky. At last the glass doors swung open and extruded the new secretary, bundled in a heavy overcoat. He was tall and stooped, and behind thick glasses his gaunt visage wore the expression of someone who had eaten a bad oyster. Nibbling hungrily on his lower lip, he then approached the makeshift podium.

The speech opened with an apology, not for keeping the staff waiting in the cold, but for having failed to grace us with his presence earlier. We put it off, he said, because rain was forecasted. But "at any rate President Eisenhower had good luck on his weather and, if he can have good luck, we can take tough luck now and then." We?

Adding "I don't want to keep you out here any longer than necessary." He proceeded to describe at length his qualifications to become what he called "seggatary of state." Those qualifications appeared to be primarily genetic: "I don't suppose there is any family in the United States which has been for so long identified with the Foreign Service and the State Department as my own family." Grand-uncle was a minister to Britain, grandfather John W. Foster ended up as President Harrison's secretary of state, uncle Robert Lansing was secretary under Wilson. Ancestors, brothers, sisters, collateral relatives—all contributed to the superior gene pool standing before us in flesh incarnate.

What came next added substantially to the chill. To his shivering staff Dulles said, "We have got to have people who are upstanding Americans of integrity, who have minds of their own and who have the courage to express their views." But "on the other hand," once decisions are made "we must all turn in, loyally, to support those policies. . . . I expect that you will carry them out loyally." (Translation: "You are supposed to be independent-minded and think for yourself—but don't even try.") In his first press release the day after the Inaugural, the new secretary had already coined the phrase "positive loyalty," meaning overt enthusiasm for announced policy. Loyalty to current policy is the normal expectation in any bureaucracy. Except that in the poisonous atmosphere which had settled on the nation's capital like a miasma, there were eerie echoes of party line, traitorous deviationists and, who knows, maybe a capitalist gulag.

In addition to feeling that he had been born to the job, John Foster Dulles also brought to it a palpable aura of piety. In 1937 he had begun a long association with the Federal Council of Churches, and in 1940 became chairman of the council's influential Commission on a Just and Durable Peace. Two years later, in the midst of Dulles's growing public visibility as a lay Protestant churchman, his youngest son Avery chose to be converted to Catholicism by the charismatic Monsignor Fulton Sheen. Although father is reported to have eventually reconciled to son's apostasy, there are reports of familial sackcloth and ashes when Avery came out of the ecclesiastical closet, as it were.

In that period Avery Dulles was a Harvard student living in "A" entry of Lowell House. As it happened, I lived there too. While he was listed in the glass-covered directory as residing on the 5th floor, none of us had ever laid eyes on him, and we were astonished when we read that he had graduated summa cum laude.

I finally got to know Avery when we were both junior officers serving on the USS *Ranger,* and he turned out to be good company. We often went together to the Sunday shipboard church service, where he once instructed me on the difference between a mortal sin and a venial one. (If you steal a chocolate bar from a shipmate's locker that's venial, but if you take $100 that's mortal—or was it the other way around?) Avery went on to become a Jesuit priest, and in time, one of the church's most influential theologians. In 2001, Pope John Paul II bumped him up over monsignors, bishops, and archbishops, and made him a prince of the church—Cardinal Dulles.

John Foster Dulles had started his foreign relations career as a junior diplomat at the Paris Peace talks in 1919. He went on to become a powerful New York international lawyer in the firm of Sullivan and Cromwell, and had been the chief negotiator of the Japanese Peace Treaty that officially ended World War II hostilities. But Dulles had an awkward smudge in his otherwise impeccable résumé. As chairman of the board of the venerable Carnegie Endowment for International Peace he had brought in as the endowment's president Alger Hiss, then one of the State Department's brightest luminaries. Hiss, who had long been suspected of spying for Moscow in the 1930's, was subsequently convicted of perjury. When Dulles became secretary of state, his earlier sponsorship of Hiss was undoubtedly nagging at his soul. Whatever the source, his approach to the personnel security issue that was already tearing the State Department apart, had an ambivalence that became recognizable as central to the Dulles political style.

The Postwar Security Climate

After four years in the wartime Navy, I had come into the pre-Dulles State Department in 1946 in a junior capacity, to a bureau headed by that same tall, charming diplomat named Alger Hiss. By 1953, it was as clear to me as it was to Mr. Dulles that Hiss had not only lied under oath, but had doubtlessly passed classified US documents to Moscow during the 1930's as charged (a fact confirmed when Soviet GRU files were later opened).

Hiss left for the Carnegie Endowment job while Dean Acheson was still Secretary of State in the Truman administration. He was succeeded in the State Department job by a mid-level Pentagon and State Department official named Dean Rusk, who would later become this country's second longest-serving secretary of state (Thomas Jefferson held the record). Rusk's first act was to request that the staff be subject to a fresh security check. Indeed, forever after friends and neighbors of anyone who had worked in Hiss's Bureau of Special Political Affairs would be incessantly grilled about personal habits, tastes, and assorted eccentricities.

My first assignment during the Acheson regime had been to help find specialists around Washington who could be readily "seconded" to help the new United Nations set up shop in New York. A couple of my finds turned out to be ex-Communists, although I had no way of knowing that. The truly bizarre thing was that when it all hit the fan a couple of years later, I was asked to investigate what had happened. I went back over my files and concluded that I was (in Senator Leverett Saltonstall's classic malapropism) clean as Caesar's wife. I received an urgent call on New Year's Eve to report my findings without delay to the secretary of state. Early on New Year's Day, the always-elegant Dean Acheson greeted me in his fancy Georgetown home huddled in a wool bathrobe. It seems the heating system had conked out. But my report appeared to do the job.

One of our chores was to put together the US delegation to the annual UN General Assembly session. This year's list included Eleanor Roosevelt. She was already the American delegate to the UN Commission on Human Rights, and at the time probably the most respected woman in the world. I received a call from security that "a problem had arisen" with Mrs. Roosevelt's security clearance over her association with some leftists, and would we please withdraw the request for clearance.

Dean Rusk, normally unflappable, lost his cool when I reported this call, and I accompanied him when he stormed over to security headquarters. When the State Department cops told him that Mrs. Roosevelt might be a security risk, Dean blew up, informing them in no uncertain terms that Eleanor Roosevelt was simply too big for garbage of this kind. Needless to say, she served the United States delegation with distinction.

Dean Rusk played a significant role as my own personal "counter-Dulles," including awarding me a grant to finish my doctorate when he headed the Rockefeller Foundation. He could not have been more different from Dulles. Born and raised dirt-poor in rural Georgia, he was balding, ramrod straight, politically liberal, possessed of a sharp intelligence and courteous to a fault. Intensely loyal and private, he swore never to write a typical Washington kiss-and-tell memoir, or to remove any papers when he left. The result was that the writings he did leave behind are rather dull and uninformative. When John F. Kennedy was elected President in 1960, he had barely met Rusk. But when a Kennedy staffer named Fred Holborn solicited names from the foreign affairs community, virtually everyone recommended Dean Rusk.

Sadly for his reputation, Dean Rusk is largely remembered for remaining unrepentant on the merits of the Vietnam War in which, as secretary of state to both Kennedy and Johnson, he had played a leading part. I remained his defender on all other counts, for three reasons. As head of the Rockefeller Foundation, he made it possible for frustrated State Department planners like me to upgrade their academic credentials. When the Dulles State Department became intolerable and I bailed out, he helped me revive some policy ideas Dulles had blocked by persuading me to lob them over the parapet via *Foreign Affairs* magazine, to which the top command invariably paid close attention. Last but not least, he was at my wedding.

THE McCARTHY MIASMA

The junior Senator from Wisconsin, a world-class bully named Joseph McCarthy, was at the height of his power when John Foster Dulles took command of the Department in 1953. McCarthy had famously said in Wheeling, West Virginia on February 9, 1950: "I have here in my hand a list of 205 — a list of names that were made known to the secretary of state as being members of the Communist party and who nevertheless are still working and shaping policy in the State Department." No one ever saw the list, and so far as I knew no Communist party members were found in the Department. But these wild allegations seemed to paralyze the leadership, setting the tone for an increasingly paranoid climate in which to do the nation's business.

For those who have forgotten, the domestic polemics of that era centered on the question "Who lost China?" and its implied corollary "I bet it was you, you traitor." China was of course never ours to lose. But some Americans had in fact sold out to Moscow, and in 1947 President Truman had established the Loyalty Review Board. As a result, life in the Cold War environment prominently featured security clearances and loyalty checks.

Tightened security was not an unreasonable precaution, since it was becoming clear to anyone who read the cables and intelligence reports, or even the newspapers, that the humorless thugs running the Soviet Union constituted a hostile force bent on destabilizing the world outside their expanding empire and damaging American interests wherever they could. If the McCarthyites had not whipped up so much overblown and destructive hysteria, one would have openly cheered the efforts to extract the few bad apples from sensitive positions. But official Washington was so nervous that its security apparatus went into overdrive, and sometimes ran out of control. Dulles had certainly done his homework on the nature of Soviet Communism. But he cynically exaggerated the threat, and in the process succeeded in making the department an increasingly unpleasant place to work.

When the much-publicized security cases of diplomats John Paton Davies and John Carter Vincent came to his desk, Dulles personally reviewed them. These two unfortunates had reported from the American embassy in wartime China that Chiang Kai-shek's nationalist regime was corrupt, while Mao's communists seemed well organized, had popular support, and would probably take over — which they did in 1949. Having been attached to the OSS in Shanghai in late 1945, that seemed to me a pretty realistic reading of the situation.

Dulles's solution in those two cases was to go for the moral double whammy. First, he concluded that in neither case could a finding of disloyalty or breach of security be substantiated. But the right wing, which saw everywhere a conspiracy that had brought down our Chinese ally, wanted those two heads on a platter. Dulles, according to biographer Louis L. Gerson, had vowed: "I'm not going to be caught with another Alger Hiss on my hands." Presumably he had this in mind when he dismissed Vincent from the Foreign Service on the ground that his professional judgment failed "to meet the standard which is demanded" of a Foreign Service Officer of his experience — without ever defining that standard. As for Davies, he underwent nine separate security investigations before a panel was found that called him a security risk. Even then, Dulles changed the language and fired Davies "for disregard of proper forbearance and caution in making known his dissents outside privileged boundaries," whatever that meant.

Another factor that made serving in the Dulles State Department such a joy was his naming of a minor-league McCarthy by the name of Robert Walter Scott McLeod to head up personnel security. I met him the day he reported in and found him pleasant and jokey. But McLeod's notion of humor also ran to telling an audience of Republican women with a chuckle that "not all New Dealers are necessarily security risks." It says something about the thick cloud of suspicion in the building that, even though my head told me my own record was bullet-proof, the search-and-destroy approach to personnel management sent a frisson of fear through the rest of me.

DULLES AND THE BIG-TICKET ITEMS

Dulles's predecessor Dean Acheson, according to biographer James Chace, wrote that Dulles's central flaw was "the ultimate sin [of] sanctimonious self-righteousness which . . . beclouds the dangers and opportunities of our time with an unctuous film." Dulles seemed given to grandiose public rhetoric that was taken seriously by others, but frequently followed by inaction, repudiation, or indignant denial — what some might call hypocrisy.

That tendency was illustrated by his clarion calls in the early 1950s for "liberation" of Soviet-dominated Eastern Europe through a strategy of "rollback." "America," he intoned, "wants and expects liberation to occur." There was some lawyerly fine print about hopefully achieving those goals bloodlessly. But thousands of Hungarian patriots never saw the fine print, and believed that our great democracy would help them throw off their shackles as we had helped European resistance movements during World War II. When in October, 1956 push came to shove and the Hungarians were bloodily crushed by Soviet tanks in the streets of Budapest, Dulles lost no time in assuring Moscow, in a speech in Dallas, that the US had no intention of getting in its way.

Another example was a January, 1954 speech spelling out his famous doctrine of "Massive Retaliation." Dulles argued that the free world needed "the means to retaliate instantly against open aggression by Red armies" so we could "strike back where it hurts, by means of our choosing." Most people thought Dulles had in mind a new strategy of deterrence based on a threat to respond to aggression, not locally with limited means, but by going after the family jewels with an all-out blow that could presumably include vaporizing Moscow. He thought that by making new threats excessively costly, the new doctrine would keep the Soviets and China from running dangerous risks.

Massive Retaliation responded to a major itch the Eisenhower administration was determined to scratch, namely the frustrating and expensive notion of limited war on the model of Korea. That bloody conflict, which they were now calling "Truman's War," was burying all too many US servicemen. The new Republican leaders feared being nibbled to death globally by Soviet salami tactics of one slice at a time, so to speak. Massive Deterrence through Massive Retaliation seemed a nifty solution

The Dulles fix soon proved to be unbelievable, as the inner contradictions became apparent of a proposal that would, in the words of Dulles biographer Townsend Hoopes: "transform the awesome nuclear capability from an instrument of last resort to one of first resort." First, that's not the way American decision-makers in fact acted in such subsequent crises as Berlin and Cuba. Second, until Afghanistan in 1979, that's also not the way Moscow normally acted outside its empire, preferring subversion, end-runs, and "indirect aggression" through proxies. And third, the Soviet nuclear capability

Testifying before Senate Foreign Relations Committee with the Genetically-Engineered Secretary of State: (left to right) Dulles, Key, and me.

would grow to the point where what we would be saying was "if you make trouble anywhere, I'm going to commit suicide." The concept was attacked by critics as dangerous rhetoric.

Later in 1954, I chanced to hear Dulles repudiate his own doctrine. A journalist named Walter Millis, who had written an influential book called *Road to War* about the catastrophic run-up to World War I, challenged the new doctrine's logic in the now-defunct *New York Herald-Tribune*. He did so on the day the Senate Foreign Relations Committee was to hold hearings on the issue of UN Charter review, for which I was the Department's action officer. Secretary Dulles was to be the chief witness, backed by Assistant Secretary for UN affairs David McKay Key and myself.

In his limo en route to Capitol Hill, Dulles was fuming. "Walter Millis totally misunderstood me," he grumbled. "Of course I didn't mean that we would use our A-bombs on Moscow if the Sovs attacked anywhere." The appropriate response would have been, "Well just exactly what *did* you mean, because that's what everyone thought you said." Key stayed discreetly silent. But since I have trouble handling embarrassing silences, I probably told the secretary that it was a brilliant concept. When we got to the Hill, Dulles, unsurpassed in both knowledge and arrogance, never once turned to his assistant secretary (or, needless to say, me).

RETHINKING THE UN

As the 1950s wore on, I managed to move into policy work and out from under the administrative cone, where my last chore had been to get rid of an employee who did large amounts of laundry in the ladies room while denouncing the rest of us as communists. As policy planner for the UN bureau, I was supposed to think, which in most eyes meant that I really didn't do anything useful. Indeed, the reaction of crisis-driven desk officers to policy planners resembled that of my children when they saw me reading the *New York Times*: "Daddy isn't doing anything, so he can come out and play with us." The grown-up version was "Linc isn't doing anything, so let's get him to draft cables on the Middle East crisis."

My view of Secretary Dulles remained strictly worm's-eye. But a few episodes provide a first-hand glimpse of the sometimes-conflicted Dulles persona. Article 109 of the United Nations Charter called for a conference by 1955 to review and possibly amend that document. I was then assigned to do some thinking on the subject, although it was clear that, with the shrinkage of America's so-called automatic majority in the UN, reexamining the Charter might open a Pandora's box.

On August 26, 1953, Secretary Dulles gave a major speech to the American Bar Association on the need for Charter revision. Hopes for the Charter, he said, required that it "be altered in some important respects." One of those respects was the great-power veto in the Security Council, which Moscow had been exploiting. His rhetorical climax was a call to America's lawyers, at the time numbering approximately 220,000, to "inventively and creatively try to solve the great problems." The following week he expanded the list of those who should advise him on changing the Charter to include "private bodies — educational bodies, religious bodies, bar associations and the like — all should be studying this problem."

The American private sector, thrilled to be assigned such a high-minded task, promptly inundated the department with phone calls, memoranda, and letters (mercifully, faxes and e-mail had not yet been invented). The obvious place to dump this growing mountain of communications was the Bureau of International Organization Affairs, specifically on my desk.

My immediate boss at the time (they changed with startling frequency) was Robert Murphy, then the most senior of the professional American Foreign Service Officers. I had first heard of him when the story broke of his clandestine 1942 landing on the North African coast, a story worth recalling in an age when Washington micro-manages field operations. Murphy was offloaded from a submarine, and put ashore in a rubber dinghy to make his way through French forces loyal to the Nazi-backed Vichy regime. His mission was to rendezvous with Admiral Robert Darlan, commander of French forces in Africa, with the objective of cutting a deal that would minimize Allied casualties in the forthcoming Allied landings in Algeria and Tunisia.

This seemingly sensible bargain ran into the historic American discomfort with the tension between morality and *realpolitik* in foreign policy. When the Murphy mission succeeded, the "Darlan Deal" became known to the American Congress and then became public. The political firestorm was immediate. ("We are fighting a world war of principle, so how dare you cut an immoral deal with the devil?" versus "Don't you understand we are serving a higher morality when we negotiate with the devil to avoid the deaths of thousands of American boys?")

Murphy had just returned from an Ambassadorship to Japan, and was marking time as assistant secretary for UN matters until, as America's first "career ambassador" equivalent to five-star general, he would assume the top professional position of what is now under-secretary of state for political affairs. I reported to him that we were being inundated by battalions of lawyers and non-lawyers responding to Secretary Dulles's call to action. I asked him if he knew what the Secretary had in mind when he gave that speech. Did Mr. Dulles really think we could do away with the veto (which was inserted in the UN Charter as much to ensure ratification by the US Senate as to keep Moscow, London, and Paris on board)? How were we (me) supposed to cope with this incoming flood? Murphy replied "Search me. Let's ask Foster." (I had never before heard anyone refer to the Secretary with that degree of intimacy, and was appropriately dazzled.)

I accompanied him to the august Secretarial Suite. After the usual pleasantries, Murphy asked me to put the questions. I couldn't very well say what was on my mind. ("How dare you launch this nutty public campaign on a matter I happen to be working on without consulting me?") Instead I asked the secretary if he could elaborate on his most intriguing point concerning the great-power veto in the Security Council, which thousands of Americans were starting to reexamine at his request.

Dulles fixed me with his usual look of disgust, chewing the lower left corner of his face with vigor. "Of course we can't do anything about the veto. I mean, we certainly don't want the UN coming in to investigate McCarthyism, do we?" My gut response was instantaneous: "You hypocritical son-of-a-bitch, I quit right here and now." Actually, I didn't say a word while digesting this extraordinary response. Instead, I returned to my modest office to search for ways of transforming the Dulles triple-axel double-looping half-gainer into soothing bureaucratic boiler-plate that would leave me blameless, if corrupted.

Early the following year, word came down that the secretary wanted a new look taken at the US role in the whole UN system in the light of changing circumstances, including the growing intake of what would eventually become about 120 new member states, few of which were likely to join America's so-called "mechanical majority." A department-wide committee was tasked to come up with a fresh strategic concept in the realm of multilateral diplomacy, and I was made its executive secretary. At last, I rejoiced, a genuine policy planning endeavor, unhampered by old thinking and open to new ideas.

Or so I believed. Six months later, after endless meetings to debate drafts which I had prepared, we came up with an agreed document. Even discounting pride of authorship, I thought it contained a sound analysis of the changing situation, along with an innovative set of recommendations for US policy adjustments. The document, with accompanying executive summary, was sent to the secretary for his consideration.

My boss (yes, another one) Assistant Secretary Francis O. Wilcox and I trotted upstairs with high hopes of commendation for a major task well done. When we were seated in the sanctum sanctorum, Dulles looked up with his customary if unintended sneer, and with the requisite lip-biting, he waved my precious composition in our faces. "No, no, no," he said dismissively. "I didn't want this. What I wanted was a gimmick to put in my speech to the UN General Assembly this fall." Fran Wilcox had seen enough dysfunctional behavior from long service as chief of staff of the Senate Foreign Relations Committee to "know when to hold 'em and when to fold 'em." But the action officer who had just devoted six months to the project made a mental note to launch a vigorous outside job search.

THE LAST STRAW: THE SUEZ CRISIS

Any thought of jumping ship had to be put on hold as the 1956 crisis mounted over Egyptian President Nasser's takeover of the French/British-owned and operated Suez Canal. What made the case particularly ulcerous was the implied threat by France and Britain to wage war on Egypt if peaceful settlement efforts failed to reverse Nasser's action. I seemed to be the only one who believed they were serious, although others began to wonder when they noticed the Brits and French (and Israelis, who had their own agenda) starting to withhold from us their normal flow of contacts and information.

In the midst of the mounting crisis, a hopeful intelligence report came in suggesting that a nervous Egypt might agree to adjudication of the dispute by the World Court. A colleague and I prepared a paper recommending that the possibility be urgently explored by the secretary. Dulles, who was noted for preaching the rule of law, rejected the legal track out of hand on the grounds that someone might try to apply it to the Panama Canal.

In early November, 1956, after the attack on Egypt (which came in the midst of Moscow's brutal Hungarian invasion), President Eisenhower, furious with his allies, forced London, Paris, and Tel Aviv to back off. With Israel profoundly shaken and Egypt flat on its back, there seemed a chance for the first time since the initial Arab-Israeli War of 1948 to come to grips with the core issues: borders, recognition, waterways, refugees, and the rest. I was one-third of a task force working in the Department's Policy Planning Staff till the wee hours to devise concrete proposals building on that possibility.

Secretary Dulles, having meanwhile disappeared to his retreat on Duck Island in Canada, returned clutching a draft embodying his solution for the Arab-Israeli conflict. It soon became the "Eisenhower Doctrine"—a plan to counter military aggression in the Middle East "backed by international communism," with nary a word about the issues driving the Arab-Israeli conflict. When US Ambassador to Moscow Charles ("Chip") Bohlen, heard that Dulles was focusing the US effort entirely on Soviet aggression, he fired off a series of urgent cables to Washington. He explained that of all the things that might happen in the region and of all conceivable Soviet moves, the least likely contingency was a Soviet-sponsored invasion of the Middle East.

With all due respect, Dulles, like British Prime Minister Anthony Eden who had planned the Suez War, was quite ill. But it was also a classic example of an ideological mindset overriding reality. It was also the last straw for one disillusioned 36-year-old idealist who was raised to believe in American virtue, trusted its leaders to do the right thing, and tried to serve both Democratic and Republican administrations, despite their respective idiocies, with the belief that civil servants could and should be non-partisan. After sixteen crisis-riddled years in and out of uniform, I was burned out and ready to accept MIT's offer to run a research project. But I never regretted my experience in that hopeful, but nerve-wracking post-war Foggy Bottom.

3 BUREAUCRACY III: 1979–80
The Atmosphere Gets Rarified

1968: A POLITICAL EXCURSION

There is a reason why my various forays into government service appear here under the rubric of "bureaucracy" rather than "politics." Every four years, many professors stand by in Cambridge, Massachusetts with bags packed, ready to help the successful candidate and hope to turn their scholarly writings into policy. Apart from being a political independent, I never was particularly attracted to partisan politics. But I did have one brief fling with a sort-of-Republican presidential candidate, courtesy of Henry Kissinger, that expanded my education about the political process.

When Henry Kissinger served as national security adviser and secretary of state, he became controversial to the point of being declared a war criminal by some. When I first encountered the academic culture, an anti-Kissinger virus had already afflicted many of my new brethren. I have to confess that at the time I never had the Kissinger hang-up that beset some of my colleagues, at least some of whom suffered from a terminal case of jealousy. Rather than finding the youthful Harvard professor superficial and dogmatic or, alternately, hopelessly 19th-century, what I saw was an extraordinarily bright and ambitious guy with an enormous store of diplomatic and historical knowledge, a sharp pen, and a mordant wit.

In early 1968, I was surprised to get a call from Kissinger, who was serving as an active consultant to Governor Nelson Rockefeller of New York as the latter prepared for the presidential sweepstakes. Henry flattered me by saying he wanted the governor to get to know me which, needless to say, worked. Shortly thereafter he asked me to draft a speech for Rockefeller on the United Nations and peacekeeping. I did that and got to sit down with New York's feisty liberal Republican governor in his elegant Manhattan townhouse to review what I had written. A few other chores followed, and I became persuaded that Rockefeller spoke for my own indecisively centrist political position.

That summer the Nixon wave swept all before it at the Republican convention in Miami, and it wasn't long before Kissinger took a right turn to become GOP candidate Nixon's principal foreign policy adviser. I gave the matter no further thought until Kissinger and I found ourselves together in England, sharing a car. We were heading from Oxford to Brill for lunch at the home of Alistair Buchan, the phenomenal British journalist-strategist, then head of the International Institute for Strategic Studies whose annual meeting we were attending. During the drive Henry rehashed the recent Rockefeller electoral fiasco, whose inside story, as seen through the Kissinger lens, went something like this:

Rockefeller lost the nomination by about 30 electoral votes. That didn't have to be. One trouble was the way the Rockefeller political staff was organized. They had rigid assignments, and mine was foreign policy. Former Republican Party Chairman Leonard Hall was in charge of rounding up delegates, and when he reported his efforts at our staff meetings, I didn't feel I could speak up. But it became obvious that he was inept, and that I could do just as well, particularly since I knew that some of the delegates were genuinely interested in issues, particularly the women delegates based in the suburbs. I decided to go around to talk to some of them, and to my astonishment picked up five delegate votes for Rockefeller.

Linc, they should have sent us out to talk to the delegates instead of leaving it to the political hacks. The trouble with Nelson is that he always delegates authority and trusts subordinates. As a result, there was no press representation for three days at the convention while Nixon held five press conferences. Now Rockefeller is being touted to be Secretary of State, although I'm not sure he would be very good at it; basically, he's a political leader. Yes, you and I could have made a difference in the outcome.

The author snaps Kissinger with host Alistair Buchan and fellow disputants: future British Defense Secretary Healey and Israeli Deputy Prime Minister Allon in Brill, England.

The lunch at Brill, attended by Israeli Deputy Prime Minister Yigdal Allon and British Defense Minister-to-be Dennis Healy, had one singular event for me. I had played a minor role in the State Department's effort to get the Israelis out of Egypt after their politically calamitous 1956 invasion of Egypt alongside the British and French, all of whom were intent on punishing President Nasser for nationalizing the Suez Canal. As we sat around after lunch, someone mentioned my involvement, and Allon came unglued. He stormed about the study, rattling the demitasse cups as he vented his spleen on the duplicitous Americans, and on me as the only available target among Americans. He held me responsible for selling Israel down the river just when they had Egypt by the short hair, so to speak.

After this encounter, I made a point of following Allon's story. To my pleased surprise, he took the sensible step of including in a *Foreign Affairs* article a map depicting a possible territorial solution between Israelis and Palestinians. His Israeli colleagues were outraged by the so-called Allon Plan, and especially by the map, which they forced him to repudiate. Later, when I was on the National Security Council staff, during one of the chronic Palestinian-Israeli standoffs I tried to get the State Department to draw up a map along the same lines. State recoiled at the idea, so I went outside the system to enlist the best Middle East analyst I knew, former NSC official William Quant, to help make it happen, but left Washington before we could pursue the matter to its conclusion. In any case, I like to think the Brill lunch had had an impact.

WHITE HOUSE YEAR

Service on the National Security Council under President Carter offered a different angle of vision into the themes of governance, rationality in decision-making, and in particular the extraordinary difficulty of doing anything resembling systematic forward planning, if only because the days just weren't long enough. Perhaps the biggest lesson learned was about the geometry of power at the top level, which I try to make sense of in the next chapter.

I had known Carter's National Security Adviser Zbigniew Brzezinski since he was a junior Harvard professor, and later as a member of the State Department's policy planning staff. It still came as a surprise when, in the spring of 1979, the White House operator tracked me down in Geneva where I was a visiting professor on leave from MIT. Since departing State years earlier, I had rejected several offers to return full-time to government service, being entirely content at MIT. I occasionally consulted in Washington but was always able to catch the next plane out of town. The position as NSC Director of Global Issues was different, covering policy questions with which I was deeply concerned. This time, it didn't take much to lure me back inside the Beltway.

Since the gung-ho days of President Kennedy and his proactive staff, the national security adviser has been a potential competitor to the secretary of state. (Thanks to the growing complexity of foreign relations, which at least in theory calls for coordination of co-equal Cabinet officers.) In the Carter administration, it was no contest: power

*With National Security Adviser
Brzezinski outside Oval Office,
the White House.*

had gravitated to the White House, as it had under Kennedy and Nixon, and relations were strained between National Security Advisor Brzezinski and Secretary of State Cyrus Vance.

Zbig Brzezinski was extraordinarily bright, charming, assertive, occasionally flamboyant, and endowed with a mind that easily translated data into coherent strategic concepts. He could readily spin ideas, some of which may have been impractical, but others brilliantly captured the essence of the matter. As a personality type, Cy Vance could not have been more different. Modest and self-effacing, he represented the best of the legal profession in terms of both talent and prudence.

The two men's policy preferences were also widely divergent. As a Polish émigré, Brzezinski was noted for his strong anti-Communism and unbounded suspicion of the Russians. If Brzezinski epitomized the realist school of international politics, Vance was at heart an idealist, deeply committed to the concept of multilateral cooperation, and determined to find common ground with the Soviets, with whom he was endlessly patient.

Since Vance had ended his earlier service as deputy secretary of defense and resumed the practice of law, he had been active in the

Madeleine Albright and Zbigniew Brzezinski at farewell party for the author in Washington, DC.

United Nations Association of the USA, as I was. As members of its US-Soviet Parallel Studies Group, we met often, and traveled together to Moscow several times during the 1970's. There and elsewhere, we and other government in-and-outers, Republicans, Democrats, and independents, had gone to the mat on a dozen occasions with our Soviet counterparts about issues such as arms control and the Middle East, issues on which the two governments were deadlocked.

I was then a good deal closer to Vance than to Brzezinski. Soon after the former became secretary of state in 1977, he and his policy planning chief Anthony Lake (later to be President Clinton's national security adviser) adopted a scheme I was pushing, (and unfortunately aborted for lack of funds), to improve State's policy planning capacity. When the White House call came in Geneva, I phoned Tony Lake to find out whether Vance would have any problems with my surfacing in the NSC camp. Vance charmingly sent back word that my presence in Washington might improve the atmosphere.

The side-benefits of my NSC tour were working with some old friends and making new ones, such as future Secretary of State Madeleine Albright, who liaised with the Congress for the NSC and played a nice game of tennis. The chemistry between me and the

Deputy NSA David Aaron turned out to be less than marvelous, so instead I worked with Ambassador-at-Large, Henry Owen, a college classmate and a pal since the age of ten.

Once again, as in State, public service proved to be enormously fulfilling. It was fascinating to be at the center of decision-making instead of the fringe. I loved the job, which gave me the feeling of actually accomplishing something tangible on matters that had been high on my own agenda. My portfolio was unrealistically long, embracing human rights policy, UN problems, refugees, Law of the Sea Treaty negotiations and a bunch of other things. I was supposed to act as policy coordinator in general, proactive policy initiator when appropriate, and White House representative on inter-agency committees.

As it had been in State but at a higher level, my work was driven by the pressure of immediate events, confirming that long-range planning isn't going to be done in either the State Department or the White House. The first piece of evidence was that, within a week of being sworn in and before I could organize my contacts and agenda, I was on Air Force Two heading back to Geneva to support Vice-President Mondale at an emergency United Nations session. It was to cope with the "boat people" who were flooding out of Communist Vietnam by the hundreds of thousands and washing up on the shores of unhappy neighboring Southeast Asian countries.

In addition, the growing threat of famine in Cambodia required the urgent raising of large sums of both public and private money, and equally urgent efforts to ensure that donated food got to the people in Cambodia rather than to either the Vietnamese occupying army or what was left of the murderous Pol Pot . There was a US coordinator for refugee affairs (first, ex-Senator Dick Clark, then Victor Palmieri), and an assistant secretary of state (Frank Loy) who had the primary operational responsibility. But the President's deep concern, plus the First Lady's personal involvement, meant that the responsible White House staff person had to coordinate the coordinators.

I spent as much time as I could over the next several months focusing on problems arising with the funding, coordination, and delivery of food to the starving Cambodians. I had also nagged the US Information Agency to publicize the massive humanitarian disasters being caused by the Soviets and their buddies in creating huge refugee populations fleeing Communist rule in Southeast Asia, Afghanistan, Cuba, and Ethiopia.

I found the effort enormously rewarding, but it had some ugly moments. Columnist Mary McGrory (sadly gone now) had greeted my appointment with a friendly column, and invited me to a party at her home where I joined columnist Mark Shields and the Irish ambassador in singing Irish ballads. But soon afterwards she wrote a column denouncing me for supporting Pol Pot, having evidently listened to peddlers of a conspiracy charging the NSC and State Department with sabotaging the First Lady's humanitarian efforts.

I shared their view that the administration had for too long blocked the Cambodian UN seat from being occupied by the new Vietnam-supported Cambodian government, which arguably had rid the country of rule by the bloody Khmer Rouge. Washington's insistence on non-recognition rested, not on the merits, but on the 1979 invasion of Cambodia by Vietnam, which not coincidentally had badly humiliated the US a few years earlier. The unintended result was to give the appearance of US support for Pol Pot, which was entirely untrue, as was the imagined internal face-off between white hats and black hats. I canvassed the key players around town to see if a policy change was possible, but it clearly was not.

Whatever individual views may have been in some agencies, the point was that the US government—including the NSC, State, and First Lady—was mobilized for the common purpose of feeding the hungry population there, or what was left of it after Pol Pot's butchery. In the effort, we had the active help of many non-governmental leaders, not to mention that delightful folk singer Joan Baez, who saw the situation more clearly than many.

The rest of my agenda also had to be dealt with. Another classmate, Ambassador-at-Large Elliott Richardson, was chief US negotiator for the UN Law of the Sea Treaty, which suddenly became a White House problem. Even before the 1981 Reagan team could put the knife into the treaty, the project faced enemies in the domestic right-wing and in Congress.

Even in the Carter administration, the treaty didn't have many enthusiasts beside me and Deputy Secretary of State (later Secretary) Warren Christopher. The budget director was leery of anything that

With President Carter, Joan Baez, and NSC press officer in the Oval Office,
the White House.

antagonized Congress, and I suspect that some of President Carter's
fellow Georgians in the White House found Boston Brahmin Richardson
a kind of alien life form. It fell to me to help Elliott steer this shaky
vessel through hostile political and bureaucratic shoal waters. Henry
Owen and I managed to keep it afloat, but only by a whisker.

UN policy was normally handled by the international organization bureau in State. But occasionally something hit the fan and rico-
cheted in my direction. On one occasion, Mrs. Carter's office became
concerned with laxity in the State Department's preparations for US
participation in the 1980 Copenhagen UN Conference on Women, and
I wound up chairing meetings in the East Wing of the White House of
the main action officers, who stubbornly refused to believe in predictions that the proceedings were likely to be corrupted by unrelated
poison pills such as the status of Jerusalem. As our fears were realized
during the conference, I took numerous early morning calls, usually
in my shower, from our delegates in Copenhagen.

Indeed, the Middle East was always good for a White House
flap, particularly when the pro-Israeli lobby got worried. On one occasion State okayed an Arab-Soviet bloc UN resolution aimed at dis-
couraging governments from moving their embassies from Tel Aviv
to Jerusalem. But Congress had voted to move our own embassy to

Jerusalem. Even though the executive branch was not going to touch the third-rail issue of Jerusalem, I had to chase down our UN people in their limos in New York in order to change State's sensible action.

On another occasion, Ambassador Andrew Young, who represented the United States at the UN in New York with great flair, fell afoul of policy when he met with the PLO representative in New York (this was before terrorist Arafat, at least for a while, became partner Arafat). Andy Young compounded his mistake by lying about it, and the upshot was that he had to leave his post. I was the designated hand-holder, and accompanied him and his successor Ambassador Don McHenry around the Washington circuit to say his goodbyes. I don't know if it made him feel better or worse when I tried to console him with the story of the 19th-century southern senator who, accused of misstating the facts, rose to intone that "a lie is an abomination unto the Lord—and an ever-present help in time of need."

The atmosphere changed drastically when, on December 27, 1979 the Soviet Union invaded Afghanistan. President Carter had to eat his earlier vow not to pay much attention to the Soviets. The whole

An unprofessional moment with classmate Elliot Richardson at the American Embassy, London.

At work in the White House.

national security apparatus, already stretched by the protracted Iranian hostage-taking of the US Embassy in Teheran, went into overdrive, and for a while I was occupied with helping mobilize international support for US actions on both fronts.

I still had the richly carpeted office in what was still called the Old Executive Office Building across the driveway from the White House, complete with red phone, marble fireplace, and balcony overlooking the West Wing. I still felt that I was doing needful things, and enjoyed the occasional face time with the always courteous and unpretentious president (another plus for Brzezinski who, unlike Kissinger, had no problem with letting his senior staff interact with the real boss). But alas, the joy was gone, and the worry lines again on the brow as relations with the only other power capable of destroying the planet went back into the tank. Some government offices may have been filled with shirkers, and some agencies should have expired under a sunset law. But I really believe that, at least where I worked, the taxpayers got their money's worth.

4 BUREAUCRACY IV: 1945–2005
The Triangular Foreign Policy Machine

AN ILLUSTRATED THUMBNAIL HISTORY

In an effort to learn more about the actual "geometry of power" within the US government, I looked at the way American presidents have dealt with foreign policy decision-making, and came up with a couple of striking conclusions. Historically, the basic geometric shape in running foreign policy has been a triangle, composed of the president, the secretary of state, and the national security adviser. I also found that every modern US administration has seen a different power relationship among those three top players.

In rare instances the triangle has become a quadrangle, and even a, well, pentagon. The latter certainly characterized the first George W. Bush administration, in which the vice president played an unprecedentedly potent role, and—as happened once before in the Kennedy administration—the secretary of defense succeeded in grabbing a major piece of the foreign policy pie. But in a longer view of history, the policymaking drama over the last half century centers on that core triangle, as can be seen with a brisk gallop through the previous eleven administrations.

It's not a long history. The National Security Council was invented in 1947, along with a staff to coordinate paper flow. The national security adviser (NSA) was formally hatched in 1953 with the title of Assistant to the President for National Security Affairs. The NSA concept is relatively new, but competitive behavior at the top is

51

not. Thomas Jefferson was at odds with Vice-President Aaron Burr; Abraham Lincoln often struggled with his ambitious Secretary of State, William Seward; and Franklin Roosevelt increasingly ignored *his* and dealt directly with fellow Ivy-Leaguer UnderSecretary of State Sumner Welles.

The basic geometry of foreign policy decision-making in the Executive Branch comes in a variety of forms, each with a mix of— for simplicity—"strong" and "weak." Simplicity also dictates two basic models. Under my Model A, activist or strong (S) presidents prefer a submissive or weak (W) secretary of state, along with a potent (S) NSA to enforce the presidential will. Conversely, Model B features a less asser- tive White House, a muscular secretary of state, and a relatively invisible NSA. This isn't math, but in a nutshell, in Model A, $P^S = NSA^S + S^W$, But in Model B, $P^W = NSA^W + S^S$, both of course, with occasional varia- tions. How do these models square with the facts?

Harry Truman was a simple man, but a better president than comparisons with his predecessor Franklin Roosevelt made it seem. However, because he lacked the usual Washington quotient of ego, he not only tolerated but positively encouraged two potent secretaries of state—the towering World War II Army Chief of Staff General George C. Marshall, and the formidably mustachioed, and brainy, Dean Acheson. According to a 1930's report, White House assistants were supposed to have a "passion for anonymity." Today this is a joke. But who can name the first proto-National Security Adviser (Sidney Souers)? The Truman trio looks like an early Model B (except when Edward Stettinius and James F. Byrnes briefly ran State).

Dwight Eisenhower, like Truman, was also sharper than appeared to the naked eye. As a former army general, however, he was accus- tomed to delegating authority. Secretary of State John Foster Dulles (though not his successor Christian Herter) was determined to domi- nate the foreign policy machinery, repelling all boarders with his sharp bureaucratic cutlass. His clout was illustrated for me when, as a junior State Department apparatchik, I had to move out so top arms control negotiator (and presidential candidate) Harold Stassen could squeeze into my little office as part of his punishment for upstaging Dulles in Geneva. Again, does anyone know the names of Eisenhower's Model B NSAs? (Robert Cutler, Dillon Anderson, Gordon Gray).

The year 1961 changed everything. A sucking sound was heard as both policy-making and information flowed unimpeded into John F. Kennedy's White House vortex. Secretary of State Dean Rusk let it be known that his goal was to "get foreign policy off the front pages." That reflected Rusk's modesty and unencumbered personality. But it was clearly not the aim of either the new president or his youthful, glandular staff.

Harvard Dean McGeorge Bundy had been recommended to Kennedy as perhaps the brightest person in the United States, which may have been close to true. Bundy presided over a new Situation Room complex in the West Wing basement, eventually complete with global communications, video conferencing, computers, printers, secure fax machines and other real-time machinery to ensure that never again would the White House have to wait for State, Defense, and CIA to decide what crises deserved top-level attention. The effect was a powerful boost to Model A.

In a rare exception, Kennedy's Pentagon acted often as the fourth, even the third corner of the top policy triangle, thanks to the high-voltage of Secretary of Defense Robert McNamara and Assistant Secretary Paul Nitze. Deputy NSA Walt Whitman Rostow confided plaintively: "We want State to take responsibility, but we can't get them to do it." Model A with a DOD asterisk was the clear winner.

It would be difficult to find anyone more hands-on than Lyndon Baines Johnson or his national security advisers Bundy and Rostow. Secretary of State Dean Rusk, whose paradigm of behavior was General Marshall, but without Marshall's enormous personal authority, remained a baffling, Buddha-like figure to the White House activists. A Model A once again had no real competition.

In the first Richard Nixon administration, the president and his NSA Henry Kissinger set out to dominate the national security apparatus. A cat's cradle of interagency committees was established, with NSA Kissinger chairing every one of them. Despite President-elect Nixon's earlier declaration that Harvard Professor Kissinger would operate quietly in the background, a media star was also born.

During the Nixon years, an underweight State Department decided to set up its own gaggle of advisory committees. As an MIT professor, I was appointed to one of them. Secretary of State William Rogers hosted a lunch for the members, and I was seated next to him. I was astonished to note his deep tan and unlined visage, which stood out among his whey-faced staff. It was public knowledge that he was being systematically excluded from the top table by the White House, and went home early. The sensible "Rogers Plan" for the Middle East in 1971 was one of his few attempts to escape from his gilded policy cage, and Kissinger relates in his memoirs how that plan was quickly squashed. Henry also confesses to mistreating Rogers, thus managing to enjoy both sin and confession. In Nixon I, Model A was ascendant.

That was pre-Watergate. In 1973, the post-Watergate Nixon appointed Kissinger secretary of state. For a while, the latter also managed to hang on to the NSA position, leaving his deputy, retired Air Force Lieutenant General Brent Scowcroft (later to be NSA to both Ford and Bush I), to manage things in the West Wing basement (the NSA now occupies a splendid first floor corner office). But the Nixon II geometric figure changed from Model A to B when, thanks to the web of deceit in which the Oval Office was entangled, we suddenly had a weak president, an NSA without sharp elbows, and a stronger-than-ever secretary of state.

President Gerald Ford, a decent man lacking an outsized ego, was America's only appointed president. For these and other reasons he relied on Secretary Kissinger. Brent Scowcroft was Ford's NSA, and the State-dominated Model B still ruled.

The Jimmy Carter administration saw the re-emergence of Model A, with a president engaged to the point of extensive marginal comments on papers that percolated upward. NSA Zbigniew Brzezinski, like Kissinger brilliant and articulate, quickly dominated the process. Secretary of State Cyrus Vance didn't throw in the towel as Rogers had under Nixon. But he was out-pointed (as was his short-term successor Edmund Muskie). In 1980, Vance did what few cabinet officers do when they feel stiffed on policy. He resigned over the Iran hostage rescue effort, against a background of prior indignities and frustrations. Sadly gone now, Cy Vance represented that *rara avis,* an uncomplicated man of principle.

Brzezinski, being a gentleman, treated Vance with courtesy, but believed that only he had what it took to formulate the big strategic concepts, which he largely did. Vance, also being a gentleman, forbore to complain publicly. Early in my NSC service, as Brzezinski, his staff assistant, and I were showering in a West Wing locker room after a tennis game, Zbig was going to have trouble finding time to appear on a Sunday talk show, then, as now, the prime weekly spot to spin policy. When I innocently suggested that Vance undertake the chore, the look from the other two naked bureaucrats spoke volumes about my naiveté.

The Ronald W. Reagan Administration is harder to analyze, given its parade of NSAs (Richard Allen, William Clark, Robert McFarlane, John Poindexter, Colin Powell, and Frank Carlucci), under a president disengaged from the details of policy. After an unedifying start with Secretary of State Alexander Haig, Jr., the decision-making model became even murkier with Irangate, when NSAs McFarlane and Poindexter cut state and defense secretaries out of major decision-making with the seeming assent of an inattentive president (Model A minus?). When the dust of scandal had settled over a weakened presidency, Secretary of State George Shultz played a somewhat stronger hand, producing a kind of Model B minus.

President George H.W. Bush brought Brent Scowcroft back as NSA, and James Baker was a strong secretary of state. But given Bush I's long experience in foreign affairs as well as Scowcroft's, the balance was narrowly tilted back toward Model A White House primacy, particularly after Lawrence Eagleburger replaced Baker at State.

The Bill Clinton administration presented the unusual spectacle of a triangle in which, for a time, none of the three was proactive. The President chose not to focus on foreign policy other than trade issues, despite campaign rhetoric foretelling drastic changes in China and Balkans policy. His first NSA was the self-effacing Anthony Lake, in the Scowcroft rather than the Kissinger mold (Tony Lake had in fact resigned from Kissinger's NSC staff in 1970 over the bombing of Cambodia). Secretary of State Warren Christopher, who had served as Vance's Deputy in the 1970's, was a fine, cautious lawyer, even more unassertive than Vance.

When the lively, outspoken Madeleine Albright took over from Christopher, it looked as if State might get out in front. But as Clinton became more involved in Middle East and Northern Ireland diplomacy, and the US had to manage military attacks in the Gulf, Bosnia, and Kosovo, his sturdy NSA Samuel "Sandy" Berger put the White House once more in charge.

*With Secretary of State
Powell, State Department
in Washington, DC.*

George W. Bush's first secretary of state was the universally-admired Colin Powell. In terms of primacy in the foreign policy realm, the presumption was leadership from State, given a poorly-informed president and an articulate but little known national security adviser.

The atmosphere changed dramatically after the 9/11 terrorist attack, which supplied Bush with the focus and drive he had lacked. A clique of hawkish ideologues had moved from think-tanks to the offices of Secretary of Defense Donald Rumsfeld and Vice President Dick Cheney. They proved influential with the President, and they voraciously ate the lunch, so to speak, of the State Department as they pushed to invade Iraq and transform the Middle East.

Bush's decision to hand the Iraq car keys to the persuasive Defense Secretary enabled Rumsfeld to brush aside the careful postwar planning done by State and other agencies that would have supplied a far more realistic view of the problems of occupying Iraq. Such costly Pentagon power-grabs did not have to happen if National Security

Adviser Condoleezza Rice had exercised her critical coordinating role toward the clashing bureaucracies. She actually chaired the so-called Principals' Committee on which both Rumsfeld and Powell sat. But pending her memoirs, one can only guess how she felt bringing Mr. Rumsfeld to heel would be punching well above her weight.

By the time Bush's first term ended, Powell had won some small victories including a White House forced by the chaos of postwar Iraq to try to recover from its earlier disdain for the UN, traditional allies, and world opinion. But Powell remained the odd man out, and my model "A" had dominated, at considerable diplomatic, financial, and human costs.

Bush's second term resembled Nixon's in making National Security Adviser Rice Secretary of State and upgrading the deputy national security adviser (Stephen Hadley) to Rice's position. But unlike the second Nixon term, the presidency was not fatally weakened, nor was a powerful Secretary of State left to run foreign policy by default. George W. Bush was not in disgrace, and Condoleezza Rice was no Kissinger. The model continued to be "A"—White House domination of foreign policy—with the same asterisk denoting the unprecedented potency of the vice president.

A footnote on secrecy in the White House. Revelations in the 1980's told of covert operations literally managed in the NSC by gung-ho staffer Marine Lieutenant Colonel Oliver North (now a right-wing darling and talk show host). I was astonished at how such things could be kept secret from fellow NSC staffers, not to mention the *New York Times* and/or *Washington Post,* which can reliably be counted on to reveal a good deal of what government insiders deem classified. As has been said, the US Ship of State is the only vessel known to leak from the top, and the president is often the main source of leakage. Cabinet officers occasionally try to undermine one another by airing their arguments via friendly journalists, and some of my fellow NSC staffers also used the press to try to win internal arguments.

Leaks aside, it would have been harder to run a clandestine operation from the Brzezinski NSC. He used an excellent device that added to the workload of overloaded directors of the so-called "clusters," but provided a healthy degree of transparency. After every workday, no matter how late at night, we dictated an "Evening Report" covering the main events of the day. The collected reports were on his—and our—desks the next morning, along with the National Intelligence Daily, NSA intercepts, and urgent overnight cables. The Reagan administration might have saved itself much woe if it had followed the practice so decisively abandoned when it took office.

Another footnote: I am convinced that no one under the age of 35 should be allowed to breathe what President Clinton's youthful right-hand man George Stephanopoulos referred to in his memoir as "that high-octane White House air." Henry Kissinger has been quoted as saying that power is an aphrodisiac. Even for the mature, it is intoxicating to flash a White House pass and glide into the West Wing for meetings in the Roosevelt Room, or the sanctum sanctorum itself— the Oval Office. For those who have not developed immunity to seductive perks, it is hard to avoid industrial-strength hubris when picking up a phone and saying, "I'm calling from the White House." Maybe the immature should have training wheels on their phones.

A final admittedly frivolous footnote: My completely unscientific survey reveals that some of the more aggressive NSAs were also ruthless tennis players—a correlation which, as Soviet theorists used to say, is doubtlessly no accident. My first-hand experience covers only two—Walt Rostow and Zbig Brzezinski, of both of whom I can say that rarely have I been pounded so mercilessly.

It may be asked how there was time for tennis in the crisis-driven Carter White House. One answer is that exercise is therapeutic in that pressure-cooker. The other is that Zbig would periodically ask me to join him for a quick game. At first, I said I was too busy. On reflection, if he could break away, obviously so could I. I lost badly the first few times, intimidated by having the executive mansion loom into my vision every time I served. Nor did it help for the court-side telephone to periodically ring, pulling my opponent off the court just as I was starting to improve (I often wondered if Zbig pre-arranged those calls). I don't have sufficient data about the other NSAs except for Bundy, who once came to dinner on crutches from an over-vigorous tennis match. Henry Kissinger certainly didn't need a tennis racquet with which to batter his opponents. But I hope other scholars complete this research so as to enrich the political science literature.

5 COLD WAR SCHOLAR I: 1957–70
The Leaning Tower of Ivory

My confessed interest in education for everyone everywhere took a concrete, albeit accidental, form when I became a full-time professor. Like much of life, it was unplanned.

In 1957 I moved back from the State Department to my native habitat of Massachusetts, on a three-year contract to run a research project at MIT's Center for International Studies (CIS). I had no real expectation of becoming anything resembling a professor—hardly a safe move for a 36-year-old with four dependents. But after all, life is a series of tradeoffs. Sixteen years of war and crisis management made my leap into the unknown seem a no-brainer.

Miraculously transformed a few years later into a professor with tenure, I lived happily ever after. That is to say, for the next thirty-four years, with time off for good behavior in Geneva, Washington, and points east, west, north and south, I had fun working with students who seemed to get younger over the years. I also did research on weighty subjects that interested both me and the government agencies and foundations which provided the wherewithal.

I had decamped from Washington with a load of accumulated frustrations and pent-up intellectual energy. Even before I had job security, I felt positively liberated by the benign atmosphere of intellectual freedom, saying and writing what I, rather than what my bosses thought. And my dance card was filling up nicely in the brave, new, and seductive world of consulting, attending conferences at glamorous sites, and pontificating in newspapers and on TV.

MIT is a phenomenal place. Great scientific breakthroughs aside, it is a nifty place to work. The faculty is encouraged to go out in the world, shed glory on the Institute (and on themselves), and bring back the benefits to enrich the educational process. No ivy is growing on either the buildings or the people, unlike the fine other school up the Charles River where I got all my degrees. Indeed, the Institute's leadership has no problem if you start a company, do consulting one day a week, or take a leave of absence in Washington. But the grand bargain is that you come back, meet your classes, counsel your student advisees, do breakthrough research, publish, and always remember where your primary loyalties lie. So instead of being furtive about ties to the policymaking community, like many academic institutions, our center was working hard to help the government do better.

THE PRE-REVOLUTIONARY CAMPUS

When I first arrived in Cambridge as a non-professor without tenure, I sat in on a seminar led by then MIT President James Killian. One of the panelists was a well-known federal judge named Charles Wyzanski, who fascinated me by asserting that every professor should be "an *ex officio* teacher of ethics." I had already encountered one of the theoretical quarrels that agitated my academic colleagues, namely whether the social sciences should be "value-free." Since our dominant professional myth was that social science is a "science," it followed logically that subjective, unmeasurable ephemeral values should not be allowed to intrude.

This notion, like so much intellectual cant, turned out to be nonsense. But change did not happen all at once. In the early 1960s, male students were wearing short hair, jackets, ties, and an air of deference to their elders and betters (I have no recollection of what MIT female students were wearing, since there were so few of them). The intellectual pace, as now, was frenetic, with the learning process likened to drinking from a fire hose.

The mention of "tenure" (later under broad attack) is worth tarrying over. Some worry that academic tenure enables incompetent professors to hang on long after the time they should have been sent off with a gold watch and a firm handshake. That is doubtless true, particularly since the universal drive for entitlements now includes professors who are no longer required to retire before they actually drop dead. This has made life even more difficult for the struggling young scholar, who may get pretty long in the tooth waiting for old Mr. Chips to pack it in.

For me, however, the granting of academic tenure was like being released from death row. It made a free man out of a nervous wreck who expended prodigious energy worrying how to support a wife and three small children after giving up security in the government for a terminal research appointment. With tenure, rather than leaning on my rake and snoozing in the sun, a period of great productivity ensued.

My salvation came in the form of being reborn as a professor of political science. But I had better confess that every time I write the words "political science" I get a little embarrassed. This is strange, since I seem able, without blushing, to pin the dreaded label "bureaucrat" on a significant part of my own career. But sadly, I have found existing theories of international relations and foreign policy to be pretty primitive, idiosyncratic, and intellectually unsatisfying, compared with the rich theoretical frameworks available in the natural sciences.

I have worked hard to overcome this bias. After all, a world-class research university should push all available envelopes in the quest for general laws and explanations. Finding more coherent theories about politics might also counter the economists' scornful contrasts between our meager efforts and their alleged theoretical richness (and Nobel prizes). The result of that ambivalence was that I tended to do theory and practice on alternate days.

Comes the Revolution

In the turbulent 1960s and 70s, it was not long before issues of right and wrong, good and bad, just and unjust, came to permeate everything I was trying to teach and research about foreign policy, arms control and disarmament, the UN, the decision-making process, and the anatomy of conflict between and inside countries. I tried hard to be objective, but by the late 1960s, my students, research staff, and outside audiences were processing my work through their own increasingly critical value systems.

In normal times, as I have suggested, life at MIT is harmonious, pleasant, intellectually but not politically exciting, and usually immune from the kind of weirdness that makes for racy novels about the Groves of Academe. But it would be misleading to say that nothing weird, unpleasant, or politically turbulent happened on the MIT campus in the Cold War era. During the Vietnam convulsion, we were treated to all three kinds of occurrences. In that climate, the ivory tower acquired a dangerous tilt suggestive of its leaning counterpart in Pisa.

Vietnam affected people on the campus in different ways. Unlike most professors, I had grown up with an ingrained trust in leadership, which was by the late 1960s and early 1970s under severe strain. Government, thanks largely to President Johnson's pig-headedness and President Nixon's mendacity, was forfeiting much of that trust. The assassinations of President Kennedy, Martin Luther King, Jr., and Robert Kennedy all fueled disillusionment and alienation. The centerpiece was growing American involvement in Vietnam, and it was Vietnam that forced at least some of us to take a hard look at what we—and the US government—were doing.

President Lyndon Johnson's dogged embrace of the Vietnam tar baby was surely his biggest mistake, one that sadly obscured his impressive domestic record. From my perspective, Johnson's second biggest mistake was the granting of deferments to college students at a time when blue-collar and inner city Americans were being drafted and sent to Vietnam to be chewed up. This special privilege had to be gnawing at the souls of my students. I'm sure that a sense of guilt explained at least some of their outsized behavior. I also suspect that, without the draft deferments, the revulsion of middle-class suburban parents to the return of their kids in body bags would have forced Washington to pull back a good deal sooner than it did.

In 1965 the *New York Times* published a letter from me supporting the US war effort, on what seemed to me the fact that the North Vietnamese were engaged in aggression and should be stopped. (I was a visiting professor in Geneva at the time, and was influenced by strong European views that the US should hang tough on behalf of the "free world.")

By late 1967, I was in Bermuda at an extraordinary meeting called by the Carnegie Endowment for International Peace to bring together Americans in the political center who were becoming convinced that the war was unwinnable, and starting to undermine our own society. The group included Eisenhower's Army Chief of Staff General Matthew Ridgway, Nixon's UN Ambassador Charles Yost, Kennedy's Deputy Defense Secretary Roswell Gilpatric, and a score of others. We produced a document that became known as "The Bermuda Paper." It called for stopping the bombing, reducing the level of violence, and pressuring the South Vietnam government to increase its own defense efforts. The *New York Times* featured our report as evidence that moderate Americans were now demanding a change in policy. When General Ridgway took the document to President Johnson he declined even to look at it.

By the end of the 1960s many of the natty dressers in our student body were in rags, alienated from "the system," and increasingly enraged by the war. Students were not the only ones to alter their appearance. Some professors soon had hair down to their shoulders (if no hair, then beards), and traded in wingtips and neckties for sandals and love beads.

One effect of the upheaval was to alter the educational process itself. The university of the early 1960s more closely resembled the 19th-century educational caste system than it did the model that would soon prevail—one that emphasized gender equality, affirmative action, and a more unbuttoned curriculum. The first two changes were overdue, although the third sometimes warped the educational process. I still wore a shirt and tie. But I did let my sideburns grow fashionably long, which made me feel that I looked really cool.

Something also happened to my general stance toward disorder, a stance the French might describe as *fesses serrées*. I still deplored the sophomoric acting out, and hated the ugly attacks on civil discourse. But I stopped reacting reflexively to challenges to authority, and began to find some merit in well-researched critiques of the conventional wisdom on history and policy. Faced with the skepticism of thoughtful students, I suddenly recalled the saying that faith can move mountains, but it's doubt that gets you an education. (Of course, as someone else said, you shouldn't be so open-minded that your brains fall out.)

I had a special problem as a teacher of undergraduate and graduate courses on American foreign policy. I tried hard to explain and interpret the Cold War world—including Vietnam—as objectively as I knew how, against an historical background broader than the Vietnam era. Some so-called revisionist historians were scholarly and on the mark. The more extreme ones, wildly popular with students and some faculty, were appalling in their distortions of history. The worst of them twisted facts to "prove" that it was not Stalin's grab of Eastern Europe, nor the scary Leninist doctrine of "inevitability of war," but rather the "capitalist-imperialist" United States of America that was responsible for not only the Cold War, but all the other bad things in the world.

Conspiracy theorists always can titillate gullible audiences with exaggerated tales of American treachery, and at that moment in history the worst of them found a dependable source of applause from students avid for sinister plots.

My particular problem was that, having been professionally weaned, not in the academic nursery, but in the wartime Navy and the State Department, I was burdened with some first-hand knowledge of what actually happened. But I must say that the best of the new wave of historians got some of it right, confirming my feeling that, in standing up to Stalin's belligerent and paranoid Soviet Union, the West had adopted counter-strategies that ultimately magnified the tension. The "good revisionists" were right about the mindlessness of the astronomical nuclear buildup based on dubious Pentagon figures on Soviet "superiority." And they were right about ultimately disastrous US support of some truly rotten Third World regimes that professed anti-communism. The Johnson and Nixon administrations didn't help either, with their obsessive manipulation of the truth.

Since MIT featured a plurality of engineering students who usually tend to political conservatism (not to mention a certain nerdiness), the radical drive came from other academic sites like biology, history, economics, psychology, and political science. The bad news for the embattled teacher-scholar was the temporary ascendancy of the ignorant, the misinformed, and the emotionally screwed-up.

Some students simply banged their spoons on the high chair. Others discovered that universities were soft targets for acting out their juvenile version of guerilla theater by occupying the president's office, chucking the dean downstairs, or noisily disrupting classes and faculty meetings. I sometimes envied the radicals their one-dimensional, black-and-white, morally unambiguous world, and began to feel that, to borrow a phrase, my knowledge was no match for their ignorance.

All of this laid a heavy hand on research like mine with a policy focus. By the end of the 1960s, my MIT research project had made a major systematic analysis of what we called "small wars"—their causes, factors tending toward violence, and ways to prevent, moderate, and terminate them. My former student Allen Moulton and I developed an eventually computerized conflict analysis system called CASCON (standing for Computer-Aided Analysis of Conflict) which eventually won a national academic prize, and was used experimentally by the UN, governments, and scholars. The number of actual wars was small, so we couldn't be as scientific as I would have liked. A larger number would have been helpful but, to borrow from another thinker, no diagnosis should require information that can only be obtained in an autopsy.

The Joint Harvard-MIT Arms Control Seminar, which Harvard professor Tom Schelling and I co-chaired during the 1960s, included people in responsible positions in Cambridge and Washington who were agreed on the urgent need to avoid a nuclear war, and were at work in areas broadly described as "arms control." Meanwhile the public rhetoric was sharpening between people favoring "arms control" and people favoring "disarmament," with some peace activists charging that "arms control" perpetuated the arms race and should be replaced by total disarmament, and self-styled realists scorning disarmament as a pipe dream.

In actual fact, the US and Soviet Union each had on the table competitive proposals for "general and complete disarmament," or GCD (in whose US development and negotiation I had been involved). But in the atmosphere of the times, that goal was clearly both unachievable and potentially destabilizing, and was not taken seriously by either government.

Given the openness of the West, the tight controls of the Soviets, and the Leninist concept of the right to cheat in order to nudge along the historical process, GCD meant unilateral disarmament by the West. Arms control, on the other hand, meant negotiated limits on numbers and types of weapons in order to preserve a deterring balance while lowering the possibility of accidental launchings or disastrous miscalculation.

Today the number of nuclear weapons has shrunk, and counter-proliferation efforts are fairly vigorous, though no one knows what to do if non-governments like Al Qaeda get their hands on nuclear materials. Indeed, a substantial number of former American military leaders have come out in favor of the safeguarded *abolition* of all nuclear weapons. Unfortunately, weapon-making knowledge can't be eradicated short of universal brain surgery, so some deterrent is needed. Otherwise, I too would campaign for their outright abolition.

Back then, the nuclear arguments reflected underlying beliefs about the two superpowers. Some on campus bought into the "moral equivalence" argument that lumped together, as equally culpable, Western democracies and Soviet communism. That was a major distortion, based in part on Vietnam, in part on Washington's eventual overreaction to menacing Soviet behavior, and in part on historic Russian fears of invasion. But I boggled at the indiscriminate lumping together of freedom and tyranny. The radicals focused entirely on American defects and were typically ignorant of the realities of the Soviet system. One wonders how many of the campus coffee-house crowd confessed error when post-Soviet Moscow opened the files, confirming truths that anyone paying tuition should have known.

The Game Gets Rough

One night in 1970, it was truly bizarre to come back to a full-blown MIT crisis from Garmisch, Germany, where I had just run a senior-level game for the Joint Chiefs of Staff that indicated the US was not likely to repeat its near-obsessive interventionism any time soon. I was met at Logan Airport with an urgent message about an impending riot at the Center for International Studies and, instead of going home to sleep off jet lag, I headed for a crisis meeting at MIT.

The ultra-radical SDS (Students for a Democratic Society) and the loonier "Weathermen" had been publicly threatening to march on the Center in order to punish us for our sins. The Center's research consisted primarily of how to aid developing countries, prevent conflicts, and understand societies like Russia and China, although at least one faculty member had been advising the US government on Vietnam. Contingency planning against terrorism in a university rather dries up the creative juices, and the SDS tactic was pretty successful, since people became testy and nervous waiting to see what might happen. In fact, if I had been advising the Weathermen and SDS I would have suggested that they keep up the threats but never make the bust, thus perpetually demoralizing their victims. But now they were going into action.

That night I sat up until the wee hours with some of our students, trying for an agreed response on the planned march to "smash" our Center. The young people most troubled were those caught between sympathy with the militants over Vietnam, and distaste for dealing with problems by blasting academic buildings, rioting, or abusing faculty members. Two of my students spent half the night sewing an enormous banner from old sheets in the fashion of Betsy Ross, spelling out the words the majority of us had been able to agree on. The emblazoned message proclaimed that we favored open discussion of all issues, wanted a cease-fire in Vietnam, supported the right of everyone in a university to dissent and express opinions, however controversial, and considered violence an unacceptable means of persuasion.

The actual day dawned wet and gloomy. At nine A.M. the MIT leadership phoned to ask that Center Director Max Millikan, my colleague Bill Griffith and I get over and address the crowd starting to fill the steps of the main building. But before we left, one of our students pulled me aside. She was a noted campus radical, but opposed what she called the "crazies." She pleaded with me not to go, saying it would do nothing but humiliate me while inflaming the mob. The three of us crossed the campus and when I reported her warning, after some hemming and hawing, the MIT high command agreed that it would be wiser to avoid a confrontation.

The climax came in mid-morning. By then it was really raining. About a hundred of us—political science faculty, researchers, students, secretaries, staff—huddled in our raincoats under the banner on the wet grass outside our building. I'm not sure if we resembled the Minutemen at Concord watching for the whites of their eyes, or Governor George Wallace blocking the doorway of Old Mississippi State to bar black students. We all wore blue armbands symbolizing our solidarity, though no one seemed able to explain the significance of the color.

Not all the political science faculty were there. A few were so outraged by the militant student protest that they rejected any notion of discussion, compromise, or common ground. Nor were all the students there. Some, even in 1970, were still in the tradition of MIT "tools" — short-haired, politically conservative and looking for somewhere else to study after the management sealed off our building.

We gradually made out the marchers, still a tiny, shapeless black mass at the other end of Amherst Street. As they came closer, we could see the leather jackets and army boots and placards, hear the screaming denunciation by a youthful Madame de Farge atop a sound truck, and feel the combination of thrill and animal fear of impending collision between two antagonistic bodies of human beings.

Above us, on the broad plaza leading into the building, were deployed MIT's battalions of deans, reinforced campus police, plain-clothes detectives, walkie-talkies, bullhorns, photographers, newsmen, TV cameras, and all the rest of the ritual counterinsurgency apparatus of the urban American university of the period. Predictably, the mob's leaders headed for the cameras as if to a magnet.

In the end, our little knot of supporters of change, non-violence, and rational discourse was virtually ignored. The marchers got their kicks from confronting, not the ambiguous liberals, but the genuine pigs (radical-speak for cops). Some did deign to face us, grinning sheepishly through their hostility. We looked in vain for the bicycle chains the Weathermen were going to use to trash our place of work and study, and perhaps us as well. They didn't smash the Center as they had promised to do. In fact, some of the potential for violence had been defused a month earlier when an anti-CIS "mill-in" recurred.

Then, several hundred students, faculty, assorted administrators, curious onlookers, plainclothes cops, photographers, and newsmen had occupied our fourth-floor headquarters, and for a day we stopped work. Some faculty went home. But some of us had stayed to protect our research papers, and wound up having a useful, if unorthodox, opportunity to explain what it was we "warmongers" actually did.

WANTED
for serving US imperialism
for planning and developing
counterinsurgency techniques at the
CENTER FOR INTERNATIONAL STUDIES

L. W. PYE   **L. P. BLOOMFIELD**

Student radicals target their MIT professors.

My own conflict research, much of it paid for by various parts of the government, had increasingly been drawn into the larger battle. Ironically, its methods and findings were starting to be used by scholars and diplomats to get a better grip on moderating and terminating localized wars that, unlike the dreaded superpower clash, were actually being fought. But the same research findings were denounced by hard-core campus radicals as a "plot to crush peasant revolutions."

These hours were a nightmare, featuring clots of disheveled-looking people wandering through our corridors and offices, some shouting obscenities at us, others gathering in knots to target their favorite war criminals, and a few just sightseeing. At the climax, a mob of activists was packed into the small fourth-floor lounge. A colleague rushed into my office to say that my work was the topic of "discussion." I went out, stood on a chair, and with great trepidation took them on.

I do not want to spend many such moments pushing Vietcong flags out of my face while trying to speak to a hostile, glandular crowd packed into a disaster-prone space with cul-de-sacs, misplaced exits, and sealed windows. About half the invaders appeared interested in getting answers from a real live foe. After a somewhat surreal twenty-minute version of Q&A, the atmosphere abruptly changed with a sudden stirring in one corner of the room. Shortly thereafter an eruption of shouted obscenities and insults ensued from that quadrant. I concluded that they—and I—had had enough, and with a feeble riposte (something like "is *that* your way of debating?"), I picked up my papers and fled.

This was university life at its worst, and if I had my way all those on campus who engaged in actual rioting instead of argument would have been kicked out. Yet in another way it was time well spent. Many who came in ignorance, rage, or curiosity found out that a good deal of what SDS and the Weathermen had been feeding them was, at best, distorted propaganda, and, at worst, lies.

A phone call the following morning solved the mystery of the sudden atmospheric shift on the battlefield. The caller was the wife of one of my young colleagues, herself an assistant professor at MIT I had spotted marching into our building. According to her, the fourth-floor debate had become so reasonable that a ringleader of the mill-in, a rather incendiary professor of modern languages, had rounded up his hard-line followers outside the hall. Claiming that this "slick bastard" (i.e. me) was pulling the wool over the eyes of the students and "reaching some of the kids," he evidently rallied them to go back in and shout me down with obscenities and leftist battle cries. My caller said she was phoning to apologize for this outrageous behavior, and to disassociate herself from the academic arsonist in question.

A postscript took place weeks later at a meeting of the Council of the MIT School of Humanities and Social Science, which routinely considered faculty promotions on their trajectory between the recommending academic department and the Institute's administration. One such recommendation was for promotion and tenure for the same professorial Robespierre who had launched his militants at me. Yes, I had learned in the groves of academe that you should be tolerant of the eccentricities of colleagues so long as they taught and wrote brilliantly. But surely this didn't exempt them from minimal norms of behavior expected of those teaching the young. Orchestrating obscene verbal assaults by students because a faculty colleague was "becoming too reasonable" seemed to me *prima facie* grounds for challenging elevation to a high position of educational leadership.

My own self-image was of a politically neutral, non-petition-signing observer of the human condition. But I felt sufficiently driven by moral outrage to throw my body in front of this particular moving vehicle. When the promotion dossier glided past the consenting boards, I requested a hearing before the MIT president and provost, which they kindly granted. I made my case to those two fine gents, who nevertheless approved the promotion and tenure. We all came out of the meeting with, in the immortal words of Gilbert and Sullivan, "the satisfying feeling that our duty had been done."

Bombs Away

The winding down of the Vietnam War did not dry up all the campus passion. In the early 1970s, the Center for International Studies had installed in adjoining offices two of the civilian stars of the Vietnam drama, both intensely controversial, and both engaged by us as visiting researchers to record their respective roles in the war in relative tranquility for the benefit of future scholars. What was unusual about it was the identity of the pair.

One was William Bundy, one of the architects of US policy in his position as, first, assistant secretary of defense, then assistant secretary of state for what at the time was called Far Eastern Affairs. Bill Bundy was actually much more than those titles imply. He was the brother of McGeorge Bundy, who had been national security adviser to Presidents Kennedy and Johnson. He also was himself one of the key "Best and Brightest" chronicled by both David Halberstam in his book of the same title, and by the anonymous editors of the *Pentagon Papers* whose illicit publication in 1971 reignited the anti-war flames.

The other scholar on our balanced ticket was the notorious Daniel Ellsberg, a former marine, who as a civilian spent two gung-ho years in Vietnam. He then worked in Washington helping to compile the Pentagon Papers, became disillusioned, secretly photocopied the document, smuggled it to the press, and wound up a hero of the war protesters.

One dark night soon after both celebrities joined us, the campus police received a phone call from someone identifying herself as a member of the "Proud Angels," which she described as an activist feminist group. She informed the cops that a bomb would shortly go off on the fourth floor of our building, aimed at the war criminal Bill Bundy. Sure enough, a fair-sized explosive went off in the fourth floor ladies room, which was located roughly opposite the offices assigned to our Odd Couple. Mercifully, no one was around at that late hour. The ladies' aim was not up to their war plans, and Bundy's office remained relatively unscathed. It was Dan Ellsberg's office that they unwittingly messed up.

I was probably the only one who came out ahead. The ladies room was furnished with some chairs and a green couch, some of which landed in the hallway through the blown-out door. I happened to have an extraordinarily enterprising secretary, who on her arrival next morning did a quick post-battle assessment. She saw no competitors, so she quietly liberated the couch to enhance my under-furnished office. There it sits today, its back still somewhat spavined, still a bilious green, but nevertheless a testimonial to the unintended good that sometimes results from bad intentions.

6 COLDWAR SCHOLAR II: 1958–71
Playing Games with Foreign Policy

The White House Situation Room was tense as the others around the small table watched the President reach for the red phone. To his right, the secretary of state had just finished drafting a statement the press secretary would read shortly in the Press Room. To his left, the secretary of defense was still working with the chairman of the joint chiefs on orders to be transmitted by the chiefs to US commands in three continents, all on Defcon3-level alert since the civil war broke out three days earlier, taking the CIA by surprise. The President signaled for silence. "We have a hotline message for Moscow. Yes, that's right. It's got to go ASAP. You already caught it on the closed-circuit TV? Okay, what do we assume for delivery time? Right. Thanks."

He leaned back, rubbed his eyes, and said in the voice of a man desperately short of sleep but determined not to show it: "That's all we can do. I don't want the US to intervene, and we can only hope the bad guys don't misunderstand and start mixing in. But if they do, we have no choice but to go in, and I want everyone to get that message!" All the President's advisers nodded in agreement, except for one. The President's chief of staff, who was present at this National Security Council meeting only as a courtesy, frowned. A former congressman who now obsessively protected his chief's political rear, when he spoke his voice was a shade too loud. "Dammit, Mr. President, we were doing the right thing before the hawks got at you. You were probably avoiding another Vietnam, and that's the way the American people and the Congress want it. So what if others get their tails caught in the wringer? Why should we?"

The argument that had waxed and waned for two days and part of one night seemed to be starting all over again. Two statutory members of the National Security Council had simultaneously opened their mouths to reopen the battle over American military intervention when the door opened and a secretary walked into the room bearing a tray of glasses filled with sherry. "Control says it's time for lunch, and would you please fill out your questionnaires before you come downstairs."

The scene, it will now be clear, was not the White House Situation Room. It was, rather, a richly-furnished suite at Endicott House, MIT's French chateau-style country retreat deep in the woods of Dedham, Massachusetts. The "President of the United States" was a distinguished business executive with some Presidential pretensions and considerable first-hand experience in government. His "secretary of state" was a high-ranking State Department official. The "secretary of defense" was an MIT professor who commuted to the Pentagon weekly to help shape strategy. The rest consisted of well-known academics and senior bureaucrats. The event was a political exercise I had christened "POLEX" that, with government support, I was developing at MIT back in the 60s and 70s in the quest for better planning and forecasting.

The story of the origins of the POLEX seemed to me worth telling for a number of reasons. First, I was appalled at how the State Department I worked for lurched from crisis to crisis, even while policy planners seemed to be ignored. Second, if greater rationality in foreign policy means better ways to try to anticipate the future, there aren't very many known ways to do that, and I found the idea of "gaming" out future contingencies to be the best way available. And finally, stories of early attempts to do that taught lessons that need to be taken seriously, and in any event make up a bit of recent history that deserves to be in print somewhere.

POLEX originally meant "Political-Military Exercise." I changed it to plain "Political Exercise" when some Vietnam-maddened students became convinced that my games on deterrence, conflict limitation, disarmament and UN peacekeeping were really secret plans to crush peasant revolutions. (I still prefer "exercises" to the more frivolous "games." But when my game-players started including a number of oversized egos, it was clear that some people considered themselves too important to simply "exercise.")

The simulation of foreign policy making and crisis management was not something I had ever heard of while I was involved in the real thing. It began for me in the late 1950s when I arrived at MIT's Center for International Studies on a three-year research appointment. Even before I had put up pictures of my wife and children and found the men's room, the Center's director, a charismatic marvel named Max Millikan, told me of his fascination with a social science experiment underway at the RAND corporation. RAND had invited in foreign policy experts from government and private life, organized them into Red and Blue teams, and for a month had them read the *New York Times* and, based on daily news, make moves to which the other team would respond.

The RAND games received mixed reviews, particularly from Washington types lured by the pleasures of Santa Monica, who ultimately found the whole thing unrealistic and unnecessarily lengthy. But the idea was novel, and I came under increasing pressure to try out something along these lines at MIT, where a couple of minor gaming experiments had already been run in classrooms.

I confess to being acutely uncomfortable with the idea at the outset. If government officials found the RAND games unrealistic, then so did I even without having seen one. The very idea of simulating reality seemed to me counter-intuitive, and to be caught doing it in public downright embarrassing. So why did I go ahead designing and directing games, to the point of being mistakenly cited in books as following in the footsteps of Frederick the Great along with more recent war-gaming notables like Herman Kahn and Thomas Schelling? Put it down to insecurity at being caught between careers, a nagging urge to be tolerant of theory-building experiments, and curiosity about the exotic world in which I had suddenly landed.

Gaming was always a sideline to my central professional concerns. But to my growing consternation I was becoming targeted with uninvited calls from governments, universities, and companies to "put on a game for us" and "show us how you do it." What follows reports on the early days of political gaming, and I would be glad to be told that all the shortfalls chronicled herein have been remedied.

1961–68: Birth of the POLEX

Today simulations of all kinds are commonplace in classrooms, government agencies, businesses, and elsewhere. But four decades ago, when I first got involved in this curious enterprise, it was virtually unheard of to "simulate" foreign policy-making.

The political game's ancestral roots were several. One was the formal *kriegspiel* or war-game pioneered in the court of Frederick the Great, commonplace wherever military forces train. Another was the "business game" used in schools of management, where the object was to acquire market share at the expense of competitors. Third was the mock trial familiar to law schools. And fourth was the psychodrama staged in mental institutions where patients, sometimes wearing masks to hide behind, take on someone else's identity and feel freer to express pent up feelings.

Compared with these, gaming of the kind I was stumbling onto is quite simple-minded. It uses human "subjects" who start with a hypothetical crisis situation described in the "scenario," take on the roles of real decision-makers, and engage in a dynamic process of interaction through an exchange of moves. The political game, unlike the war-game (which I have never run) doesn't have "victory" as its goal. Like the real world of diplomacy, it can include intimidation, disinformation, and economic or psychological warfare to gain influence or power, or defend against assaults on one's diplomatic position. But the main effort is to negotiate, resolve conflicts, buy time, defuse crises, prevent war, and somehow come out looking good—not so different from real-life laborers in the diplomatic vineyard.

Along with a bunch of student games and some esoteric quantitative experiments with the technique, a dozen or so professional-level MIT games took place under my direction during the 1960s and 1970s, all financed by the government, whether the Arms Control and Disarmament Agency, the Navy, or the quasi-governmental Institute for Defense Analysis. Virtually all the games were tied to my research projects on the UN, arms control, deterrence, peacekeeping, and conflict. In that era of generous government financing, the final decisions on spending the money were mine—ah, those were the days. For various reasons (including the plush setting at MIT's Endicott

Running MIT's first professional-level political game at Endicott House, Dedham, MA.

House) I was able to attract government officials at mid-level and higher, as well as some of America's leading academics, congressmen, and business leaders.

Given my obsession with better planning, it was gratifying to be able to use members of the State Department's Policy Planning Staff for virtually all my games. This resulted from a visit to Secretary of State Christian Herter, in company with MIT's Max Millikan and Walt Rostow, during which I described with some embarrassment the political games I had been lured into running. (That had to be the last era in which academic entrepreneurs like Millikan and Rostow could effortlessly exchange ideas with the top command in Washington). When I asked the secretary for cooperation in gaming policy problems, the courtly Herter expressed mild horror at the likely reaction in Congress to his Department "playing games." (I was privately in spirit with the Congressional know-nothings on that.) He promised, however, that some of his policy planners would regularly take part, which they did.

In 1961, as the Berlin crisis was ominously building, which resulted in the Wall, my classmate Henry Owen called from the State Department Policy Planning Staff to ask if I would put on a game on

Berlin. I didn't think MIT should become a sort of vending machine, and in any event the Defense Department, with Tom Schelling's capable help, was beginning to develop its own "pol-mil" gaming capability, so I begged off.

The Pentagon games differed from ours in being highly classified and they focused on a military problem, whereas I kept on hand a couple of military officers on assignment to MIT or Harvard in case a military situation developed, but only as a sidebar. Government sponsors occasionally pressured me to classify our games, but in my new state of academic purity I self-righteously declined, resulting in some noisy cat-fights. (In publishing our results, I did, however, agree to protect the identity of government participants, particularly those who at least figuratively wore trench coats and false beards.)

The State Department was molasses-slow in catching up to this potentially valuable policy-planning tool. However by 1986, with the blessing of Secretary of State George Shultz, the Department decided that it had for too long piggybacked on Pentagon games. I was invited to return to State for a few weeks to help set up a permanent gaming capability, which since then has done some remarkable things under its industrious director Fred Hill. It is a valuable policy planning tool, but an organizational orphan, highly valued by some key officials but operating with about one-twenty-fifth the budget of the Pentagon's political-military gaming operation.

WHY DO IT?

Through a painful learning process, I wound up realizing that the POLEX could do some things better than the usual one-man essays, hierarchical discussions, or inter-agency committees. Neither a game nor anything else can predict the future. But I found that, at its best, a good game could provide:

- Better anticipation of the reactions of foreigners to a US policy move than the consensus-driven discussion process, or the pernicious Washington tendency to look in a mirror and say "Aha, that's what those foreigners would do!"

- A chance to pre-test policy initiatives in a safe environment.

- A way to force the worst into a process that often presupposes a best outcome. (I wish some politically fearless games had been run on Iraq in early 2003 rather than letting the White House and Pentagon assume a rosy outcome.)

- Loosening up of stereotyped assumptions, by placing Americans and foreigners in the other's shoes.

Each of the above should be written on the blackboard 100 times by would be gamers. Getting a good sense of reactions abroad to a US policy scheme is probably the single most important challenge to both intelligence and diplomatic services, but on the record is often wrong, sometimes disastrously so. The closest thing I know to an actual foreigner is a well-informed US expert getting into the foreigner's shoes. The second indispensable use of games is to save political leaders from seeing only best case outcomes of their preferred policy. To come anywhere near these ideals, a game has to be meticulously planned, with clear objectives and skilled participants. It just isn't good enough to say, "Let's throw 'em a crisis and see what happens." That's fine for a high school advanced social studies class or a freshman college course. But the nation won't be well-served until the modest efforts of the State Department's new gaming facility become the model for leadership retraining at the top.

Games can show beginners—and, for that matter, non-beginners—that while a politician can land in the headlines overnight, it can take months to land on a beachhead, build a new coalition, or mobilize public opinion. Games can help persuade "rational" Westerners that our earnest initiatives and pure motives can be misinterpreted when filtered through a different mindset. Games can sober up enthusiasts for a favorite policy by revealing the negative reactions likely to come from non-enthusiasts. And games can take another look at a prematurely discarded policy alternative.

There were plenty of bumps along my own learning curve, including a nightmare experience with my first professional-level game in 1958 when I first got to MIT. At that time the geniuses behind the Xerox machine hadn't finished inventing it, so we used the old Thermofax machine. You stuck a page into its maw, the machine heated up, and something happened in its depths that slowly transferred text onto curly brown paper. Still enamored of Washington's bureaucratic ways, I had arranged that each team would have color-coded message forms, so team moves would not only be in writing, but subject to Control's prior approval before distribution.

This worked while the teams sat around in their team rooms discussing their proposed goals, strategies, and the rest of my checklist. But soon they started drafting messages to other teams on our beautiful message forms. Lines began to form in front of my desk. As they stood there cooling their heels, those who in real life were accustomed to snappy service glared at me and my increasingly frantic Control group.

As we stuffed their message forms into the overworked machine to get them into the game's bloodstream, the Thermofax jammed, the paper overheated, smoke issued from its orifices and the whole contraption threatened to burst into flames. A merciful veil has fallen over memories of what ensued. But without a doubt, this was the low point in my checkered avocation as a gamer.

POSSIBILITIES AND PITFALLS

No matter how powerful a computer, no one I know has come close to crafting a satisfactory artificial model of the decision-making process, the policy machinery, or the international system. This means that a productive game has to depend on the model of reality the participants already carry inside their heads. It follows that for policy purposes, you need experienced players most likely to possess the most sophisticated, complex, and authentic model available. You obviously don't expect this of a college freshman. If a student role-player during the Cold War decided to "lob one into the men's room in the Kremlin," it could be written off to youthful exuberance and profound ignorance. But what a good classroom game does is to begin to form inside that eager head the beginnings of understanding of how the system works, i.e. an entry level model.

Another issue is whether games always have to be about crises. That was the natural mode, since if there was no crisis why would busy people take part? Some game directors got antsy when their game became quiet, as in an early Naval War College game I helped direct. The admiral in charge became distressed because the three- and four-striper students got so caught up in diplomacy they never got around to war-fighting. But the State Department games I organized show that much can be learned from gaming out vital non-crisis issues like oil supplies or fresh water shortages, as well as from starting a game with a planning session that considers future possibilities, and only then a decision phase in which the teams are confronted with a crisis.

Occasionally a game elicits insight that finds the way up the chain of command to decision-making levels. But the insight seems to emerge in the game's dynamic interaction, rather than being closely tied to the starting scenario. The connection came to light when political scientist Robert Mandel went through my MIT game records.

His sobering finding was that, in retrospect, the scenarios prepared in advance to start the game, however "plausible," bore little relation to what subsequently happened in the real world. But when he looked at what transpired once a game got going, he found that the interactive process sometimes produced outcomes that accurately prefigured the real world. Three examples:

- A game on civil strife in Angola correctly anticipated Portugal's bailout from its African colony.

- In a simulated Arab-Israeli blowup, Egypt in the end turned away from its then Soviet ally, which provoked a charge of unrealism, but a couple of years later Egypt actually expelled the thousands of Soviet troops on its soil.

- Finally, in the Moscow game described later the "US" team played a surprisingly realistic—although disconcertingly tough—hand, at one point launching overflights by Sixth Fleet jets in the crisis-ridden Sinai Peninsula. As the visiting game director, I blew the whistle on that move as unduly provocative. ("The US would never do something that rash in a crisis.") A week after I left Moscow, real Sixth Fleet aircraft did just that.

ROLE-PLAYING AS METHOD ACTING

My most striking lesson was related to the extraordinary transformative power of role-playing. I ran my first MIT classroom games early in the 1960s—a period of growing student alienation. One of my students in a graduate seminar was a mouthy young British socialist who had nothing but contempt for the US. I ran a little game in which each student was assigned a role simulating a US decision-maker, with my disaffected Brit randomly assigned the role of US secretary of defense.

Through several more periods, the class played out a typical Cold War crisis. My British socialist, who was quite bright, played a very intelligent hand as secretary of defense, and afterward admitted to a far better understanding of the pressures confronting his real-life counterpart. He also hated me for what I had done to him, and remained permanently unforgiving.

Something similar happened later in snowy Minneapolis. At the urging of the wise and entrepreneurial Harlan Cleveland, then the dean of the Humphrey Institute at the University of Minnesota in the early 1980s, I put on a game for the fellows of the Institute. Unlike my British Socialist, they worked in state and municipal organizations. Also unlike my fellow jet-setting conference-goers, these folks dealt directly with real problems facing real people. With the help of the university's food experts, we focused the game on a hypothetical international crisis stemming from a severe worldwide grain shortage in a period of poor crops.

Among the bureaucrats, social workers, journalists, and others were a couple of nuns from a local Catholic order. One of them wound up, like my benighted socialist, playing the hand of the US Defense Department. Like my Brit, she had to deal with challenges based on strategic rather than humanitarian considerations. But unlike the Brit, her innate humanitarian sense was clearly violated by the temporary day job I had given her, and she fled in tears.

Lest it be thought that this was a gender matter, in one of my MIT games the US Team was chaired by war-hero turned CEO, General James Gavin. A liberal Massachusetts Republican politician, George Lodge, was assigned a role on Gavin's team to ensure that domestic considerations would be taken into account. Lodge, a decent, idealistic guy, was so offended by the hawkish route taken by his team, that as a matter of conscience, he resigned from the team, and from the game.

A cross-cultural confirmation of the same potent psychic effect was supplied by a game I ran for the Soviets in Moscow in 1970. When the newly-established Soviet Institute of the USA and Canada invited me to Moscow to lecture on US foreign policy, no one said anything about a game. After I was securely in his hands, the Institute's canny director Georgi "Yuri" Arbatov insisted that I put on a game to "show us how you Americans do it." Exhausted from giving day-long lectures, I demurred on the grounds that the Soviets had surely been putting on political (or at least political-military) games for years. Anatoly Gromyko, who worked at the Institute, volunteered to check with Daddy. He reported back that, according to Foreign Minister Andrei Gromyko, all previous Soviet efforts were war-games, and this political game would be a first for them.

In my irritation with yet another example of exploitation of the working class (me), I insisted over Arbatov's objections that the topic be the Middle East ("much too sensitive"). The previous night, over excellent vodka and stringy chicken, I had concocted an unpleasant Middle East scenario. The next morning the Soviet professionals looked pretty skeptical when they were assembled, briefed, and formed into teams that transformed them into Arabs, Israelis, "Arab radicals," and Americans, as well as the Soviet Politburo.

The real region at that moment featured a war in Jordan, 20,000 Soviet troops in Egypt, and Israeli air raids over the suburbs of Cairo, all of which added to their general nervousness about this leap into the unknown (not to mention the watchful stares of the anonymous, stony-faced guys sitting in the back of the room). It seemed axiomatic that the experts, all of whom were doubtless Communist Party members, would be watching their rear ends closely.

But something extraordinary happened. In less than an hour, the players stopped being flustered and began to get inside their roles, seemingly unbothered by either the presence of a probable American spy (me), or their own spies in plain clothes lounging in the back. (The only exception was the team playing the USSR, which was obviously inhibited from any departure from official policy and played a dull, safe hand.) What really blew me away was that the four staffers who had strenuously objected to playing "Israel" soon began to do so with a vengeance, plotting devious ways to thwart Moscow and its pro-Arab clients, while our "Arab Extremists" team worked hard to engage the USSR in a war with Israel.

When it was over, my hosts had substantial second thoughts about an American professor coming to Moscow in the middle of a real Middle

East crisis and running their first political game—on the Middle East, no less. Arbatov asked me pointedly if it would not be embarrassing for me to have it known that I came to Moscow and ran their "first planning game on the Middle East." When I expressed no concern, he finally blurted, "Linc! Please do not publish game!" When Anatoly Gromyko and Deputy Director Vitaly Zhurkin came to visit my home in Cohasset a couple of months later, they told me the game—and all future games—were now classified "Top Secret." I more or less agreed not to publish all the details, but described it all to our American Ambassador in Moscow and, back in Washington, to both State Department and CIA audiences, as well as my colleagues at MIT.

The degree of player commitment in a good game continued to be a source of amazement. One of the innovations in my two-day (sometimes three-day) professional games at Endicott House was closed-circuit television to enable the Control group to continuously monitor the playing teams (a technique that subsequently became standard in government games). The setting was enticing to overworked policy officials who, although dealing with familiar if artificial policy issues, were ensconced in the lap of luxury unlike most government offices. Our amenities included a bartender on duty after hours, gourmet dinners, and relaxed evenings in the stately lounges. I couldn't believe my eyes when, on such an off-duty evening, an idle glance at the TV monitors revealed one of the teams meeting clandestinely (or so its members thought) in order to plot ways to get ahead of the game.

Role-playing seemed at times to have this effect on even the most hardened professionals. Several of America's best Soviet experts of the day such as Marshall Shulman and Alexander Dallin took part in one of our first Endicott House games. Since the working style of Kremlinologists tended to be analytical, our Soviet team had trouble settling into this format. However, by the second day we observed that each time a member of the Soviet team headed for the men's room all the others insisted on tagging along.

By the morning of day three, it became apparent that if the Soviet team members didn't trust each other, they also no longer trusted the Control team that was running the exercise, and began keeping us in the dark about their strategies and planned moves. These were smart men and doubtless having some fun while grinding out highly authentic moves. But their professional expertise also got caught up in an unfamiliar force field.

The same was brought home to me when, during the late 1960s and early 1970s, I became involved in some senior-level political-military Pentagon exercises under the Joint Chiefs of Staff. One unusual game code named Epsilon was staged in October 1969, at a US military base at Garmisch in the foothills of the Bavarian Alps. What was unusual about it was that the players were drawn exclusively from the American ambassadors stationed in Europe plus the four-star generals and admirals attached to NATO and the US European Command—in other words, no major carrying the general's briefcase, or foreign service officer opening car doors for the chief of mission. In fact, for security purposes, the whole bunch of prima donnas was carted around Garmisch in an unmarked black bus (whereas, as game director, I had a car and driver all to myself).

Epsilon focused on the subject of Yugoslavia, and our "Soviet Team" chairman was General Andrew Goodpaster, then NATO supreme commander. The game lasted for a couple of intense days, and produced a counter-intuitive outcome in the form of a "NATO" failure to send the requested military assistance to a Yugoslavia beleaguered by the Soviets. When the game wound down, I accompanied the good general to his helicopter, which was idling in the courtyard. As he entered the chopper, Goodpaster stopped, turned around, and said, "You know, Linc, we really should have been tougher, because I'm really not sure they got our message." Something made me ask, "Who do you mean by 'we,' Andy?" "Why, the Soviets of course." I was sorely tempted to haul him out until he could be deprogrammed.

GAMES VERSUS REALITY

Sometimes the bright line between the game world and the real one became blurred, with awkward results. An example was the 1963 game the State Department ran in-house—its only such venture until the mid 1980s when its own gaming facility was created. Two feisty assistant secretaries of state—Walt W. Rostow and G. Mennen "Soapy" Williams—decided that the department should take a fresh look at the policy dilemma created for the US by Portugal's continued grip on its territories in Africa. Rostow, having tried (unsuccessfully) to save "Iran" from going down the drain at one of my early Endicott House efforts, suggested gaming it out, and I was invited to come back to State to help organize it. The heart of the US policy dilemma was the insistence of the US Navy that military bases in the Portuguese-ruled Azores were indispensable to US security, which effectively blocked any attempt by other agencies to reconsider the mounting political cost to the US of supporting dictator António de Oliveira Salazar's Portugal.

The game was classified, and cleverly code-named "Operation Porter," standing for Portuguese Territories. This deception took the press corps about three minutes to decipher, particularly since the press room was located about ten yards from our game site, and the assemblage of well-known policy officers was easy to observe. As things worked out, the game quickly surfaced the tension between State's Bureau of European Affairs, which insisted we support NATO ally Portugal, and the Bureau of African Affairs, which in that era of worldwide decolonization saw the handwriting on the wall for the remaining Western colonies in Africa. As a good game can sometimes do, it came close to rescuing Uncle Sam from the horns of his dilemma. But that ace got trumped—as chronically happened in real life—by the Navy's insistence that US security required hanging on at all costs to its naval base in the Portuguese-owned Azores. For the record, over a quarter century after Angola and Mozambique became independent, the US still has a base in the independent Azores.

At the same game, a very competent officer from the White House National Security Council staff played a key role on the US team. Unfortunately for him, as he sat immersed in game-generated "top secret" cables and intelligence reports, a call summoned him to an urgent meeting at the real White House on US policy toward South Africa. When last seen, he was frantically trying to sort out in his head the distinction between the authentic-looking game messages and what was really happening.

A final example of games getting mixed up with reality was a peacekeeping training exercise by the newly-created International Peace Academy (which has gone on to train hundreds of peacekeepers and mediators for UN missions, often with the help of simulations). This one, held at the headquarters of the Austrian Diplomatic Academy in Vienna, was IPA's maiden effort. The challenge for me as game - director was to apply the technique to a widely-assorted group of mid-level and senior officers drawn from the foreign and defense ministries of 28 different countries in several continents, most of whom had never heard of political gaming. Even after giving several lectures on the subject, I was not at all sure they were persuaded.

The topic we chose was the once and future impasse on the island of Cyprus between the dominant Greek Cypriots and the minority Turkish Cypriots. The assignment of game roles turned out to be not all that difficult. For example, it seemed logical that our rather tough Polish army colonel would make a splendid Turkish Cypriot chief. Others were similarly assigned with an eye to avoiding close proximity to their own nationalities.

Our preparations went smoothly until the line between simulating reality and real-world diplomacy suddenly got blurred. IPA's management had given the host Austrian government a list of the participants' names and titles for its information. One participant was Osman Orek, who was listed as "Defense Minister, Republic of Cyprus." The trouble was that he had actually ceased to be defense minister of the Republic of Cyprus when the Greek Cypriot government, in cahoots with Athens, ran a coup in the course of which Defense Minister Orek was unceremoniously carried from his office still aboard his official chair. But so far as he and the leadership of Turkish Cypriots—and Turkey itself—were concerned, he was still "Defense Minister," although of what, was not completely clear.

The next thing we knew the Greek government in Athens had filed a formal complaint with the Austrian government in Vienna, and both capitals suddenly had their diplomatic knickers in a twist. Osman Orek took it all in better humor than the governments, with one exception. In his mind, there was simply no way that an assortment of Asians, Africans, Europeans et al, however proficient in their own national services, could possibly understand the Turkish Cypriot mind and culture, and he warned me that this flaw would cripple the whole effort. Despite his deep misgivings, Orek played the game with skill as a UN mediator. When it ended, he sought me out and in an astonished tone of voice exclaimed, "They behaved just like Turkish Cypriots!"

GAMES WITHIN GAMES

Games should be faithful to an explicit purpose in the mind of the game designer. But sometimes a game turns out to contain an unplanned element over which Control has no, well, control. That happens when a participant—or sponsor—has a hidden agenda that can skew the game in a way unforeseen by the management.

A serious subtext lay behind a top-level Joint Chiefs of Staff's political-military game on the then, as now, controversial issue of building an anti-ballistic missile system. The objective of the Pentagon game was to probe the difference that the threat of an anti-ballistic missiles capability might make in the strategic balance with the Soviets. Surprised at being invited to chair the United States team, I was told the topic was so sensitive among the services that an outsider was needed. What I didn't know at the time was who was selling what, and who was supposed to buy it.

This was one of those funny Pentagon games in which a colonel-level working team met for the best part of a week talking through the scenario, responding to Control team inputs, and considering the alternatives available to the US. The format, based on the way Washington normally operates, involved bringing in senior officers once a day to be briefed by the team chairman and then making the basic decisions.

The problem arose because the working-level team members lived around the clock inside the hypothetical world defined by the scenario which shaped their thinking and actions. But the chief of staff of the Army, the undersecretary of state, the head of North American Air Defense, and other heavy hitters on the senior part of my team had time only to hastily read through a briefing document en route to the game. When they were told what we were doing, they had trouble reconciling the world they had just come from and the world of the game.

So far as an extraneous agenda is concerned, when the ABM game ended the four-star general in command of NORAD, Air Force General "Bunky" Reeves, turned to Army Chief of Staff General Harold K. Johnson, and said "Johnny, you've got to get me that ABM system." I came later to suspect that the Army had simulated this particular game in order to persuade the Air Force that the Army's proposed ABM system was the way to go.

Chairing Control Group at Joint Chiefs SIGMA 1 Political-Military Game, the Pentagon.

This, by the way, turned out to be the only political-military game at the Pentagon up to that time that ended in a thermonuclear exchange, and the joke making the rounds in the Pentagon was that it took a disarmament expert from MIT to come to Washington and start a nuclear war. Actually, the game went nuclear not from any doing of mine, but from the prodding of the leading civilian on the US team — Undersecretary of State Foy Kohler — aimed at overcoming the typical conservatism of the military. I'm not the only one to notice this phenomenon. Former Air Force Chief of Staff Charles A. Gabriel was quoted as saying: "In all the war games we run . . . the military are by far most cautious. The civilians are more aggressive when it comes to playing a scenario involving escalation."

A truly horrendous example of an unforeseen personal subtext occurred in another top-level JCS game. That game revealed a deep flaw in the notion that the US team should be the official with the most expertise on the region. Unfortunately, I had been invited to direct the game, which postulated a new crisis in Southeast Asia, that confronted the US with choices based on an assessment of US interest.

The time was the early 1970s, and the man selected to head the US team was a retired senior diplomat who had served as the American ambassador in Saigon. He was obviously still burning with resentment at Washington's lack of support for him and the forces.

Somehow, despite the headlines in every American paper about the way this troubled nation was convulsing, he managed to persuade the US team to intervene in Southeast Asia with American military forces. This was nothing short of bizarre at a time when the US was not only withdrawing its forces from Vietnam, but when American society was being torn apart by deep-seated dissension. Of all the critique sessions I have presided over following a political-military game, there is no question that this was the most agonizing. The Pentagon had arranged the attendance of the entire civilian and military top command with the exception of President Nixon and National Security Adviser Henry Kissinger, who was skeptical of the whole gaming business anyway. Sitting on the front row of the briefing room were Secretary of State William Rogers, Secretary of Defense Melvin Laird, their Deputy Secretaries, the Director of Emergency Management General G.A. "Abe" Lincoln, and the chairman and members of the Joint Chiefs of Staff. As I summarized the actions taken by the "United States," they all stared at me as if I had just escaped from a lunatic asylum. I don't know if the Cabinet types ever came back again, but I must say I don't blame them if they didn't.

The main lesson of that game, of course, is that you're likely to get a more authentic simulation of American political leadership if you head the US team with someone off the street, rather than the expert who is in love with the region being gamed and obsessed with a desire to reverse the course of history.

A final example of an unplanned subtext was a game I was talked into running at MIT by an extraordinary Renaissance-type guy named John Craven. Craven was a physicist with a law degree and a deep knowledge of grand opera, whose day job then was as Chief Scientist of the Navy's cutting-edge Polaris nuclear submarine program. He phoned me out of the blue and asked if I would run a game for the Navy. I was interested in deterrence, and was close to saying yes when he went on to explain that what he really wanted out of the game was a number, i.e. the minimum time it would take for the White House to communicate with a flotilla of nuclear-powered submarines at a moment of crisis. (Communicating under water is far from easy, and a major effort at the time was aimed at large, very low-frequency antenna arrays; one aborted scheme was to wire up the whole state of

Wisconsin underground, which was nixed by the farmers who feared the radiation would cause their milk cows to dry up.)

I told Craven we would be glad to have his financial sponsorship for our research on deterrence but that we didn't do numbers: we were still experimenting and the POLEX wasn't that scientific anyway, etc. John Craven is the personification of persuasive, and I wound up agreeing, with a strong disclaimer about anything quantitative emerging.

As it turned out, we did come up with a number. But it was not, as Washington assumed, the time it took to issue a firing order. Probably because of my own bias toward arms control, the number represented the time it took in a nasty superpower crisis for the president to order a flotilla of subs to surface so they could be counted from satellites for high-speed reassurance to avoid nuclear miscalculation by either side. (The number was something like 10 minutes.) I thought no more of it until Craven called two weeks later to congratulate us on providing the data that clinched the decision to build a low-frequency antenna station in Cutler, Maine at a cost of $150 million as I recall. I boggled at crediting our game for anything of the sort, but there was little I could do about it except to congratulate myself.

THE BOTTOM LINE

Political gaming, as the late Adlai Stevenson said about flattery, is all right so long as you don't inhale. If done well, it can be effective in enhancing the quotient of rationality in America's foreign and national security policy. Games can help initiate juniors into the complexity of the decision-making process, and allow seniors to try out alternative policy approaches without falling in flames. Given our national tendency to ascribe Western "rational" mindsets to others, it is instructive to use experts on foreign cultures to help get a handle on likely foreign reactions.

At their best, political games represent a way to glimpse some of the potential pitfalls in managing this nation's affairs. Games should not be used only by subordinates, but where they are most needed—by people at the top who hold our fate in their hands. If done right, they might help avoid future disasters.

7 THE REAL WORLD I: 1970–89
The Soviet Union from Tyranny to Turmoil

A light snow was falling—the kind of indulgent snowfall that gave the sharp, ugly edges of Cold War Moscow a romantic 19th century patina. I walked past the Manege, where the Czar's fancy horses were once put through their paces. The back street leading away from the Kremlin was almost deserted at that time of night. At least I hoped it was, because I didn't want any of our KGB minders to follow me. It was 1976, I was going to a rendezvous that could spell trouble, and our delegation would not appreciate a private adventure that added further problems to the frustrating day-long sessions.

Irena was one of the exotic points of light in the drab Moscow scene. She was in her mid-twenties, taught English on the side, and on my previous visit had been assigned as my "aide." Her day job was party secretary of a Communist cell at one of the Ministries. Unlike her less exotic counterparts, Irena, who was short and pretty, wore extreme makeup and a big hairdo, sported miniskirts and foxy leather boots, and disappeared for hours at a time while her colleagues were slaving away. She loved to party, and skated close to every edge except the official one: her fun-loving side promptly disappeared at any criticism of the Party. I read her as frivolous, somehow immune from the rules, and shrewdly gaming the system that offered her a fast track upward and onward.

I was heading for an address that came with a message that morning asking if I would come alone after 10 P.M. for "a very important matter." Normally I would have mentioned it to others. But something about Irena's tone constrained me, and here I was heading toward just the sort of compromising situation all previous trips to the Soviet Union had taught me to avoid.

In those police state days, a Moscow back alley in the middle of the night was probably the safest place in the world, so I had none of the normal American fears of being mugged. Still, as the storybook lights of the Kremlin disappeared in the distance, I had growing misgivings about a potential trap. The feeling grew as I searched for the numbers on the grim façades of Stalin-era apartment houses lined in a sad row like so many battle-weary soldiers.

The numbered doorway led not up but down, into a dingy, unlit basement hallway. I knocked on the door. It was opened by a somber-looking young lady in a long, loose-fitting garment. She wore no makeup, and her hair was tied up in a bun. It was Irena. Standing behind her were two other Russians in their twenties or thirties, looking nervous. It became clear that they had decided they could not stand the oppression any longer, wanted their freedom, had quit their party-related jobs, and were anything but the kicky system-busters I had taken Irena for. They were all planning to defect, and wanted advice and help.

For the next three hours, the propaganda-inspired questions tumbled out: "Can you really live anywhere you want in America?" "Don't you need a propiska (permit) to move from one place to another?" "If I make enough money can I buy my own truck?" "Can I drive it anywhere I want?" "Will I have to pay a bribe for a license?" "Do they persecute Jews/Catholics/foreigners?" "Is it true they lynch the blacks?" "Is the US really planning to bomb Moscow?"

The toughest of all was Irena's private question to me: "Will you carry my jewels out of the country for me so I can get them from you if I make it to America?" Emigrés couldn't take more than 50 rubles out of the country, and women were subjected to a body search by a gynecological nurse. But someone who tried to smuggle their stuff out could also be in deep trouble. With great misgivings I did just that, and Irena somehow managed to emigrate. She told me later that when her group was staged through Vienna, they were taken on a walk. When they came to one shop, they stopped and stared in silence, several openly weeping. It was a butcher shop. The shop window was hung with all varieties of meats — fat chickens, hams, cuts of beef, sausages — everything that had long gone missing from the shop windows of the Workers' Paradise.

I tell this story to put a human face on the tyranny that had gripped Mother Russia since the fateful day in 1917 when Vladimir Ilyich Lenin arrived in St. Petersburg in a sealed train from Zürich to launch the revolution that brought the Bolsheviks to power and transformed the twentieth century. This episode took place about midway into the final two decades during which the Soviet Union was slowly dying from a metastasizing cancer of the system. My little midnight adventure was a small sip from the cocktail of fear, ignorance, feelings of revulsion, and stirrings of hope in a generation that Communist rulers had sought to indoctrinate through control of information and mobilization of the young.

Like all Americans who worked and raised a family during the 1945–89 Cold War, I was acutely aware of the challenge to both our security and our values from a hugely militarized and hostile version of Karl Marx's theoretical utopia. From its birth in 1917, the Soviet Union had proclaimed its determination to bring down the "capitalist-imperialist" world around it, and it devoted seventy years to actively undermining that world.

As a foreign policy specialist and political scientist, I shared with many colleagues in both government and academe a special fascination with the differences between the two systems—democratic and "scientific socialist." Democracies are governed by a variety of forms of popular participation. The USSR went for comprehensive top-down governance under the ironic banner of "all power to the people."

Of course there was no tradition of democratic rule under the preceding Tsarist regime, and the Soviet Union perpetuated the traditional Russian model of autocratic rule backed by the army and secret police. But the Bolsheviks went a vast distance further in their structure of governance centered in an all-powerful and self-perpetuating Politburo endowed with total power. To control a country of peasants and intellectuals stretching across eleven time-zones, the Soviet Communists invented a unique geometry of governance in the form of two parallel structures at all levels—government and Communist Party.

These twin governing structures ran from the top all the way through every institution and every region, down to the street level where all incoming information was controlled by the government, children were indoctrinated from infancy, and people were expected to spy on their neighbors. That system was exported to wherever Soviet power and influence ran, through Eastern Europe and Asia.

The preceding chapter told of my efforts to help Americans and others to get our arms around that unfamiliar political species through role-playing games in which experts simulated the behavior of Soviet and other decision makers. I also told of a political game I ran for the Soviets in Moscow in 1970. But nothing can replace first-hand eyeballing of things learned from cables, books, and simulations of the real thing. I had an opportunity to do that in eight visits to the Soviet Union between the Cold War frost of 1970, and the vintage year 1989 when the Russian earth moved underfoot, the Berlin Wall tumbled down, and the Soviet system and empire soon thereafter collapsed, along with the whole structure of false utopia and genuine brutality.

This chapter is drawn from a journal I kept during my visits to the Workers' Paradise. Many of the furiously contested political, military, and other issues between Moscow and Washington we wrestled with during those visits have passed into history. What follows skips much of that, and focuses on changes I observed at the human level over twenty years—changes in how the system controlled (or couldn't control) life, along with changes over time in the morale of a sampling of Soviet officialdom.

I couldn't directly eyeball their military and intelligence establishments, which were obviously enormous. What I could do was collect impressions over that final twenty years of things like the quality of life, the mood of the people, and other evidences of how individuals dealt with their plight in those final decades of one of the 20th century's most terrible and most compelling dramas. For a more frictionless read, I have changed the real-time present tense of my journal to the normal past tense.

During much of that period, incidentally, some high American officials believed that the USSR was getting stronger and would win the historic contest unless we undertook a mighty military buildup. In the 1980s President Reagan did just that, including pushing his unrealistic dream of an invulnerable anti-missile dome over the United

States. I think the Reagan build-up and rhetoric did help to demoralize a Soviet leadership that began to feel hopelessly outclassed. But I am here to testify that the rot was inexorably spreading even as some paranoid colleagues back home feared a powerful Russia having its way with a weak United States of America.

1970: FIRST IMPRESSIONS

In 1970, the US was getting bogged down in Vietnam, President Richard Nixon and National Security Adviser Henry Kissinger were starting to focus on China as a counterweight to the USSR, and the Cold War remained the context for world politics. The newly-established Soviet Institute for the USA and Canada — the so-called "Arbatov Institute" — was allowed to bring in a guest under carefully-controlled conditions. My initiation into a daunting and depressing world I had only known from diplomatic cables, intelligence reports, research, and headlines, was as a lecturer on US foreign policy and my MIT conflict research. The Institute also invited as my briefcase-carrier, my son, Lincoln Jr., who had just graduated from high school and was on his way to Harvard (and would later become an Assistant Secretary of State).

Moscow was a stark contrast to the bustling, noisy, quarrelsome diversity and high-style, carbon-monoxide-polluted atmosphere of the laid-back West. Comparisons sprang to mind of Communist East Berlin and Belgrade, both of which I had recently encountered. All had the same gray look and smell, the same unfinished, shoddy concrete structures, and empty roadways. At least my arrival as an invited guest helped me avoid the nightmare encounters with bureaucracy other visitors experienced. When we got into the car the driver took windshield wipers out of his pocket where he had stashed them ("Otherwise gone," he explained).

We were lodged in the official "guest house" of the Soviet Academy of Sciences. If the Intourist Hotel was allegedly three stars, this dump was no stars. Massive culture shock characterized our first supper in the hotel "buffet," which included shouting battles between a customer and the beefy custodian of the abacus (i.e. the cashier), as well as the indifference of the help. Also, Moscow was having a major cholera scare, so we drank nothing that didn't come in bottles.

Our constant companion was a friendly, bright young bear of a guy named Andrei Kokoshin. He had been extracted from training for the Soviet Olympic rowing team to become a graduate student at the Institute. Andrei was a delightful, if temporarily brain-washed, companion who later wound up as defense adviser to President Yeltsin and parliamentary hot-shot in the Putin era. A gray and ugly city, Moscow looked better in the vivid sunlight if one skipped the peeling paint on shabby side streets. There was virtually no traffic, but everyone wanted a car. The Institute's Deputy Director Vitaly Zhurkin said you can get a Russian to agree about pollution, but his heart wasn't in it—the car comes first. He claimed housing had improved slightly over five years ago, when it was still one family to a room. Now only half of the families were jammed into one room. The lucky others occupied flats boasting one or two rooms plus communally shared kitchens and baths.

Zhurkin said restaurant service had improved, and sure enough, a nice-looking young waiter even smiled at me once. A drive was on for better social amenities, and "our men are encouraged to become waiters" as compared to an earlier time when any able-bodied young guy's self-image had been that of engineer, pilot, or coal-miner.

The universal posture of waiting was typified by the orderly line winding around Red Square and ending at the Lenin Mausoleum— the favored attraction for Russians on their Sunday off. (What else was there to do?) The three-hour wait didn't seem to deter people who came a long way to view the remains. We got VIP treatment and went right in, which was slightly embarrassing. In the freezing cold chamber, the embalmed Lenin under bright fluorescents resembled an oversized special in a refrigerated supermarket meat department.

Stalin, who earlier had lain frozen alongside Lenin, had been made a non-person in 1956 when Prime Minister Nikita Khrushchev came clean about his many crimes, and the great tyrant was suddenly demoted to a nondescript tomb outside the Kremlin wall. But he had now mysteriously acquired a statue, and my handlers complained that American news magazines had created "havoc" over this, calling it re-Stalinization. They also insisted that only unfriendly foreigners paid attention to the order in which Kremlin leaders lined up atop the Lenin mausoleum to review parades in Red Square. I said

Lined up to view the cryogenic Lenin in Red Square, Moscow.

we learned a lot from that shifting lineup of gray, scowling, overweight guys in square coats and hats.

Moscow was cold and grim, but Red Square at night could be fabulous with its golden Kremlin towers and St. Basil's psychedelically-striped onion bulb towers. Above all, the city was clean. The well-maintained parks were full of docile, well-controlled crowds, who were barred from the huge traffic-free spaces on the roadways by militiamen, one of whom stopped my taxi and fined the driver on the spot—a common form of low-level graft. At dawn, old women with corn brooms swept the snow out of the gutters. But there was absolutely no litter, and resolute ladies set off after any kid who dropped a piece of paper (which wasn't often, given the lack of paper). Foreigners rarely visit Russian homes, but Ambassador Victor Issraelyn and his pretty wife, on home leave from the Soviet Mission to the UN and sufficiently corrupted by the West, were very gracious with me and Linc Jr.

Mostly, the institute worked me hard. Arbatov was cordial, canny, charming, and cold-eyed, and his deputy Vitaly Zhurkin cautious but extraordinarily candid (after the USSR collapsed he was the favorite Russian at many Western policy gatherings). The institute had eighty professionals, including Foreign Minister Andrei

With Deputy Director Zhurkin and Director Arbatov (both at left) at the USA Institute, Moscow.

Gromyko's son Anatoly, who was on vacation. Anatoly came back for my first lecture and stayed for the whole week.

On our second night Arbatov gave us a dinner at Arkhangelskoe, near Iusopov's palace on the Moscow River. Afterwards he took me for a walk along the dimly-lit woody paths, followed at a distance by his deputies and my guy. He dilated expansively on his Central Committee connections, worried about Nixon's temperament, and claimed that collective decision-making "produces sane policies conforming perfectly to Soviet interests." He hinted that the Kremlin hierarchy could "order some work done" by his Institute, but that it wouldn't be publicized. His line was that he couldn't change Soviet policy, and moreover "we are not a bunch of pacifists, and don't believe in phony fraternizing." But if the balance in an internal Kremlin debate about US relations was close, he could weigh in on the "right" side.

Arbatov was a master of alternate good cop-bad cop postures. In his office, brandishing an article by my classmate Henry Owen, he launched into an angry diatribe against US "Cold Warism" that picked up considerable steam. I began to worry about his blood pressure — and mine — but soon realized that his was phony while mine was real. Bad cop seamlessly switched to good cop as his minions produced a gorgeous caviar-heaped lunch for the two of us. All was suddenly detente, a successful visit, businesslike relations, etc. Until the demise of the regime, he was the Politburo's main man in dealings with Americans.

The full meaning of the "Don't You Wish Everyone Used Dial?" commercial was exposed at every public encounter. There was also a lot of public rudeness, and smiles were rarely returned by the preoccupied, harassed, set faces grimly focused on personal survival against heavy odds. A sense of defeat seemed to combine with a crafty, dogged save-yourself strategy. In the average café, the food was unspeakable and the service even worse. Flies were everywhere, and no screens nor any real selection in the shops. The military and police commanded ample resources, and it seemed to be that only the people got screwed— evidently the end-result of "power to the people."

I was getting exhausted from giving lectures scheduled for an hour that stretched till the end of the day, and began to feel like an exploited worker under the heel of my (communist) bosses. When with tongue not entirely in cheek I went public with my discontent, I was cheered by some staffers. The institute had furnished me with an escort, car, driver, and 250 rubles of spending money—four times what a teacher earned in a month. But after day-long performances, everything was closed and there was no way to spend the rubles. The last straw was a request that I show them how to organize a political-military game. They boggled at my Middle East scenario, I churlishly said no scenario, no game, so we did it my way.

After I pleaded to be taken to a proper bar and fed a proper drink, my tiny entourage proposed a special treat at the Hotel Rossiya—the monstrous new hotel near the river. Most entrances were locked so getting in was a challenge. Even this new building looked dilapidated, particularly the men's room, and the wait to be seated at one of the many empty tables was half an hour, plus another forty minutes to get fed.

The next day included a "protocol" visit to the Soviet Academy of Science. Vice President Rumyantsov, a pleasant older guy with a hearty laugh and the smell of power, was in charge of social sciences in the USSR. His qualifications? Editor-in-Chief of *Pravda* and member of the Central Committee. The Academy was a national icon and was housed in one of Catherine II's palaces. I sat in an enormous conference room overlooking spacious gardens, and admired angels dancing on the high frescoed ceiling as tea with stale cakes was brought in. We talked past each other about the nature of the social sciences in the two societies, and after forty-five minutes I politely stirred. But he insisted that we keep talking, so I told him what some adventurous (and free) American social scientists were doing. He looked skeptical.

When Linc Jr. and I visited Ambassador Jacob Beam, we found the Embassy offices shockingly shabby (a grand new embassy was built but remained unoccupied for years while KGB listening devices were dug out of the walls). Jake Beam, characteristically taciturn, seemed unusually pessimistic, one reason for his malaise being that Henry Kissinger had recently been in Moscow to negotiate with the Kremlin without notifying the Embassy that he was in town—a splendid way to demoralize your ambassador.

Taken to lunch at the Praga, a uniquely good restaurant featuring fake Moorish architecture, the American guests were offered *bowls* of Volga River caviar, along with cold sturgeon, good Russian beer, excellent black bread, and shashlik. Caviar was generally unavailable to Russians, and my hosts longingly watched me consume a huge dish of the same. I pressed them to help themselves to Linc Jr.'s, which he had politely refused, but they declined so I had to choke down a second large bowlful of the heavenly stuff.

Son-and-heir (now christened Linc Lincovitch, meaning son of Linc) and I were then taken to the "Park of Sport and Culture" for tennis. The court was stony, and a loudspeaker blared scratchy Beatles numbers, but I managed to sweat out some of the beer. (Thirty five years later Russians were winning Wimbledon and the US Open.)

The long lines in front of shops were unnervingly silent. People carefully examined every inch of our clothing; American *djins* (i.e. blue jeans) fetched several hundred rubles in Red Square. I could have changed dollars there for lots more rubles than the absurd official rate, but was massively deterred by the possibility of a police "provocation."

By the time I gave my last lecture at the Institute a warm feeling had set in, and at least half of the staff found ways to let me know they wanted to visit MIT. After my farewells, the driver took us to Spasso House, the ornate Czarist villa that housed the American Ambassador and family, where we had drinks on the terrace with the Beam family. The cholera scare had produced dehydration, and Linc Jr. downed several cold cokes in rapid succession. I put away two of them before falling happily on a vodka martini.

With US Ambassador Jacob Beam at Spasso House, Moscow.

Jake Beam was pleased that I was able to go to the mat for something like fifteen hours on US foreign policy with a group of Soviet specialists and officials, and he especially liked the fact that in my "political game" they were forced to play it our way. But he was very suspicious of Arbatov, whom he saw as a tough, hard-bitten, and unyielding critic of the US. (Dissident Andrei Sakharov once told another dissident that Arbatov was "an old whore," while his deputy Zhurkin was "an honest man.") I agreed with Beam, but confessed to also find Arbatov bright, charming and an interesting companion.

During our last night in Moscow our otherwise agreeable young escort Andrei Kokoshin denounced the poet Yevtushenko because he didn't follow the line, and Linc Lincovitch tackled him when he opined that "freedom to criticize ends where the system is involved." We drank vile-smelling mineral water from Georgia (reputed to be Stalin's favorite) and not-bad dry champagne from the Ukraine. We walked back to the hotel through dark streets along the Moscow River, where I freely admitted the superiority of the crime-free Soviet capital.

Though invited for fourteen days and rewarded with an offer to go "anywhere in the Soviet Union" as my reward, we opted to stay only eight days (I felt like the W.C. Fields' contestant whose first prize was one week in Philadelphia, and the second prize was two weeks). We decided on Leningrad and were promised the Red Arrow train. The latter was famed for its plushness and samovars, and we gladly sacrificed opening night at the Bolshoi. Just before departure, it turned out we were not taking the Red Arrow but the standard Moscow-Helsinki Express.

The railroad station was a scene of total confusion—mobs of angry tourists, shrugging officials, and total lack of information (mercifully Vitaly Zhurkin was with us). We boarded the train to find that the three of us shared a four-bed compartment with a lady in her late 80's, whose family laid her out as if for last rites. After locking the outer door, Zhurkin nobly took the other upper berth, leaving me below across from our ancient charmer. At 4:30 A.M., grandma poked me in the ribs to get up and let her out. (Vitaly said she thought we had locked her in to rape her.) There was no dining car, only one little closet with two indifferent females selling tea and salami to a vast crush of people. In the aisle, no one let anyone else pass.

Leningrad was still obsessed with its ghastly wartime ordeal, and didn't let its children forget it. When we visited the line of the furthest German advance, our guide recalled eating shoe leather during the siege. The cemetery, with 800,000 souls underground and Chopin's Funeral March aboveground, was vastly moving. But downtown, busloads of Finns arrived on a one-day tour to get drunk before returning to dry Helsinki.

At the Leningrad airport, hundreds of people milled about on the tarmac in front of the ancient airport building—which was locked. Flights were announced, then cancelled. In the little café building the johns had no seats and no toilet paper. Our ancient plane finally wheezed in to Moscow at midnight. Aeroflot's international flights got most of the caviar, and the next morning, en route to Bucharest, I ate both of ours.

1972–89: Time-Lapse Snapshots of Slow-Motion Change

Most of my subsequent visits to Moscow took place under the umbrella of the United Nations Association of the USA. We were not government officials, even though most of our members had been in government and would probably be going back in. The counterpart Soviet group was the Soviet United Nations Association, obviously under close official control. The two UN Associations provided a convenient cover for unofficial talks that paralleled official negotiations, and under that protective coloration for two decades we looked for wiggle room on stalled topics. The Cold War was on and for a decade the Soviets clung tightly to the official line. But on occasion the UN Association format made it possible to get a little ahead of officialdom by discussing possible compromises, and floating new ideas.

Before those meetings our little group usually got briefed in Washington on the state of play in bilateral negotiations—not to receive instructions, but to avoid sounding stupid when we debated policy issues. Washington often asked us to push for something they were concerned about, but we always spoke as individuals, and there was rarely a group position. In fact, sometimes our individual chores were parceled out in Moscow while we waited for our hotel rooms to be ready. Our absence of coordination and lack of instructions astonished the Russians, who always arrived with cleared position papers. This could be bothersome for both sides. Yet there was something marvelously American about our organizational sloppiness, which in any event gave an accurate impression of cacophony in the US policy community.

The two groups were clearly not symmetrical. We Americans had no official responsibilities, while the Soviets did. It could be said that we sometimes pretended to be close to our government, while they pretended not to be close to theirs.

The UNA-USA Panel included former or future rainmakers like Cyrus Vance (President Carter's secretary of state), C. Michael Blumenthal (Carter's secretary of the treasury), William Scranton (former senator, governor, and Republican Presidential candidate), retired general Brent Scowcroft (President Ford's national security adviser and later President George H.W. Bush's), and Charles Yost (President Nixon's ambassador to the UN). It also included Marshall Shulman (Carter's ambassador-at-large), Helmut Sonnenfeldt (counselor of the Kissinger State Department) and, oh yes, me. The staff work was managed with phenomenal competence by Russian-speaker Toby Gati (who became President Clinton's principal Soviet expert and assistant secretary of state for Intelligence and Research).

On the Soviet side, the delegation was usually led by the ubiquitous Georgi Arbatov and another academician or two, and it invariably included Arbatov's deputy Vitaly Zhurkin. Another frequent participant was Yevgeny Primakov, Middle East expert, *Pravda* columnist, head of the Institute of Oriental Studies, KGB officer, and eventually Boris Yeltsin's Prime Minister.

Most of the day-long discussions focused on nuclear arms control, on which official negotiations had waxed and waned for four decades. We spent endless hours on European security, on the chronically-deadlocked Arab-Israeli conflict where we backed opposite sides, and on sharp differences about UN peacekeeping. We also had an economics panel of US business leaders with whom the Communists were always more comfortable.

1972: RIGID MOSCOW, FREE-FORM TBILISI

On our 1972 visit, the political atmosphere was marginally improved by the Nixon-Brezhnev agreement on principles to moderate the struggle. Sadly, the new "détente" was soon undermined by policies that confirmed each side's suspicions. Very little had changed since my debut visit two years earlier. Windshield wipers were still stuffed in the driver's pocket when he left the vehicle, and the road traffic was sparse. The few small Moskvitches and Fiats on the road cost 4500 rubles each—a two or three year salary for most Russians. Resentful Muscovites said there was plenty of traffic—and everything else—in black-market-ridden Soviet Georgia. Some new housing was visible, but the rule was still nine square meters per person.

Our delegation was installed in the 6000 room Hotel Rossiya, where I had a small suite with a black-and-white TV and a tiny fridge (which never did make ice). The multiple buffets and restaurants were so badly laid out one had to walk forever to find one. Each wing on every floor had the standard *deshurnaya*—the unsmiling ogress who kept one's keys and monitored one's morals, accompanied by clusters of fellow ogresses, all declining to return a greeting.

A few more chic types than in 1970 were visible around Red Square, but the giant GUM department store still had long lines of sullen, badly-dressed customers waiting to buy the shoddy, overpriced junk. Lenin's Mausoleum was closed, so tourists from the provinces stared at each other.

Dinner at the Rossiya was atrocious, but the band was lively and one couple actually did the frug. I had stumbled on an ethnic celebration, and stayed to admire the energetic folk dance by a chorus line, none under two hundred pounds. On the streets, people still looked over my clothes with exquisite care. Some new fashions were visible, but men's and boys' hair was still very short, no jeans were in sight, and napkins and towels were still tiny and paper-thin. The streets were sqeaky-clean and the underpasses spotless. Why so little petty crime, antisocial behavior, or disregard for regulations? Civic pride and a citizenry massively encouraged by a zero-tolerance attitude toward any of those offenses.

Soviet TV "news" remained literally unbelievable, featuring a steady stream of heroic Soviet workers, heroic Vietnamese workers, heroic children, heroic bureaucrats, and un-heroic American imperialists. Weather remained a state secret, presumably because the West would use it for a sneak attack from the air, so the weather announcer provided only temperatures. The two TV channels were government-run, but one could switch from propaganda to officially-approved plays, operas and ballet, some of which were quite nice.

The KGB followed us everywhere, which seemed very inefficient. The current spook, standing six foot three and wearing a trenchcoat, stood out like a sore thumb. We went to a ballet in the Kremlin, and at intermission time Bob Kleiman of the *New York Times* mentioned that he and his wife were taking the night train to Leningrad. With my 1970 horror story in mind of chaos at the station, I urged them not to even think of tackling it without a Russian-speaking guide. The spook's head was towering above the crowd, so a couple of us went over and asked him point-blank to help the Kleimans. He was supposed to be undetectable, and was visibly shaken. After the blood returned to his face, he gulped and mumbled that he would.

It was the aforementioned black market-ridden Soviet Georgia which I picked for my post-meeting reward. The contrast between the two centers—Moscow and Tbilisi—was, to put it mildly, stunning.

1972: THE GEORGIAN OASIS

My visit confirmed my second-hand impressions of alienation of this nominal part of the Soviet Union from its distant rulers in Moscow. Like many other pieces of the Russian empire, Georgia was ethnically and religiously different from the Slavic, Orthodox majority and had a rich history extending back to pre-historic times. When, after the Bolshevik takeover, Lenin announced that "nationalities" were free to secede, Georgia accepted with alacrity. When Lenin changed his mind, the out-raged Georgians fought — and lost — a bitter war with their conquerors. Russians were delighted that they could buy anything they could afford from the "black-marketeer Georgians." But the Georgians (like the Chechens today) never forgot, particularly when contemporary Russia encouraged secession movements in two Georgian provinces.

Domestic flights to Georgia and the Caucasus used a minor Moscow airport with no provision for foreigners. My flight companion to Tbilisi (which means hot water) was a pleasant young French TV sales engineer, who told me that I spoke French with a Russian accent. In Tbilisi, in a nice corner suite overlooking the river, the ice trays worked. But as in Moscow women workers in the hotel angrily screamed at each other. The streets were packed with people of every age chatting away at all hours. Everyone smoked.

A huge statue of hometown boy Joseph Stalin dominated the main drag, despite his having been dethroned at the 20th Soviet Party Congress of 1956. Street signs were supposed to be bilingual, but were all in Georgian script. And Georgians lived up to their reputation for exuberance, with the consumption of alcohol nothing short of astonishing. Dinner in the hotel dining room featured an unending succession of standing (swaying) toasts, and next morning half the men were drinking champagne at breakfast.

My suspicious Intourist guide took me to the Palace of Friendship, where I was received by the overseer of non-existent Georgian foreign policy. My minder translated the obligatory welcome speech by the Foreign Minister about peace and friendship, followed by my obligatory insincere response. We were joined by the Deputy Foreign Minister, who was commanded to produce gift books along with some dusty postcards and an even dustier candy box. I inadvertently dropped a French word, and discovered that both officials — but not my minder — spoke some French. We had an animated conversation in French while my increasingly agitated handler glowered.

Next was a private showing of an incredibly boring propaganda film. From a seat behind me the Deputy Foreign Minister whispered in my ear that he stayed up late to hear jazz programs on the Voice of America. His favorite "jazz musicians" turned out to be Doris Day and Fred Astaire. He also told me risqué jokes in bad French.

I was taken out one evening for shashlik. Half the restaurant's customers were smashed, and constantly leapt to their feet with shouted toasts while musicians produced sobbing Middle East tunes. The next morning I discovered that someone had broken into my room during the night and cleverly opened my locked suitcase.

That evening my young French engineer friend staggered into my hotel dining room. Two days ago he was bright-eyed and dewy-cheeked, ready to help Georgia modernize its TV. Two days of Georgian hospitality had transformed him into a hollow-eyed wreck. He said his telecom hosts worked two hours, and partied the rest of the time, averaging fifteen toasts at both lunch and dinner. French honor was at stake, so he had to join them, finally becoming deathly ill.

I ordered dinner for us in broken Russian, and we were joined by a Finn who seemed to understand four languages but spoke none. A drunken diner at an adjacent table covered with bottles of Georgian wine gathered up an armload, lugged them over to our table, and started on the toasts. When it all started up again I feared that my new friend, his face filled with horror and his eyes awash with tears of self-pity, was going to die. But once more he managed to save France's honor.

As the only foreigner on the Tbilisi-Moscow return flight, I was unable to decipher any of the announcements. The plane had no reading lights, no ventilation, no oxygen masks, and no luggage racks. Farmers with fresh vegetables to sell in Moscow loaded up the flimsy overhead string nets with their heavy wooden crates, whose sharp edges brushed precariously across my scalp. Most passengers didn't bother to buckle seat belts on takeoff or landing, and the tough-looking security guard stood during the trip while putting moves on the stewardess, who also stood. In Moscow I found that Bob Roosa (former Deputy Treasury Secretary) had a ticket for me to the State Circus, which was surely the most tasteful, energetic, and enjoyable circus I had ever seen.

1974: Détente Comes Undone

In 1974, détente was coming under increasing strain, thanks to Soviet fueling of Third World conflicts and American temporizing on promised economic aid. The Soviets were worried about bomber gaps, missile gaps, and military budgets, but they were determined to sound confident (exactly like their counterparts in Washington).

In what sounded like a policy shift, Primakov wanted the two superpowers to control nuclear proliferation through the International Atomic Energy Agency. Also, their economy must have been hurting, because they said they wanted to join the World Bank and create joint ventures with Americans. Direct investment in the USSR was now OK, but profits had to be called "royalties," "commissions," or some other euphemism.

They also floated the idea of an agreement combining the non-use of force (they'd like to win without getting hurt) with no-first-use of nuclears (which the Pentagon short-sightedly opposed). The session got hung up on their proposed "Indian Ocean Zone of Peace," and Primakov and I were asked to work out a compromise draft. We came up with something that made no sense, since Americans wanted an end to Soviet meddling on the Indian Ocean's southern shores, while the Soviets wanted our nukes out of Diego Garcia Island.

At a fancy luncheon hosted by the Foreign Ministry, there appeared something we rarely saw—a decent-looking steak, whose immersion in mud-colored gravy only slightly diminished my anticipation. Just as I reached for a fork, the host began his welcoming toast. Ten minutes later, as the beautiful entrecote turned into a congealed mass, he was just warming up. I could have wept.

There were no telephone directories since phone numbers, like the weather, remained classified. The latest quip asked, "What's the difference between a joke and an anecdote?" Answer: "An anecdote only gets you three years."

1976: Inside the Politburo

In the fall of 1976, détente was evaporating fast as Moscow tossed gasoline on Third World brush fires, and Washington reneged on promised economic aid. Republican Gerald Ford was voted out and Democrat Jimmy Carter in. One of Carter's early pronouncements was that, unlike Nixon and Ford, his policies would not be dominated by the Soviet Union. Whoever decides such things in Moscow had asked that ours be the first private American group to get on a plane after the election.

Chaos remained the order of the day in Moscow hotels. The Intourist elevators dropped just enough to produce panic. TV, still black and white, never mentioned the arrival of American grain but instead ran old footage of Sheriff Bull Connor's dogs beating up blacks in Birmingham. But the food was an improvement over the Rossiya, featuring caviar and blinis washed down with good Russian beer.

Some new construction was underway, but housing was still limited to nine square meters per person. There was a new gas station on the huge Leninskaya Prospekt but few cars. People repaired their own cars, and still pocketed windshield wipers while they were parked. Snow drifted down, and heavily bundled-up shoppers who looked frozen stood impassively in long lines for shops that may or may not have fresh vegetables, hats, stockings, shoes, vodka, or television sets. Paper napkins were still tiny and toilet paper abrasive. When a new book appeared on a street stand, a mob formed. But Russian-made shoes, always the source of instant identification at the UN, seemed a bit more normal looking.

Occasionally something concrete may have stemmed from our endless discussions. The new Soviet prototype "Backfire" bomber had been setting people's hair on fire in the Pentagon on the assumption that it represented a new threat to the US. The Soviets insisted it could only fly one-way, which meant it couldn't attack us. Our delegation to Moscow this time included James McDonnell, the air pioneer who became chairman of McDonnell-Douglas aircraft. He listened patiently to the Soviet denial that Backfire could ever be configured for a round trip to North America and back. Scratching his head thoughtfully, he drawled, "Waal, give me a couple of days with that plane and a few of my mechanics, and I guarantee that bird will be able to fly roundtrip." The discussion ended abruptly and we heard little more of Backfire.

Our delegation had a rare session with Boris Ponomarev, member of the Central Committee. One had seen the long Zil limos, curtains drawn, zooming in and out of the main Kremlin gate while militiamen frantically signaled everyone to get out of the way. Inside, the interior was palatial, but the areas where the superleaders worked had been modernized, and were discreet, hushed, and intimidating.

Six of us sat at a long table across from Ponomarev, his interpreter, and a couple of Central Committee aides. Photos were taken, tea, cookies, and chocolates offered. But what was billed as a purely ceremonial half-hour stretched to an hour and a half, as we asked increasingly pointed questions and he replied with increasingly strident boilerplate. I was fascinated to stare at one of the most powerful men in the world, accountable only to a handful of associates who could instantly make him a non-person. Like a Chinese meal, it left us hungry an hour later.

The value for them was clearly different. The next day the official government newspaper *Izvestia* had a headline story about our "friendly talk" with Ponomarev. Jack Matlock, the competent low-key US Ambassador, said he read this as a signal of Moscow's interest in having the incoming Carter administration drop its anti-Soviet election rhetoric and return to the Nixon/Kissinger detente that had deteriorated during the Ford administration.

But the Soviets, insisting that "you can't abolish the class struggle," argued the necessity of militarizing local "struggles for freedom" and "helping regimes threatened by fascism." One of their generals we met with claimed that the Soviet navy was defensive but ours was offensive. Sure. Ambassador Matlock said US-Soviet relations were either on a plateau or going downhill.

China was becoming a three-Excedrin headache for them, which may explain the slight improvement in the tone of our meeting. They typically started out by claiming that the US (with Chinese collusion) was erecting a "wall" against the Motherland ("encirclement"). But they also wanted us to somehow reduce China's military capacities, arguing that we had more influence with Beijing than they did. One high official explained relations with their great sister Communist state by pointing to North America on a wall map: "Please picture Mexico with a hostile government, possessing nuclear weapons, and claiming a quarter of the United States." Me: "Gulp." Official: "How would you feel?" Me: "Not very good." Russian: "Ah, you've got it!" It was bizarre that some Americans still believed in a cohesive "Sino-Soviet bloc."

The Hotel Intourist claimed to stock the *International Herald-Tribune* but it was never available. Bendix CEO Mike Blumenthal demanded of our hosts, "How do you expect us to do business in a place where we can't even buy a newspaper?" The current joke: The new Five-Year Plan lays out what we won't have for the next five years.

No trip to Moscow lacked its *Catch 22* story. Mine took place at the *Berioska*—the dollar shop not available to Russians—where goodies were sold to foreigners with hard currency. My purchases included a bottle of Stoly vodka. I took my slip to the cashier, and found I could now pay with MasterCard! Then it was back to each counter to collect one's purchases. The saleslady brought out two bottles of vodka. Me: "I only wanted one." She: "My slip says two." Me: "I really don't want two." She: "You have to take them." Me: "A refund then, please." She: "We don't give refunds." Me: "May I see the manager?" She (after lengthy disappearance): "The manager is out." Me: "Please try." She (in an accusing tone): "You paid with a credit card!" Me: "OK, give me a credit and I'll buy something else." She: "You have to buy it at the same counter where you got the vodka." Me: "What else do they have?" She: "Chewing gum." Me: (Unprintable). She (Shrugging).

I finally spotted a tin of English chocolates, which cost fifty kopeks more than the vodka. Me: "I'll take this." She: "That will be fifty kopeks difference." Me: "Here are 50 kopeks." She: "We don't take kopeks." Me: "OK, here's a dollar." She: "We don't have any change." And so it went, into the snowy night.

1978: SMALL CRACKS IN THE MONOLITH

Two years later, in 1978, some tiny cracks appeared. A high-ranking Soviet privately described his own recent book as "propaganda." The good news was that some of our arguments reportedly impressed General Secretary Brezhnev. The bad news was that they wanted us to stop nagging them about Soviet interventions in Africa, which was "part of the historical process."

They were more preoccupied than ever with China, and afraid of US "collusion" with Beijing, quoting Zbigniew Brzezinski to prove our hostile intent. The endless arguments on the SALT nuclear weapons reductions followed the familiar playbook in which the Soviets wanted agreement on broad general principles, while the US wanted to see the fine print. Much of this argument went on to the backburner a year later when the Soviet Union invaded Afghanistan.

What was different this time? A couple of things. The hotel this time was the Sovietskaya—an ancient (1908), baronial (long velvet curtains, sweeping staircases, elegant marble pillars) watering hole of Moscow's Tsarist merchant class. When I tried the fire escape doors on my floor they were locked. Someone said the management preferred losing its guests to losing control over them.

As I climbed the grand staircase, I heard "Linc!" hissed from behind the curtain. The strained visage of a young USA Institute researcher Olga peered around the long drape. "We can only talk by the window." As I moved behind the curtain she whispered, "I can't breathe. I have to get away. They are making me tell lies!" "Who is making you tell lies?" "My thesis supervisor." (She named the second deputy director of the Institute, who we knew was KGB.)

Rock and roll had finally penetrated, and on a stage at the end of the huge hotel dining room a small but energetic group, framed by two gigantic speakers, performed throughout dinner. The amplification was full-throated, making it impossible to converse over the inedible food, so I danced with Olga between courses while she poured out her anger and frustration. She eventually made it to the US, where she became a successful entrepreneur, like many of her well-educated Russian cohorts.

1980: THE SOVIETS BEGIN TO FEEL NERVOUS

The election of Ronald Reagan as President in 1980 would soon plunge bilateral relations, already frosty, even deeper in the ice. The Reagan rhetoric was tough, notably his characterization of the USSR as "The Evil Empire." But it went well beyond rhetoric. As US military strength was ramped up, nuclear jockeying in Europe threatened a perilous game of chicken over intermediate range nuclear weapons. The later opening of Soviet records revealed that some Soviet leaders actually believed the US was planning to launch a disabling military strike. On the US side, things became hairy as Moscow seemed to be making preparations against that mythical event. Some read those reports as indicating a possible Soviet preemptive attack against us— precisely the worst-case escalation scenario in which mutual misreading of intelligence could lead to a catastrophe.

Happily, the cloud lifted, and Reagan in fact wound up appalling his advisers by momentarily agreeing with Soviet Premier Gorbachev to scrap all their nuclear weaponry. The Washington hawks' fear of being overmatched by the Soviets was ironic in a period of growing rot within the Soviet system, but it is not clear that everyone in Washington understood or attributed significance to the process, which was undramatic and even invisible alongside the official bluster and threat.

Ours was the first private American group to be invited to Moscow since the Soviet invasion of Afghanistan in December, 1979. It was small—former Governor William Scranton, General Brent Scowcroft, industrialist Ivan Selin, Sovietologist Hal Sonnenfeldt, Toby Gati, and me. Before the US election we had been invited for briefings from senior figures in the Carter administration (which I had just left) and the Reagan campaign. The Carter people asked us to push their stalled arms control package and to warn Moscow that an invasion of Poland would put an end to détente. The Republican team wanted us to make clear that a Reagan victory would confirm Moscow's worst fears.

It did that without our help, as we discovered on arrival in Moscow right after the election. Moscow's nightmare had come true, and the Soviets were nervous, pessimistic about the future, resigned to a costly US military build-up, and wistfully hopeful that Reagan would "turn out to be like Nixon." One high official summed it up when he urged that Washington avoid overreacting to "normal Soviet moves" which were "just for security" and intended only to "offset US superiority." The Soviets showed an extraordinary amount of interest in us, as did our Embassy and the world press, which followed us around and packed our final press conference.

I got to make the US opening statement, in which I ventilated my strong belief that détente had been wrecked by Soviet insistence on taking unilateral advantage while expecting us to act as passive victims of the historical dialectical process. Scowcroft told them that SALT II (Strategic Arms Limitation Talks) prescribing nuclear arms cuts was now off the table. (Sonnenfeldt added that the SALT process would have no resurrection or Easter Sunday, and Arbatov got even with pious President Carter by quipping that that was better than being born again.)

With former and future National Security Adviser Brent Scowcroft in Moscow.

The Soviet team now unembarrassedly included key Central Committee officials. Valentin Falin, former Soviet Ambassador to Germany and one of the smartest senior *apparatchiki*, made the remarkable confession that Moscow was not sinless. But he added that he had found the Carter administration unpredictable (which it was), and complained that the White House never seemed to notice when Brezhnev said Moscow was not trying for military superiority. Their civilians now appeared free to discuss sensitive technical military matters they used to leave to the uniforms. Primakov bizarrely argued that the Soviet invasion of Afghanistan was a "stabilizing act."

A closet dissident told me that respect for the US was lost when we didn't hit Iran after their seizure of our embassy, a mistake Tsarist Russia did not make when the Persians once attacked their embassy. He even claimed that if we had been tougher on Iran, Moscow wouldn't have invaded Afghanistan. Businessman Selin (who became undersecretary of state) tried fruitlessly to arrange a serious discussion with Soviet management systems experts. He quipped that the Russians had just smiled when, in my somewhat overheated opening statement, I had "asked them for unconditional surrender," but "had hysterics" when he asked to meet their systems analysts.

Our Spasso House visit was the first US-Soviet gathering in the eleven months since they invaded Afghanistan. Courtly Ambassador (and IBM founder) Tom Watson was extremely gloomy, offering a

fairly apocalyptic toast, the gist of which was, first, that if God had designed the two most antagonistic powers, it would have been us two;
and then, that our two countries were on a collision course; and finally, only drastic action could avert a smash-up. His deputy chief of
mission Mark Garrison whispered to me that Watson had arrived hop-
ing to be the détente ambassador, but had been almost totally isolated
since the invasion of Afghanistan.

That's at the "macro" level. What about the "micro" level? A
nascent women's movement had sprung up, and miniskirts began to
make an appearance. But women's lib was frowned on. (As one typical chauvinist put it, "Man should be the boss, women belong in the
kitchen.") The women worked at jobs all day, getting home when
their husbands did—but were still expected to do all the shopping
and housework. The common quip remained, "We pretend to work
and they pretend to pay us."

Faces on the street were grim as ever as shoppers contended
with long lines at the *Produkt* (grocery) store. There was no meat outside of Moscow and little inside, with potatoes available only in the
"free (i.e. black) market," while over-privileged Scowcroft and I com-
peted vigorously for Ivan Selin's stock of fresh caviar. Women danced
together at bars, teenagers resembled the US of the 1950s. The latest
joke: Two years ago a popular film was *The Taste of Bread*; a new one
will be called *The Smell of Meat*.

1984: THE UN IN LENINGRAD

In 1984, I found myself in St. Petersburg (still Leningrad) as a member
of the US delegation to a regional UN disarmament conference. The
Soviet officials present were still shaken up by the US military buildup,
Star Wars in particular, and one Central Committee staffer somberly
allowed as how "we must start thinking in an entirely new manner."

The UN meeting was full of platitudes and fantasy but, as
sometimes happens, was offset by a ludicrous sidebar in the form of
a reception given for the delegates by the mayor of Leningrad. The
room was set up with a podium and a table in the center laden with
officially-available delicacies including caviar, whole sturgeons, and
good vodka in tiny glasses. Just as I headed toward it with joy in my

heart, the mayor began his speech of welcome. Along with my polite fellow delegates, I retreated back against the wall.

As the Mayor droned on, I noticed Vitaly Zhurkin edging up to the table. Looking sideways at me, he hissed "Linc, come!" Emboldened by higher authority, I again sidled toward the table, this time backwards. I reached behind me in the general direction of the caviar and came up with a fistful of delicacies, which I managed to put in my mouth while smiling encouragingly at the Mayor. As he resolutely droned on, I was surprised at how much one can eat facing backwards while the faint of heart look on disapprovingly.

1989: "THINGS FALL APART; THE CENTER CANNOT HOLD" (W.B. YEATS)

My final visit, once again with the "parallel" US and Soviet groups, took place in 1989 on the cusp of the system's impending implosion. Premier Michael Gorbachev had a growing reputation abroad as a Communist leader who was different. He had already made two major speeches at the UN that could have been given by any US President with a few name changes.

There were certainly ideologues left over from the Stalin era who would have loved to smash those who had thwarted them, and they had been highly visible during my early visits. But by the late 1980s, senior advisers to the waning leadership were trying desperately to appease the US, by finding non-humiliating ways to modulate the adversary relationship that had poisoned the last half-century. At our meetings the Soviet pretense of non-government status was stripped away, and the "unofficial" Soviet delegation included serving officials like now Deputy Foreign Minister Vladimir Petrovsky (who said he had written Gorbachev's two astonishing UN speeches) and division head Andrei Kozyrev (who quickly became President Yeltsin's Foreign Minister).

Despite Gorbachev's policies of *glasnost* (openness) and *perestroika* (economic restructuring), life was pretty rotten for his people. The bottom line was that *glasnost* worked, *perestroika* didn't. The food crisis was severe and, as one party member put it, "we are expected to eat *glasnost*." There was little food in the shops and not much of anything else, though meat was still available in the bitterly-resented "special stores" for the *nomenklatura* (party élite).

During a break I visited some shops. The butcher shop was appalling—a few stringy chickens, some cans of generic smoked fish, and a mob of sullen customers. The drill was still to line up to pay the cashier in advance, then line up to order something only to be told *vsyaw* (all gone), then line up again to retrieve what was left of one's order and have the receipt checked.

This time they put us up at the Cosmos, a gigantic new hostelry. Standing around for forty minutes in the enormous lobby waiting for the arguments over rooms to cease revealed things old and new. Old: no one was admitted to the hotel without explaining the reason or showing a pass—except VIPs (like us) who were passed through the clot of non-door-opening doormen, slovenly militiamen, taxi drivers, and anonymous layabouts, all of whom blocked hotel entrances. Lobby kiosks sold the usual *brak* (junk) for rubles, the rest for hard currency. Calculations were still made with lightning speed—on the abacus. New: one drab corner was brightened by a wall of shiny new slot machines, made in Spain, and activated with tokens costing one US dollar. In another corner, a neon-lit bar sported a huge illuminated "Heineken Beer" sign. The thrill of seeing non-communist foreign papers on display was only slightly dampened by the fact that they were a week old (even at the kiosk in the Foreign Ministry the *International Herald Tribune* was five days old).

One sign of improvement on the consumer front was the new crop of "House of Fashion" shops. There were now plenty of blue jeans on the street, plus Nike running shoes (on closer inspection, the swoosh logo was fake). Upgraded women's fashions appeared to run to pink hair and figured mesh stockings, though the female majority still wore babushkas and heavy wool stockings. After abolishing the *dezhurnaya* custom in hotels and experiencing a crime wave, every floor once again featured the dragon ladies responsible for keys and morals. But this time they seemed a little younger, prettier, and less forbidding.

My room was equipped with a new Soviet-made *color* TV, its empty cardboard carton still on the floor. Instead of one TV channel for propaganda and the other for culture, there were now five, one pounding out rock, another lively conversations that not so long ago would have brought a prison term. One program sympathetically depicted a crowd of worshipers, some quite young, at an Orthodox church ceremony. An English-language program on Radio Moscow called *Up the Market* described its target as "businessmen around the world." My room even had a small fridge, and several sizes of real towels, colored and uncolored, though toilet paper still resembled #4 sandpaper.

With childish faith in the new freedom to speak up, I dropped my 20-foot long shortwave radio antenna out the window for improved reception, and waited nervously for the militia to send me to the nearest Gulag. The *Voice of America* in English came through weakly, the BBC strongly and Radio Moscow like gangbusters. You could be telephoned by direct dial—but not from here. Instead, hours were spent, third-world style, trying to connect, occasionally reaching an operator who told you in poor English that all international circuits were busy.

Red Square at night, dramatically illuminated in a light snowfall, was still one of the premier sights of the world. Across from the Kremlin, the GUM department store was architecturally still a splendid baroque pre-mall, but no longer crowded thanks to an almost total lack of goods on the shelves. Gorbachev's anti-alcoholism drive meant no vodka at receptions, none sold before two P.M. and less visible public drunkenness.

Some of the younger guys who sought me out in the corridor during the breaks to talk about multi-party democracy shared the general outrage at Gorbachev, and spoke of Boris Yeltsin the way some Americans once talked about Eugene McCarthy or even George Wallace— as a handy protest against everyone else. At the Foreign Ministry's Institute of Diplomatic Studies, the Rector Richard Ovinnikov (who had been around the UN for years) and his deans told me they couldn't use any of the old textbooks, which were "full of lies." But they still had no new ones and, for the occasion of my visit, at each place at the table lay bad photocopies of my recent articles. Two faculty members announced that they taught my "theory of conflict," which I didn't know I had.

It was hard to believe one's ears along the Arbat listening to "Hyde Park" style speeches in which nothing seemed taboo except direct public criticism of Gorbachev. The themes, repeated like a new mantra: "We were lied to, secrecy ruined socialism, Marxism-Leninism hasn't fed us, we lied to the young people who now distrust everything, we will do almost anything to collaborate with you and get your help which we desperately need."

Russian-speaker Toby Gati and I spent an extraordinary hour driving all over Moscow with a pickup driver who put New York cabbies to shame with his explosion of rage that he said reflected the feelings of all the workers he knew. It went something like this: "The country is in the hands of a Mafia. Gorbachev, Schmorbachev—they are all alike, crooks and parasites who promise everything and grab it for themselves. *Perestroika* is a joke, nothing has changed except for the worse. If an election were held tomorrow, no worker would vote for the Communist party, which would be thrown out on its ear. It's all words. Gorbachev made promises but delivered nothing. Yeltsin is the only one who speaks for the people. (Now shouting) I'm sick to death of their deceit, promises, and privileges. I could take it if everyone was poor and equal, instead of poor and unequal. But we have no food and no goods, and they get everything."

The questions are obvious: Why did we keep going to Moscow, hardly a garden spot? Were we ever able to influence events? Indeed, could *any* private group lacking responsibility and authority have impacted the deeply-fraught relationship between the world's two nuclear giants? Is the virus of personal freedom communicable?

Maybe some of our groups were affected by this experience as they moved into positions of high authority (for example Cyrus Vance, who became secretary of state, and Evgeny Primakov, who became prime minister). Maybe hanging out with undisciplined, free-speaking Americans had a positive impact on at least some Russians, although it doubtlessly confirmed some in their prejudices. When we came up with something particularly useful, it was passed up to the top, starting with our earliest joint effort on preventing nuclear proliferation which reportedly helped the nuclear non-proliferation treaty negotiators.

But the real answer is that I don't know what influence such "dual-track" efforts had. All I can conclude is that during a protracted period of high tension, frustration, and occasional terror, one had to believe that, given the enormous stakes, it was worth the effort.

8 THE REAL WORLD II: 1976
The Middle East: Kings, Bombs, and Touch Football

For anyone interested in international relations, American foreign policy, comparative religion, or issues of war and peace, the Middle East is the place for you. Westerners have tried for decades to export to the Arab Middle East their various brands of governance, but with few if any examples of success. More recently the United States revived, with a literal bang, its periodic historical urge for political proselytizing, with the laudable but problematic aim of bringing reform to a region traditionally ruled by feudal, monarchical, or autocratic leadership. The US-led overthrow of the Saddam Hussein regime in Iraq in 2003 had the explicit goal of spreading liberal democracy throughout the entire area, most particularly in the hostile states surrounding democratic Israel. As for the outcome, as so often in American history only time will tell.

For a political scientist, a fascinating aspect of Arab governance is the relation between mosque and state, notably in Saudi Arabia. There, the deal struck between the rising Saudi royal family and the puritanical religious movement led by zealous followers of an 18th century cleric named Muhammad al-Wahab, made Wahabism the official ideology of the kingdom. The result is a political geometry featuring a reluctantly modernizing monarchy co-existing in parallel with a fanatical Islamic establishment. The first of the three stories later in this chapter illustrates both the nature of that rule, and the gap in understanding between that culture and ours.

Another favorite form of governance in the Arab Middle East is all-powerful autocratic governance at the hands of tribal chiefs such as the murderous Iraqi Tikriti Saddam Hussein, and the brutal dynastic rule of the Alawite Assads of Syria, both members of the fascistic Baa'th Party. A glimpse of that unlovely model of brutality and cynicism can be had in my third story in this chapter.

In the Persian/Arabian Gulf, rather than those two familiar models of governance and power arrangements, one can find a third genre. Typified by Kuwait, some Gulf states display a greater degree of political and cultural sophistication, and even glimmerings of political democracy, doubtless fostered by centuries of contact with the outside secular world via trade routes from three continents. My Kuwait vignette suggests a degree of what the Italians call *dolce far niente* that would be unthinkable in either of the other two political cultures.

Those stories point to larger issues that make the Arab Middle East such a chronic challenge for American foreign policy-makers. But no discussion of the Middle East, however brief, can make sense without a focus on its very centerpiece. The Arab-Israeli conflict has been unique in its effect on regional stability, and in its nagging centrality for US administrations.

Certainly no other part of the world has been the subject of so many political-military games. Those games hopefully improved our understanding. But alas, they cannot claim to have succeeded yet in advancing the prospects for an enduring peace. Indeed, that conflict has for a half-century threatened to cause American diplomacy to fall in flames over and over again as Washington has tried in one way or another to deal with the always smoldering and sometimes raging conflagration that has been consuming the two Semitic cousins.

On a more personal note, in an unplanned way, some significant pieces of my professional life have involved the Middle East. It all began in the early post-World War II years in the State Department, when the Arab-Israeli conflict suddenly took center stage. My education continued as I became a student of conflict trying to analyze the struggle between Israelis and Palestinians—the two inheritors of Britain's League of Nations Mandate for that holy/unholy place. Part-time involvement continued when I returned to Washington to serve in the National Security Council. As an MIT professor, I found myself in the Middle East several times lecturing for the State

Department in the role of scholar with an independent, but presumably not too embarrassing, interpretation of US foreign policy. And among the senior-level political gaming exercises I have run were several on the Middle East, including one in Moscow.

For Americans, the Middle East presents two quite different story lines. One centers on the Gulf. (I learned the hard way not to call it the "Persian Gulf" in Saudi Arabia, and not to say "Arabian Gulf" in Iran.) Modern American policy in the Gulf has its own complex narrative: two wars with Iraq, a love-hate relation with Iran, and an insatiable thirst for Mid-East oil. That part of the story has obviously been worth a book or two.

In my musing on US policy plus the three illustrative yarns that follow, the focus is on the other half of the Middle East story—the turbulent piece of real estate known to historians as "The Fertile Crescent" and to some geographers as the "Near East." For our purposes that means Israel and its unwelcoming Arab neighbors. (By the way, how many realize that to say "Near East," "Middle East," or "Far East," is to unconsciously parrot old-time British labels describing distances from London?) Whatever you call it, it is where a bitter and bloody conflict has played out for a half-century between Israelis and Arabs, with the United States sometimes in the role of referee.

Everyone is by now painfully aware of the litany of issues on which the "Middle East peace process" has regularly foundered: final boundary lines, the fate of several million Palestinian refugees, and control of places sacred to both Jews and Muslims (not to mention Christians). But I have long been convinced that, underneath those specifics, the deep estrangement between Arabs and Israelis rests at its very essence on the profoundly different historic narratives—the potent mix of memory, myth, and reality that each side carries inside its collective head.

The dominant historic memory of Israelis is the Holocaust in Europe in which six million Jews were slaughtered. Anyone who threatens Israelis is seen through the agonizing filter of that experience. The dominant historic memory in the minds of Near East Arabs looking at Israel is Western colonialism from which the Arab world only recently escaped. It is this huge psychological disjunction that, subconsciously or consciously, lies beneath the positions each has brought to one failed negotiation after another.

The rise to power of extremists in both camps has undermined the most basic aspiration of both sides, further poisoning the atmosphere. Palestine's Hamas faction has terrorized and slaughtered innocent Israeli civilians while demanding the extinction of Israel itself. Right-wing Israelis have asserted divine claims to the entire Palestinian-populated West Bank and even proposed expulsion of its people. Even without those extremes, Palestinian rhetoric has always denied Israel the feeling of permanence and security it most desires, while typical Israeli attitudes toward Palestinians (and indeed all Arabs) often echo the feeling of superiority typical of colonial overlords toward Rudyard Kipling's "lesser breeds." But the reality is that multiple personal tragedies have been inflicted on both peoples, with murderous Palestine suicide bombings followed by brutal Israeli leveling of homes and grabbing of land, in a mindless cycle of death and destruction.

A final point to ponder is the extraordinary way in which, unlike Americans, the ancient tribes in the Middle East are not mobile, do not accommodate easily to different cultural styles, and marinate in their long history. In the bloody 1980–1990 Iran-Iraq War, both sides had a burning memory of the battle of Karbala in the year 637, when Arabs conquered the Sasanians who ruled what was then Persia. Religious Israelis measure their divinely-ordained presence in the region at over 3,000 years.

For all these reasons the two estranged Semitic cousins talk past each other, and for an outsider to explain each to the other, or to counsel moderation was all too often to speak in a vacuum.

The Middle East in American Politics

Both the Israeli and Arab worlds have a preoccupation with the United States that borders on the obsessive. Israel is totally dependent on the US for economic, diplomatic, and moral support. Egypt, Jordan, Saudi Arabia, and the Gulf states have also been dependent on the US, whether for defense, money, arms, or oil purchases. Dependency breeds resentment, reinforced by a deep-seated suspicion that Washington is engaged in a gigantic conspiracy in which they are caught like flies in a web. The assumption that everything the US does is really a sinister plot prevailed long before the invasion and occupation of Iraq. As Henry Kissinger once noted, "In the Middle East, the part of the world where mirages are a natural phenomenon, nothing is ever as it appears."

When I lectured in Israel, my *bona fides* seemed based on my writings, which they had extensively marked up and annotated for purposes of challenging me. If there was suspicion, it was of American overtures to the Arabs behind Israel's back. In Arab countries, my credentials had less to do with academic achievements than with the fact that I had worked for the US government, was undoubtedly connected to the CIA, and was therefore useful to cultivate. (I have sometimes wondered if there *is* truly one God in the region, namely the CIA.) Americans should probably be flattered that incompetence is often mistaken by foreigners for a devious plot.

Every US administration has tried its hand at resolving the Arab-Israeli conflict. In 1947, the US was midwife to the UN's Partition Plan, which divided Britain's Palestinian mandate into Arab and Israeli states. Ever since then, the United States has been the indispensable third party as its diplomats, Sisyphus style, doggedly pushed the rock of peace up the mountain of conflict, only to see it roll down again and again. Results-oriented Americans have been chronically frustrated by the parties' multiple suspicions, as well as by the way history and religion combine to override sanity.

There is another chasm, that which separates Middle East and Middle West, so to speak. This is the foreign policy sector in which US domestic politics most consistently override any pretension of even-handedness. The pro-Israeli lobby is formidable, as officials in both branches can attest. Its unbroken string of political victories in both Congress and executive branch have inspired the Arab-American community to work toward a more effective lobby of their own in Washington. But that may not help the Arab cause, for four reasons.

First is the strong American attachment to democratic Israel, bolstered by deep sympathies engendered by the Holocaust. Second, the influence of the modest-sized American Jewish population is multiplied by the pro-Zionism of the huge evangelical Christian community. The millions of Americans who take the Book of Revelation literally, support Israel as a step toward their apocalyptic vision. These fundamentalist beliefs have reinforced the consistent pro-Israeli tilt of US policy. Third, American military strategists have preferred to place their chips on high-tech, militarized Israel as a sophisticated, reliable ally—a Sparta that supplies a US anchor in an unstable but crucial region.

The biggest factor of all is the way nineteen Arab Muslims on September 11, 2001 profoundly changed America by hijacking civilian airliners and launching them as missiles. If some Americans are still privately anti-Semitic, the post-9/11 anti-Arab prejudice has been blatant. What is particularly tough on Arab-Americans is the lack of distinction drawn between peaceful Muslims and fanatical Islamists. If a bombing occurs, Arabs are automatically suspected, on the same premise that lies behind the apocryphal Scottish "Drunkard's Law" (if a known drunkard is seen in the vicinity of a crime, he is presumed guilty).

This combination of factors has kept Israel as a vital national interest through ten US administrations. But it was not always so, particularly back in 1947 when London dumped the combustible issue of Palestine's future onto the lap of the just-born United Nations. The notion of a Jewish state in the Middle East had no constituency in a State Department whose regional experts were exclusively Arabists, and the Zionists' only constituency was in the White House. Presidential responsiveness to Israel has in fact always been ahead of the State Department, which has the rest of the world to deal with. But that difference was most stark during the early years of the UN when President Truman overruled his State Department on issue after issue concerning the Middle East.

The matter came to a boil in November 1947 over the plan to partition Palestine into Arab and Jewish states, with Jerusalem to be internationally governed until a final status could be negotiated. The regular US delegation to the UN General Assembly in New York dealt with all pending issues on the agenda—except this one.

Unprecedentedly, the White House set up a parallel US delegation in New York under future Secretary of State Dean Rusk to ensure that President Truman's policies were not sabotaged. Rusk later told me that under those extraordinary pressures he saw delegates emerging from the conference room and throwing up in the nearest

wastebasket. As a junior officer, I happened to sit with the US delegation on the day when, in an atmosphere of unparalleled tension,
partition of Palestine was narrowly approved and the six Arab delegates marched to the podium to proclaim that "this means war."

As low-level fighting began, policy warfare escalated in this nation's capital. The diplomats in the Near East bureau headed by the
fabled Loy Henderson bitterly opposed US recognition of Israel as
something guaranteed to exacerbate already-strained relations with
their Arab clients (some in that bureau and elsewhere in the department were also outspokenly anti-Semitic).

Internecine battles in Washington continued up to a second
moment of high drama when, late one night in May of 1948, Israel
proclaimed its independent statehood. Chief US delegate Warren
Austin, the venerable Senator from Vermont, had under State Department instructions just assured the UN Security Council that the
US would not act precipitously when word arrived of a White House
announcement of recognition (actually the Soviets beat us to it by
minutes). Poor Senator Austin was also responsible for one of the few
inadvertently light moments when, in the midst of one heated debate, he reportedly pleaded with the Muslim and Jewish delegates to
"act like good Christians."

Contrary to popular belief, the US did not become Israel's sole
backer until France's President de Gaulle, irritated over Israel's preemptive attack on Egypt and Syria in 1967, ended France's role as Israel's
arms supplier. Since then, the US has consistently tilted towards Israel
even while trying to appear evenhanded in its default role as mediator (default because even Arabs resentful of its pro-Israeli tilt have
depended on Washington to pressure Israel when necessary). Secretary of State Henry Kissinger came closest to squaring that policy
circle when he conducted his famous shuttle diplomacy between regional capitals in the aftermath of the 1973 War. In the process, he won
the confidence of the hardest case in the ranks of Israel's enemies, the
late Syrian President Hafez al-Assad (the joke making the rounds was
that thenceforth, when Assad discussed political science, he did it
with a German accent).

Presidents Carter and Clinton and their secretaries of state,
through prodigious personal efforts, produced what looked like highly

positive results in orchestrating negotiations between Israel and Egypt's President Anwar Sadat, and with Palestine's leader Yasser Arafat—only to see the stone roll downhill again.

The Bush II administration, faithful to its well-known ABC policy (anything but Clinton) initially downgraded US involvement in the conflict. But like its predecessors, it later felt compelled to become engaged, if fitfully. Bush called for a Palestinian state, but refused to negotiate with Arafat. He joined the European union, the UN and Russia (the "Quartet") in yet another plan that became known as the "roadmap." With the *intifada* and the Iraq War, the long road to even a partial peace resembled a badly-built rollercoaster. The death of iconic revolutionary and spoiler Arafat in late 2004, the election of Mahmoud Abbas as Palestinian president, and a new openness to negotiation by long-time Israeli hardliner, Ariel Sharon, seemed to create yet another possible doorway to the negotiated peace long sought by the now-exhausted sides.

No one ever described this problem as either simple or clear-cut and neither has US policy invariably been crystal-clear. In early 1948 when, following the UN Partition vote, fighting broke out in earnest, the allies we had pressured to support the plan complained that we were not putting our money (troops) where our mouth was. An urgent State Department meeting brought together all available American drafters of the UN Charter, who were somehow persuaded to conclude, on narrow legalistic grounds, that the US had no obligation to enforce the partition vote—the outcome State had devoutly wished for.

In 1956, President Eisenhower forced Israel to give up its conquests from the Suez War, pledging that it would not allow the Gulf of Aqaba to be blockaded again. But eleven years later President Lyndon Johnson reneged on the pledge that everyone—including this officer—had made to the Israelis. In the middle of the 1973 war, President Nixon (a.k.a. Henry Kissinger) blocked resupply to Israel in order to keep its troops from going too far into Egypt, and Israel henceforth made strenuous efforts to substitute indigenous production for American military technology.

The Arab states that wanted to end their unwinnable war with Israel continued to believe that their only leverage was through Washington and in time, Egypt, given a huge annual US subsidy, became a useful if grudging diplomatic helper. Jordan, which had taken the wrong side in the 1991 Gulf War by supporting Iraq, rekindled its friendship with Washington and recognized Israel, despite that policy's unpopularity on the Amman street. It has never been safe to bet on outcomes in a place that has experienced six major wars over the last half-century, and is unique in that both sides are often right — and both just as often wrong. But we can help, and we can hope.

Kings, Bombs, and Touch Football

The contemporary American impression of the Arab Middle East is as a non-stop horror show — turbulent, fanatical, and hostile. If a century ago romantics imagined a sandy landscape of nomads and poets, the American architects of the 2003 Iraq War had a new vision of a transformed Middle East: peaceful, democratic, "American." All three images, like everything else about the region, constituted a mix of truth and fantasy. Impressions of three key Middle East countries in a somewhat earlier time might help toward a more nuanced perspective.

In the spring of 1976, I toured the Middle East for the US Information Agency. The following three accounts may suggest some modest insights: royal misconceptions that bedevil US relations with the Arab world; the *dolce far niente* enjoyed by Kuwait before being attacked by Iraq; and the surreal nature, then and now, of Baathist Syria.

Kings

The Kingdom of Saudi Arabia has been ruled since 1932 by four of the forty-five sons of Abdul Aziz ibn Saud, who founded the dynasty after conquering assorted tribes of the Arabian desert. Before the 1970s only a handful of Americans knew that a fellow-American named Kelly had found oil there, and that a conflation of oil companies called Aramco was busy turning sand into gold. But by the late 1970s when I visited Saudi Arabia, Americans had a vivid memory of long, angry lines at the gas station when the Arab members of OPEC tried to cut off America's accustomed gasoline fix.

A still-earlier generation of Americans had heard of King ibn Saud when, in February, 1945, they read that President Franklin Delano

Roosevelt had taken a meeting with the King on the cruiser USS *Quincy,* moored in Egypt's Great Bitter Lake, on FDR's way home from the Yalta Summit with Churchill and Stalin. The President and King did lunch, and what really electrified the folks back home were pictures of whole sheep being roasted over glowing charcoal braziers on the *Quincy's* fantail, transforming the American warship into a kind of floating Arabian Nights eatery.

Ibn Saud died in 1953. His successor, son Saud (who similarly fathered forty-five sons) was dumped by the royal family in 1964 after almost bankrupting the kingdom. Next came modernizer Faisal, who was assassinated by his nephew. He was followed by industrializer Khalid, cosmopolitan Fahd, and de facto ruler Crown Prince Abdullah, after which the Kingdom would soon start to run out of eligible sons of the founder. Khalid ibn Abdul Aziz, known as a self-effacing and conciliatory ruler, was the king I got to meet.

It was a fascinating time to be there, midway between nomadic past and hi-tech future. The country was being torn up in a monumental effort to substitute the twentieth century for the medieval era that came before. Everything was under construction, with dust and rubble everywhere. Unfinished buildings looked out on a procession of air-conditioned limousines and taxicabs driven primarily with the horn. Tall cranes vied with donkey power, and expensive Swiss watches were peddled alongside wandering goats. It was a unique three-class society, with an upper class of four and a half million Saudis who didn't work with their hands; a middle class of foreigners imported to run the technical systems; and a working class of a million Yemeni, Pakistanis, and Egyptians.

The overloaded leadership seemed to be experiencing the worst of both worlds. On one hand, they were buying into the evils of industrialization (automobiles, for example, came in tagged "for export only," meaning they had no emission-controls and thus induced a smog-drenched atmosphere). On the other hand, the royals were finding it increasingly harder to preserve the rigid socio-religious traditions of the ascetic Wahhabi sect of Sunni Islam. In Riyadh, where the religious police were everywhere, "blue cinemas" were showing pornoflicks, in exchange for which the dens of iniquity agreed not to advertise or otherwise proclaim their presence.

A visitor couldn't help wondering how a deeply conservative society could survive this kind of onslaught. In the year 2005 the answer is problematic, but in 1976 there was still a kind of internal strength sorely lacking in the Shah's Iran across the Gulf. For one thing, the Saudi royal family supplied built-in relief valves in the form of public audiences where people could seek redress. For another, the rulers eschewed the cult of personality then rampant across the Gulf, where every newspaper was obliged to carry a daily front-page picture of the Shah and his Empress.

Riyadh was only then becoming the capital, with most foreign embassies waiting in the far more cosmopolitan Jidda for their new Riyadh abodes to be completed. When I headed for the Mathera palace in Riyadh, my sole purpose was to pay my respects to the father of one of my long-time MIT students. Minister of Court Ibrahim al-Sowayal had been Saudi Ambassador in Washington for twelve years, and despite not being a member of the royal family had already served as foreign minister and agricultural minister. (He told me that King Faisal gave him the latter job because he had the best garden in Jidda.)

After some chit-chat punctuated by infusions of sweet coffee, my host left the room. When he returned, he seemed a bit revved up and asked me if I would like to meet the King. The answer was obvious, and my pulse quickened as he marched me into the high-ceilinged audience room through the simple chambers and corridors characteristic of the (at least outwardly ascetic) Wahhabis. Despite the unexpected arrival of the German Chancellor, not to mention an influx of Swiss itching to do some high-level business, I was accorded a private audience.

The King and I (that sounds familiar) sat in adjacent deep armchairs with an ornately-carved gilt table with a telephone between us, and looked sideways at each other, which accounts for what appears to be a painfully stiff neck in people pictured in that unnatural posture. King Khalid, who toyed with a ring on his pinky finger as we spoke, had kindly deep-set eyes and the aquiline nose of the Sudeiri branch of the royal family. The plain white *kaffiyeh* on his head was held in place with a black wool band, and he wore the standard *abayeh* gown, except that the edging was gold. Standing in front of us

The King and I: Audience with His Majesty King Khalid in Riyadh, Saudi Arabia.

was the royal interpreter, a tall, good-looking guy with cold eyes named Khalid Anani. His English was superb, and I learned later that he was US-trained. Sitting silently off to the side was my American embassy minder John Rock. A row of courtiers sat or stood at the far end of the huge chamber, about seventy feet away.

I explained to His Majesty that I was here to learn about his country because I thought it important for US-Saudi relations to improve, better understanding achieved, etc. He remained courteously impassive until I offered to explain some American views of things if that would help contribute to the cause of peace.

King: "Excellency, why does the US permit Congress to interfere in American foreign policy? For example with respect to Turkey, your domestic Greek lobby has forced the US to turn its back on its faithful Turkish ally who fought so well alongside you in Korea." Score one for the King.

I responded that as a result of recent scandals with which I was sure the King was familiar (President Nixon had resigned in disgrace two years earlier), the Congress was temporarily in a position of ascendancy, throwing the American political system temporarily out of balance.

King: "Excellency, we think Nixon's troubles were caused by a plot on the part of a minority of Americans, obviously Zionists, who wished to make trouble for him." Uh-oh, back to square one for that. (It was nothing short of bizarre that a few months later in Moscow a Central Committee *apparatchik* explained to me in a similarly paranoid vein that their hero Nixon had been brought down by the American enemies of détente.)

There just wasn't time to straighten the whole thing out. But before I could work up a short answer, the King asked me why we didn't improve our system by making terms of Congressmen shorter, and that of the President longer so that everyone could get to know and trust him. He explained that, in his country, when a new hospital was built or a new aircraft designed, people wanted someone else to try it first, and surely it was the same with presidents. (He forbore to mention royal tasters, who I imagine had first crack at any poisons that had infiltrated the royal cuisine.) I said that some Americans wanted it the other way around—longer terms for Congressmen so they didn't have to run full-time, and conversely shorter for the President, who could concentrate on his job for one six-year term. His Majesty looked suitably baffled at such a ridiculous constraint on someone who had succeeded in taking power.

About midway through our conversation, the King pushed a small button lying on the table, which produced a servant with a pot of tea. When the latter bent over, it was easy to spot a holster containing a small revolver. (The characteristic Arab *djellabah* was in fact originally designed to fall open at the front so weapons could be quickly drawn.) What I couldn't understand was that the royal bodyguards—big, fierce-looking guys wearing great curved swords—were all sitting in the outer chamber at least fifty feet away.

When the King agreed that my embassy minder could take some photographs, the latter stood up, moved in front of the King, unzipped his flight bag, and pulled out—a camera. It could as easily have been a submachine gun, and I didn't see how anyone could have done a thing about it, which seemed surprising after the assassination of his brother Faisal. Didn't they remember the old Arab saying in which a Bedouin asks the Prophet, "Should I let my camel loose in the desert and trust in Allah?" After due consideration the Prophet replies, "No, first tie up your camel, then trust in Allah."

TOUCH FOOTBALL IN THE GULF

My next stop was Kuwait, hotter than Saudi Arabia, but brighter and more colorful, an impression fortified by the miraculous appearance of drinks on Gulf Air as soon as we were wheels-up from abstemious Dhahran. Kuwait, in those years before Saddam Hussein tried to gobble it up as his 19th province, seemed almost carefree by contrast to its royal neighbor to the south. It featured spacious squares, noise, smiling people, a women's movement (which had come close to getting the vote) and broad ethnic diversity. Thanks to soaring oil revenues, Kuwait was extraordinarily rich, to the point where public telephones required no coins for calls.

Indigenous Kuwaitis constituted only forty percent of the population, the rest being Palestinians, Lebanese, Egyptians, Jordanians, and Iraqis. Palestinians had no political rights, but something close to equality with Kuwaitis in the commercial sphere. (When they were expelled in 1991 in punishment for the PLO's support of Iraq's invasion, it left a major hole in the working structure.) The pecking order among non-Kuwaitis gave the Kuwait Sheraton a loftier reputation than the Kuwait Hilton, since the Hilton employed Egyptians (branded as "lazy and don't care"), while the Sheraton hired Palestinians (lauded as "hustlers"). Kuwait may have been considerably more relaxed than Saudi Arabia. But both countries, equally distant from the Arab-Israeli front lines, seemed prepared to fight to the last Palestinian. Their private explanation for supporting the then-radical PLO sounded a good deal like the intimidated merchants in Al Capone's Chicago who had to pay protection money to avoid being bombed.

One morning I gave a talk to the Kuwaiti Development Board, which was then dispensing enormous sums of money to projects in the Arab world. The dozen members of the Board sat around a small table, a telephone in front of each. While I was giving my talk, the phones periodically rang, and much serious business was transacted, interrupted only by an occasional encouraging smile in my direction.

Among the many ways in which travel has broadened my skills was by teaching me how to give a speech to an audience of whom half are talking on the phone. (I found it helped to mentally replay the scene in *Dr. Strangelove* when the Joint Chiefs of Staff, a red phone in front of each, are tensely dealing with an escalating nuclear crisis, and we then hear General Buck Turgidson muttering into his instrument, "Of course I love you, Baby, but I told you never to call me here.")

At the American Embassy's welcoming reception in Kuwait City, a couple of lively younger guys stood out among the more sedate guests. One was a Kuwaiti political scientist named Faisal, dressed in the traditional long white *dishdash,* the other a Palestinian political scientist named Tawfic, dressed in a suit. After we had chatted for a while, they retreated to a corner to consult about something. On their return, they issued an invitation to "spend the night in the desert." I must have looked blank until an Embassy officer whispered to me that such an invitation was rare and not to be declined. My mystification was not diminished when I was instructed to bring bathing trunks. For the desert?

The next afternoon I was picked up by Faisal in the ubiquitous Toyota pickup, except that his was new and shiny. Tawfic seemed to be in charge of a couple of boxes perched in the back. We drove south until Kuwait City, with its signature striped water towers, receded from sight. Sand stretched in every direction as far as the eye could see. Faisal hung a left, and soon we were driving along the water in an officially-posted forbidden zone that appeared deserted. We suddenly came upon a community of small concrete structures lined up along the beach. They were illegal vacation "cottages" owned by wealthy Kuwaitis. On the sand in front of each, a strange wooden platform supported on rickety-looking stilts rose up six feet or so.

Party time along the Persian/Arabian Gulf south of Kuwait City, Kuwait.

We stopped at one such concrete box, which had neither doors nor windows, and unloaded the crates. I was instructed to disrobe and don my bathing shorts. Faisal stripped off his floor-length robe and revealed a T-shirt that proclaimed "Go Jayhawks." Tawfic's T-shirt celebrated another famous American university. They produced a football, and the next thing I knew we were playing a downsized version of touch football in the Persian/Arabian Gulf as the sun set in the west, tankers slipped past like silent ghosts and the tide steadily rose.

Twilight transformed the waterway into a palette of deep rose, purple, and blue. We eventually went indoors to change into shorts and shirts. My teammates emerged with the boxes they had brought from Kuwait City, along with a square of elegant oriental carpeting. They climbed up the narrow ladder to the platform and laid the carpet on the flooring, followed by the boxes. The sky darkened and without transition was filled with stars, many as bright as planets. We waded out, ascended the ladder, and settled on the carpet under the heavenly canopy. The rising water beneath gurgled and sighed as waves from passing ships carried the tide up the platform's stilts.

My hosts opened the boxes and set out a roast chicken, ham, hummus, tabouli, salads, nuts, dates, figs, fruit, breads, gin, tonic and ice on a finely-embroidered tablecloth. We spent the next hours gorging on the Arabian feast, drinking non-Arabian gin and tonics, telling stories, and eventually falling asleep under the stars, to dream of the Thousand and One Nights and of an oasis in a place that had experienced much history and would experience a great deal more.

But academics didn't necessarily have it all that easy. One of my subsequent performances in Kuwait City was a talk on the policy planning "games" I had been developing at MIT. The games were a sidebar to my research on conflict and arms control, but happened to be sponsored by the US government and participated in by officials as well as academics. The chairman for the evening was the undersecretary of state for foreign affairs, an imposing royal named Rashid al Rashid. When I had finished, he stunned me by tearing into the academics present, including my touch football buddies, excoriating them for being alienated rather than devoting themselves to helping their society and government "as MIT obviously does." I suddenly longed to be back under the stars, lulled to sleep by the magical tidal music of the Persian (Arabian) Gulf.

BOMBS

When in 1963 the Baath socialist party took power in Syria, it was militant and uncompromising, hostile to Egypt's President Nasser (a fact that is important to my story), and warm toward the Soviet Union. General Hafez al-Assad, known originally as a pragmatist, took over in 1970 after his Baathist rivals got a bloody nose blundering into Jordan's expulsion of the Palestinian guerrilla army which had lodged itself in that country.

Syria, competing with Iraq for the title of tough guy on the block, had severed relations with Washington after Israel's victory in the 1967 June war, and relations began to mend only seven years later. The US Embassy in Damascus had been functioning for only two years, when I was fortuitously accepted as the first officially-sponsored American lecturer in Damascus since relations were broken. I was already in the neighborhood, scheduled to hit Bahrain and Qatar for the weekend before a final turn in Teheran, and when the Syrian government gave its OK, Washington rerouted me to Damascus, where I spent the Mother of All Weekends.

My immediate host was the embassy's public affairs officer (later Ambassador) Kenton Keith, who four years earlier had persuaded the Turks that the US had something else to offer (me) beyond the seductive Orson Welles films that drew huge crowds in Istanbul. When I hit town, Keith hastened to lower my expectations. Not only were the Syrians unlikely to show up on general grounds of unfamiliarity with the US cultural hustle, but there were additional complications.

Palestinian activism in neighboring Lebanon had become a threat to Syria's self-image as the hegemonic "Greater Syria," and President Assad's army had just launched an all-out assault on the forces of his faithful ally Yasser Arafat. The armor both sides were throwing against one another had all been supplied by the Soviets. Astonishingly, the invited Syrian élites did in fact show up for the welcoming reception, over a hundred of them, and it wasn't long before the canapés, the booze, and the decibel level began to be indistinguishable from places where we were friends rather than adversaries.

The next morning I paid a call on the US ambassador, a quiet professional named Richard Murphy whose briefing was a model of cogency. When I asked him about his contacts with President Assad, he said they were rare. He added that even when he did see him, "Mr. Assad is a man of long silences." Only a pro could endure that for long. Next was the obligatory tennis, played on a clay court whose ochre tones blended in with the surrounding treeless hills and houses. Like all tennis in the region, it was too hot but generated needful endorphins. But unlike tennis in Western-linked Saudi Arabia and Kuwait, long-severed Syrian ties with the West had generated a desperate scarcity of tennis balls, so lobs were hit with great care.

The centerpiece of my visit was to be a downtown luncheon speech to which high officials and leading academics were invited. Dick Murphy warned me that, thanks to the sudden escalation of the war, very few Syrian officials were likely to show. With an hour until lunch, I lay on my bed in my guest room trying to figure out how, in case anyone did show up, I could speak freely without causing a new break in relations. Suddenly a noise outside the window grew louder. It began to sound like an angry mob, and shortly thereafter approximately a thousand screaming Syrians passed on the street directly by my window. Most were young and, I learned later, unemployed and therefore available as extras for a government-produced mob scene.

A minute later, an enormous explosion close by that almost blew me out of bed was followed by cries and associated sounds of bedlam. The noise was the Egyptian Embassy being firebombed by the mob a hundred and fifty yards from where I lay (the carefully controlled reporting to the outside world spoke only of "some students marching on" the Egyptian Embassy). Fortunately, the Egyptian offices were vacant, it being Saturday. Unfortunately, a family lived on the top floor, so the attack was not entirely cost-free.

Why, you might ask, should Syria firebomb the embassy of its ally Egypt, with whom it had even been politically united in the short-lived United Arab Republic (UAR)? Well, for one thing relations were now strained. For another, in a city which, like Moscow at the time, kept foreign newspapers, periodicals, and other independent news sources from its citizenry, what better way to send a pointed private message to one's ally for his eyes (or ears) only?

It now appeared certain that this particularly noisy form of Middle East communication spelled curtains for any high-level Syrian gathering to hear an MIT professor pontificate on foreign policy and global interdependence. If the war and the firebomb did not constitute enough of a deterrent, consider the sudden arrival in town of the Saudi and Kuwaiti Foreign Ministers on a belated peacemaking mission aimed at reconciling Cairo and Damascus. Or the simultaneous arrival of Soviet Prime Minister Kosygin, his visage covered with egg over the use of Soviet armor against each other by both his clients. (Murphy later told me Kosygin had not been allowed to leave the airport.) Or, to top it all, the sudden appearance in downtown Damascus of Idi Amin, Uganda's mass murderer.

It was in this fatalistic mood that the Ambassador and I arrived midday at the Hotel International and descended to the basement nightclub, where all was in readiness for his party. We were just figuring out how the handful of Americans present could possibly eat all the food and drink all the wine when, one after another, they came — Deputy Ministers, Foreign Office department heads, newspaper editors, the Rector of the University and his deans — in short, the full guest list. The fact that their country was at war seemed to call for an all-out assault on the bar. As the party got livelier, a train of servants marched in bearing an enormous meal.

For the next couple of hours, while they tucked away all that lovely food and not bad wine, I was on my feet speaking and answering questions, not about interdependence, but (What else?) US Middle East policy and regional prospects as one allegedly independent outsider saw them. The US Ambassador sat there grinning until I asked him to help me answer some questions about US policy, and then we both stood dodging verbal bullets while the Syrians sat there stuffing their faces. Astonishingly, no one mentioned either the escalation in Lebanon or the fire-bombing.

That night someone threw a party, for which I was more than ready. I wound up chatting with the only foreign journalist to get on top of the story, even if she couldn't send it out. Just to complete the weekend's cast of characters, the freelancer was Francesca Hilton, daughter of Zsa Zsa Gabor and hotel magnate Conrad Hilton.

On Monday morning I headed for Teheran, where no one seemed to be conscious of sitting on a powder keg that would blow sky-high in two years.

9 THE REAL WORLD III: 1961–93
The Rest of the Map

Foreign travel began in earnest after I finally became a professor at MIT in the early 1960s. I went on some overseas junkets during subsequent decades as a solo lecturer or conference participant, easily seduced by the amenities. The conferences were usually held at classy resorts or fancy villas that a rich plutocrat had donated to a nonprofit foundation in exchange for a tax deduction. Four of the short vignettes in this chapter describe events of that variety.

The rest of my travels were a very different kind, all but Yugoslavia with Uncle Sam as the sponsor, paymaster, and tour director. In its global quest for hearts and minds, the State Department and US Information Agency occasionally offered up an academic as a minor cultural road show, vaguely akin to more popular offerings like symphony orchestras, ballet troupes, or the all-time cultural magnet—a can of Orson Welles films. In the 1970s and 80s I was invited to put on this kind of dog-and-pony show in thirty-five countries.

Why, you might ask, would Washington want to put a freewheeling academic before foreign audiences to hold forth on, of all things, US foreign policy? I think they figured that any undermining of relations would be outweighed by a demonstration of the virtues of a free, if not particularly well-disciplined, nation.

My own reasons for going are easier to understand. By any account, the arrangement was cost-effective, if only because being ushered through foreign airports by an embassy officer bypassed the frequent police and customs' horrors. More to the point, the embassy set up policy briefings and sessions with the ambassador, scheduled lectures and other public appearances, arranged meetings with key locals and media, organized transport, hotels, and tennis—in short, took care of everything I would otherwise have had to manage (and spring for). In return, the system exploited me shamelessly. But the tradeoff was worth it.

Those thirty-five government-sponsored gigs, along with several unrelated overseas adventures, generated a few stories about inter-cultural encounters that help illustrate some of the problems that beset well-meaning Americans who try to explain their country in an age of expanding US global presence. I have tried in these little vignettes to indicate how each related to the core themes that have run through my professional life, and what lessons I learned (or should have). But I will also confess that they were selected because I thought the reader might enjoy them.

1961: A MARVEL OF AMERICAN TECHNOLOGY

This story conveys a not-so-subtle reminder of the private resentment even our best friend abroad harbors toward its rich, technologically dom-inant American cousin when the latter starts boasting. The unadmir-able but human quality the Germans call *schadenfreude*—literally joy at someone else's bad luck—appears here when a hot new US invention misfires in front of a waiting audience. The appropriate lesson—mod-esty with friends (though not necessarily enemies) about this country's extraordinary power—sadly remains unlearned half a century later.

The Soviet spacecraft "Sputnik" (meaning fellow traveler) went into orbit in October, 1957 at a time when US rocket tests were pro-ducing spectacular TV pictures of launch pad fires and mid-air U-turns followed by fiery crashes. Despite the defensive sour grapes ("Heck, all the Russkies did was put a little grapefruit into orbit"), the US went into technological overdrive, not only putting astronauts into orbit, but a man on the moon as well. Early in the process some heavy thinkers began trying to figure out what the deeper meaning of the space age might be.

The American Assembly, created by Dwight Eisenhower when he was briefly President of Columbia University, decided to organize a conference on the social-political-economic-military implications of outer space. As a newly-minted academic, I was asked to edit the volume of papers to accompany the meeting, as well as to co-chair the session with the Assembly's head, the marvelously crusty former Brown University President Henry Wriston. Not to be outdone, the Europeans shortly thereafter proposed something called the European-American Assembly on Outer Space, which was held in England at the seaside resort of Brighton.

My co-chair there was the extraordinary Alistair Buchan, founder and head of the International Institute of Strategic Studies (and son of John Buchan, a.k.a. Lord Tweedsmuir who wrote *The 39 Steps*). Buchan (to whom I was known forevermore as "the Bodger," for reasons having to do with a stapling machine) was great fun to work with, and the conference went swimmingly. On the final day, we were all invited by the Lord Mayor of Brighton to a reception at a remarkable place called the Royal Pavilion. The Royal Pavilion is a grand and surreal Orientalist architectural confection created in 1822 for King George IV by John Nash, who also designed the gorgeous Royal Crescent that looks down on the city of Bath.

The Lord Mayor, heavily hung with seals of office, greeted us warmly. I saw him standing in the Great Hall chatting with American banking tycoon John McCloy, then the undisputed leader of the American "establishment," and the opportunity was irresistible. I had brought along my new Polaroid—that magical instant camera recently invented by an American genius named Edwin Land. The early Polaroid was very large, very heavy, and called for some fairly complex maneuvers. You inserted the film after removing it from a largish box, and after two minutes pulled out a piece of paper covered with noxious gunk, followed by a second paper on which, in a couple of minutes, a picture miraculously materialized. The only downside was that one was left clutching a handful of evil-smelling debris.

Taking advantage of this fortuitous moment to display the latest wonder of American technology to a dazzled international audience, I lined up the Lord Mayor and McCloy, who both smiled while I clicked the shutter. A crowd eagerly formed around the increasingly debris-laden photographer, and after the stipulated time I triumphantly pulled the crucial piece of paper from the box and held it before them tantalizingly as we awaited its magical climax. We waited. Then we waited some more. The paper remained blank, snow-white, empty.

Some guests drifted away with ill-concealed smirks, while more forgiving souls took pity and hung around. After checking everything that could conceivably go wrong, I re-loaded, lined up the Lord Mayor (McCloy having sensibly headed for the bar), and gave it another try. This time, excelsior! The Lord Mayor's figure, chains and all, slowly emerged. Unfortunately, his face remained entirely blank. The only plus from this exercise in public humiliation was the secret joy I was able to give our non-American friends as another experimental US rocket did a U-turn and nose-dived into the turf.

1968: WHEN THE YUGOSLAVS LOVED NATO

If the Soviet Union was the declared opponent of the US and its Western European democratic allies, Yugoslavia was a unique piece of the otherwise monolithic Soviet empire, and even its domestic invention of workers councils was a deviation from the power structure devised by the Bolsheviks in Moscow. The Western alliance came to experiment with a more nuanced relationship with this deviant regime, but the relationship was extraordinarily ambiguous.

Soon after World War II, the Soviet Union had taken over all of Eastern Europe and much of the Balkans—except Yugoslavia. Yugoslavia had been taken back from the Nazis, not by the Russians, but by a couple of squabbling homegrown factions, one of which was led by Josip Broz-become-Marshall Tito, who then seized power. Before long he broke free from the Soviet yoke and, in a long-running historical irony, his Communist government became famous for thumbing its nose at Communist Big Brother in Moscow. The Soviet leadership had to live with the schism, the "bone in the throat," as they put it, through the next half-century. Taking its own deviant path to Socialism didn't mean that Yugoslavia was any friendlier to the United States and the West. What it meant was that Belgrade could be just as nasty to Moscow as to Washington.

A little over a decade later, Soviet-ruled Czechoslovakia, like Yugoslavia, tried for a modest breakout from Moscow's control with a movement the Czechs called "socialism with a human face." In September, 1968, the Soviet-run Warsaw Pact shocked the world by sending its divisions into Czechoslovakia to stamp out the heretical "Prague Spring." When the Yugoslavs saw Soviet tanks pushing into Prague, they felt their nightmare was coming true: the Soviets wouldn't stop in Czechoslovakia, but would keep marching south to remove once and for all the bone that had lodged in their throat since the Federation of Yugoslavia had strayed from the true faith and trodden the path of ideological apostasy.

Yugoslavia promptly went into a state of mobilization, complete with antiaircraft batteries pointing skyward from newly-dug revetments around the airport. Yugoslavia, like Israel, kept in ready reserve a substantial citizen army, each member of which had standing instructions to grab the uniform, gun, and map from the closet, and head for an assigned cave in Montenegro where they were expected to hold out to the last Russian. The citizens' army was placed on full alert. Like the rest of Yugoslav mobilization, the alert was concealed from the outside world by tight censorship.

That happened to be the moment I arrived in the capital city of Belgrade to give some lectures. It was a coincidence, the invitation having been extended well before the crisis. Despite the dicey atmosphere, my program went on as planned. Until, that is, my hosts asked me to pay a call on the senior Yugoslav diplomat I recalled as one of the most virulent anti-American propagandists it had been my misfortune to have to listen to at the United Nations. Ambassador Alex Bebler was in retirement. But with the greatest reluctance I allowed myself to be dragged to his house. Before I could even get my coat off, this old calumniator of the US, NATO, and the West in general looked at me intently and asked, "If the Russians attack, will NATO help us?" I had to sit down, so great was my astonishment. The Soviets fortunately remained content with a renewed grip on Czechoslovakia and did not keep heading south.

Two later events put that little encounter in 3-D for me. The first took place the following year when I directed a political-military game in Garmisch, Germany for the US Joint Chiefs of Staff. The game focused on an excellent "What if?" question: What was the likely US response if the real-life Yugoslavia were again threatened by the Soviets and asked for NATO help? In that game, the senior American diplomatic and military leadership in Europe unanimously declined to send NATO to the defense of hypothetically-threatened Yugoslavia. The second sequel supplied the ultimate irony when, thirty years later, NATO finally did arrive in Yugoslavia. But its arrival took the form of US-led NATO bombing of Belgrade into ending its brutal suppression of ethnic Albanians in the Serbian province of Kosovo.

1970: Caught in the Berlin Wall

The city of Berlin, left deep in the Russian zone of divided Germany after World War II, was the very heart of the Cold War. Not only was Germany split into allies and Soviets, but so was Berlin, producing a virtually unique power arrangement and several hair-raising crises between the nuclear-armed powers. Many political-military games—and war games—were run in the US to try to anticipate reactions to unforeseen events. One of my most powerful learning experiences was that no matter how much one had studied this case, first-hand exposure taught a powerful lesson about the unexpected personal threat.

During the Cold War, West Germans lived cheek by jowl with the East German Communist regime and its notorious Stasi secret police snoops and enforcers, all backed by heavily-armed Soviet occupiers. I got briefly mixed up in this powder-keg when West German intellectuals and politicians organized a "Peace Research Organization" in West Berlin under the leadership of one of America's most noted political scientists, the late Karl Deutsch. As one of many efforts to stay linked with the democratic West, the organization had invited some scholars from the democratic world to a weekend conference at a very German villa featuring mounted stag-heads looming over the sweeping staircase above a monstrous fieldstone fireplace. It was located on the shore of Lake Wannsee where, in 1942, Hitler's exterminate-the-Jews program was crafted.

In 1970, democratic West Berlin was still defended by a small "trip-wire" force of élite US, French, and British military units. I had met the Deputy US Commander in Europe, a pleasant air force general named David Burchinal, at a stateside meeting where he had issued an open invitation to me to visit Berlin. I wrote him that I would be taking part in this conference, and when my wife, Iri, and I landed at Templehof Airport, we were surprised to see a US military vehicle draw up alongside our plane to whisk us to the VIP lounge. As part of the chit-chat there, I answered questions about the consulting I was doing for Deputy Secretary of State Elliott Richardson. A phone call was also made by my military greeter to Burchinal's headquarters in Stuttgart. That pleasant social occasion at the airport is painfully relevant to what happened on our final Saturday in Berlin.

While we were at the West German conference it was arranged that, right after the meeting ended on Saturday and before we flew home to catch up with our three young children, the US military would take us on a tour through East Berlin. The reluctantly-agreed-to US-Soviet protocol was that once each day the Americans and Soviets could symbolically show their flag in the other's Berlin sector, in the form of a spin around the other's turf in a military police vehicle. That Saturday we would be passengers in the daily show-the-flag run. A few hours before plane time, we arrived at Checkpoint Charlie at the Berlin wall, in front of the famous sign warning that one was leaving the US Sector. Our bags were packed, and it seemed like a terrific opportunity for a brief peek at the very heart of the Cold War in Europe before going home.

We couldn't board the MP sedan right away, since no civilians were permitted to be in official vehicles passing through the barriers and tank traps that cluttered the roadway between the two parts of divided Berlin. While the MP car drove alongside, we thus walked along the heavily-barricaded East-West divider till we reached the East German checkpoint, and would only regain the security of that vehicle when we emerged on foot in East Berlin proper.

When we arrived at their little building, the East German border guards were not particularly charming, but they were businesslike. Their rules required everyone to change West German marks into East German marks, and they were emphatic that we not only spend their marks in the Soviet Sector, but also have in hand evidence of such expenditure. They pointed several times to a wall poster detailing the perils and hazards of violating their currency rules. (We were aware that not much earlier, to make a political point, the Soviet KGB had imprisoned another American professor, Frederick Barghoorn of Yale, on phony grounds.)

At Checkpoint Charlie, West Berlin, just before The Bad Trip.

As promised, the dun-colored MP sedan was waiting for us when we emerged at the Soviet sector, and we had a fascinating, if sobering, ride through this ugly communist stepsister of lively, prosperous West Berlin. But what became chillingly evident was that no shops were open on Saturday, and there was nowhere to spend our East German marks, not to mention showing evidence of the same. As the implications became clear, a tiny worm of anxiety began to make its presence known in my digestive tract. Our sergeant-driver did an illegal U-turn and returned post-haste to the East German side of the Wall, where Iri and I dismounted while the car drove through to Checkpoint Charlie in the US sector.

This time the atmosphere was sour and unfriendly. The border guards made it alarmingly clear that, unless we actually spent our East German marks in East Germany, we would not be permitted to return to the West. They then took our passports to photocopy — and declined to return Iri's. One of them suggested dropping our East German marks into the lock-box on the floor ostensibly for East German

Doing the Communist goose-step in East Berlin.

charities. But this would of course leave us with no evidence that we had spent their funny money in their miserable country. In short, *Catch 22.*

The next thing I did leaves me with a vivid memory of panic combined with a sense of the absurd. Free to walk around but not return to the West, I went outdoors to try to signal to Checkpoint Charlie. There was a foot of snow on the ground, but even standing on tiptoe on the snowbank, it was not certain that I would be visible through the crossbars of the Soviet tank traps. The climax of my panicked performance was to jump up and down as high as I could in the snow while waving my arms with extreme vigor.

After what seemed like an eternity, the top of a US MP vehicle came into view, its red rooflight rotating. As it drew alongside the communist checkpoint, our sergeant hissed between clenched teeth, "What in the hell is going on?" I waved him on and ran to join him at the East German border. An experienced cold warrior, he had no trouble understanding the challenge of finding something — anything — to buy in a tightly shut-down East Berlin.

We careened through the empty streets at high speed, finally spotting a regional railroad station. Sarge jammed on the brakes and I leapt out. Inside, a mob of people, bundled up against the cold, filled a cavernous, dimly-lit hall. In front of the one open kiosk stretched a long line waiting to buy newspapers and cigarettes. When I finally was served, I pointed to some miniature bottles of schnapps wrapped in dusty tinfoil and bought them all. Receipt in hand, I stumbled through the sullen crowd, jumped into the car, and hung on as we made record time westward.

When we reentered the East German checkpoint, the atmosphere had changed once more. The border cops, who seemed to have received new orders, were now full of a kind of forced amiability. They displayed gold-toothy grins at my purchases, which I pressed on them along with my precious receipt. Iri's passport was returned, and we were sent on our way with heartfelt, if insincere, wishes for a *gute Reise*.

The scene back at the American checkpoint was one of minor pandemonium. A hotline was open to both Washington and the US Command in Stuttgart. High-powered telescopes on the second floor, invisible from ground-level, were trained on the scene of our recent action. The working assumptions on the US side had been three: the Communists were looking for another "incident" to manufacture; the work I was doing for the deputy secretary of state gave them a bonus excuse to use the word "spy"; and the East German police had monitored every word of the conversations in the airport VIP lounge when we arrived.

We caught our flight back to Boston with only minutes to spare.

1972: THE CYPRUS STRADDLE

The situation in the divided island of Cyprus was one of the most popular topics for political games. Pre-1974, it was a question of power relationships between the Greek and Turkish ethnic inhabitants of an island that was simply in the wrong place geographically, closer to Turkey rather than to its majority Greek homeland. The geometry of power was four-way, including the two Cypriot peoples and their two unfriendly sponsors. After 1974, when Turkey invaded and created an unrecognized Turkish Cypriot "state," it became an unresolved conflict to which US diplomacy, along with that of the UN, failed to settle the matter but helped keep it relatively peaceful.

The governments of Cyprus and the US had instituted, as an annual cooperative event, a daylong session in the capital city Nicosia on the subject of American foreign policy, and the US Information Agency asked me to be the target for this particular year's bilateral batting practice. The session was co-chaired by American Ambassador David Popper, an old friend from State Department days, and the Cypriot foreign minister, a man named Spyros Kyprianou who went on to become that country's unsuccessful president. The island was divided (as it still is today) along the so-called "Green Line" monitored by United Nations peacekeepers. No Turkish Cypriots showed up at the meeting, only Greek Cypriots and American diplomats and reporters.

The seminar was evidently a success, if a bit grueling for the sole "lecturer." The next day, in company with Popper, I paid a courtesy call

After visiting President Makarios in Nicosia, Cyprus.

to Cypriot President Archbishop Makarios, a famously wily character once described by Secretary of State Dean Acheson as "that bloody and bearded old reprobate." Protocol dictated that we follow that visit with one to the Turkish Cypriots on the other side of the Green Line.

We did so, and our host at the luncheon meeting was the formidable, and unfortunately durable, Turkish Cypriot leader Rauf Denktash. His "cabinet," which filled the table, included Osman Orek, whose participation in a peacekeeping game I ran in Vienna two years earlier had created a minor international incident. Orek seemed to have forgiven me for what had befallen him in Vienna. He was once again a happy man in his role as "Defense Minister," this time not of Cyprus, but of a shadow regime that would be declared the "Turkish Republic of Cyprus" after the Turkish invasion two years later.

Denktash, who is nobody's patsy, lost no time in challenging me. "Okay, Professor, you've been on the island for two days, so you're an expert, right? What do you recommend that we do?" I knew what lay behind his sarcasm. Casual visitors tended to scold both sides for not collaborating on practical matters of common concern such as sewers, roads, etc., not to mention putting aside their ancient grievances and learning to like each other. I heard myself replying that the best thing they could possibly do was to build some high walls between themselves and the Greek Cypriots.

The Turkish Cypriot leadership was thunderstruck. The notional President demanded to know how I could possibly recommend something so sensible. I couldn't give them the real reason, which was that as a conflict analyst, I had studied their mutual bloody-mindedness for years. I gave them the second-best explanation, which was that I was living temporarily in Geneva as a visiting professor, and was impressed with the way the Swiss had stopped killing each other several hundred years ago. The cantons into which Switzerland is partitioned are self-ruled, distinct from others in language, ethnicity, or tradition, and have a variety of restrictive internal rules such as work permits and required retirement residence. My hosts were clearly fascinated, and I felt I had delivered a blow for common sense.

Unfortunately, when I returned to Geneva I came close to ruining a Belgian dinner party when an elderly Swiss notable flew into a rage at the notion that the Swiss were separated by walls. Late in the

1990s, when I repeated the story to a group grappling with the still intractable Cyprus problem, the UN Cyprus mediator Diego Cordovez exclaimed "Aha, so that's where Denktash got this idea he keeps bugging me with about building walls!" The lesson for me was that there are some cases, including this one, in which US and UN diplomacy may even succeed one day—after the Greeks and Turks in Athens and Ankara realize where their best interests lie.

1975: CLEANING UP AFTER KISSINGER IN MEXICO

Nineteenth century English historian Thomas Carlisle argued for the decisive role of the "great man" in history. Determinists like Karl Marx argued the contrary. Occasionally a charismatic figure emerges whose fingerprints can be spotted on historical events. Henry Kissinger for a time looked like one of them.

Many Americans—professors, diplomats, presidents—have followed in the wake of Henry Kissinger, either basking in reflected glory or, in this particular case, caught in the turbulence. For me, the particular occasion was another USIA/State Department gig as an itinerant professor of international relations. I arrived in Mexico City shortly after the American Congress had passed a Trade Bill, one piece of which was aimed at punishing the oil-producing countries that had boycotted the US during the OPEC oil embargo following the 1973 Middle East War. Fair enough—except for the fact that several members of OPEC had not stuck it to Uncle Sam but, on the contrary, had supplied us with their oil. Among the good guys were Ecuador and Venezuela. But the new US law made no distinction between black hats and white, or, for that matter, sombreros of any color.

My invitation was to give the inaugural address at the opening of the new Mexican diplomatic academy, which promised to be a splendid occasion. But the Trade Bill was a major fly in the tequila. Outrage was universal throughout Latin America at the "discriminatory law" passed by the great brute of a Gringo to the north. The Mexican papers featured huge headlines decrying the "Trade War" we had supposedly launched against the little guys to the south, and I couldn't help wondering how interested they were likely to be in an MIT professor's musings about international relations.

The fancy invitation said the speech would be followed by an *"ambigu,"* which I subsequently added to my French vocabulary to connote a cold collation of, I hoped, delicious Mexican hors d'œuvres. The new *Instituto de Estudios Diplomaticos* occupied a fine building with a charming, hacienda-type patio that put the interior architecture in touch with the colorful, if deeply polluted, heart of Mexico City. I was cordially welcomed, and took my place on the dais in the spanking new auditorium.

As I looked out at the audience, I noticed that much of the front row was vacant, which I assumed reflected the universal strategy of sitting in the rear in case it proved necessary to make a hasty exit once the speaker is sized up. After the blunder of trying to tell an American joke to a non-American audience, the session got going in a promising fashion, and I seemed to get their attention with my good news-bad news analysis of international relationships. My MIT research team and I had just finished a report to the State Department on interdependence, and I thought our Mexican friends would enjoy our conclusions about how a seemingly dominant Uncle Sam was actually quite dependent on others for some things.

I was just getting into high gear when there was a stir in the audience and a door in the back of the auditorium opened to discharge a procession of black-suited figures, who descended the stairs and filled the vacant seats in the first row. The chairman turned to me and whispered, "That's the Foreign Minister." Simultaneously energized and intimidated, I pressed on to my peroration, and looked at His Excellency Emilio Rabasa for signs of enthusiasm. When the chairman called for questions, guess whose hand shot up?

Turning for approval to his subordinates who filled the hall, the Foreign Minister launched into a lengthy diatribe, the gist of which went something like this: "Your Secretary of State Henry Kissinger—a man I thought was my friend—was recently in this country. At our meeting at Tlatelolco he promised me NO MORE AMERICAN SURPRISES on Mexico and the rest of Latin America. I believed him! How, therefore, Erudito Bloomfield, can you explain the offensive against all of Latin America launched by your government in its discriminatory trade bill? How do you explain the unceasing discrimination by Americans against Mexico—and now Ecuador and Venezuela too?

HOW DO YOU EXPLAIN MY BETRAYAL AT THE HANDS OF HENRY KISSINGER?" To the delighted cheers of the Mexican foreign service establishment as well as their friends and relations, the Foreign Minister sat down, beamed at me, and awaited my response.

I must have somehow responded, although a merciful veil has fallen over memories of the next few moments. The meeting finally ended, and I was accorded a nice round of applause, doubtless for furnishing a fine stationary target for their *jefe*. Everyone then pushed his or her way out of the auditorium and down the stairs in order to tackle the promised *ambigu*. By the time I was escorted downstairs, the Foreign Minister was standing in a flood of TV lights elaborating his grievances to a wider Mexican audience.

I could glimpse through the ravenous mob a long table set out with piles of delicious goodies plus a large ice carving of a swan. As I headed in that direction to abate my hunger and drown my sorrows, the Foreign Minister reached for my elbow and dragged me to the corner he had just occupied. For the next quarter hour I responded to questions from Mexican TV, while the delicious collation in my honor dwindled down to a few scraps, and the ice swan lost its tail-feathers.

My other stop was the picturesque Cuernavaca, where for two days I provided a non-stop seminar on foreign affairs to a group of courteous Mexican officials, none of whom demanded to know why Secretary Kissinger had betrayed them. Motto: do even more homework before taking on this kind of mission. Or at least run a game about it before you go.

1975: ORIENTAL SNAPSHOTS

Japan is an excellent place to test the usual American presumption that other people are basically like us when you get to know them, or that, with lots of study, Americans really understand the mindset of other cultures. This is the best argument of all for policy games in which the "other" is faithfully represented by individuals with deep first-hand knowledge of how other people think and act. Japan is an excellent site for the test because our close political and economic relationship is matched by uniquely opaque style and approach on the other side.

A Washington-sponsored speaking tour of Japan and Korea took place at the height of the OPEC oil embargo against the countries, such as the United States, that had not openly denounced Israel in the 1973 Middle East War. Japan was virtually one hundred percent dependent on imported oil, some from Indonesia but mostly from Iraq, and its kimono was in an understandable twist over energy prospects.

The Japanese dilemma was in the forefront when I addressed an audience of Japanese officials, journalists, and educators at the American Embassy in Tokyo. In the Q&A period one question stood out: "Can you give us any reason why Japan should not build a strong blue-water navy to ensure that our oil imports are protected?" I fell straight into the trap. Pointing to a world map on the wall behind me, I traced the tortuous route the tankers must take to get from Japan to the Persian/Arabian Gulf. I pointed to the South China Sea, the narrow Strait of Malacca, the Indian Ocean, the Arabian Sea, and the Strait of Hormuz at the mouth of the Gulf. "What," I asked, "would you do if, after spending 30 billion dollars on building warships to protect your tankers, the Iranians or Omanis sank a couple of block-ships in the channel? Wouldn't your enormous expenditures have been in vain?"

I looked out at my audience, confident that my superior logic would spare them from wasting a fortune. With a polite hiss or two from around the room, the senior official who had raised the question smiled. "Ah yes, Bloomfield Sensei. That is why instead we are sending our Foreign Minister to Baghdad to negotiate a new agreement on reliable oil supplies for Japan." The smiles and nods around the room made the point even clearer.

Many of the issues of that day have been overtaken by events. But one footnote highlights the occasional cultural dissonance between East and West. My last provincial lecture was in the city of Fukuoka, where I overnighted en route to Seoul. Everything worked well until I tried to order breakfast in my hotel room. The telephone conversation went like this. Me: "Where is the breakfast I ordered?" Voice: "You want breakfast?" Me: "I already gave my order." Voice: "You want water?" Me (becoming agitated): "It's not here!" Voice: "One beer?" Me: "That's not what I said." Voice: "One bread?" Me (gurgle).

1977: In Vino Veritas: Helsinki, Istanbul, and Lisbon.

That master of the thoughtful witticism, Adlai E. Stevenson, who was President John F. Kennedy's ambassador to the UN, once described that job as a combination of "alcohol, protocol, and Geritol." Indeed, one chronic feature of the often testy relationship between the State Department and Congress has been the deep suspicion on the part of some Members that American overseas diplomacy is conducted in an alcoholic haze. That represents at best a misunderstanding, at worst a nasty expression of anti-foreignism.

Governance and its offshoot diplomacy are serious matters. But there is a human side, and the fact is that important parts of the negotiating process take place informally or might not take place at all. Except for some rigorously Muslim countries, alcohol is one of the lubricants of diplomacy, just as it is in corporate life, the media, possibly courtship, certainly seduction. But I digress. The following three glimpses of the diplomatic life by a part-timer have in common a sampling of the role of that indispensable lubricant.

On a high-speed weekend speaking tour of Scandinavia, I raced from one-day performances in Stockholm and Oslo to a two-day stop in Finland, starting with the capital city Helsinki. Downtown had architectural echoes of Tsarist Russia borrowed from neighboring St. Petersburg—yellow state buildings with white columns, which were nice, and blocky apartment houses in Stalinist gray, which were ugly. Given Finland's history of uneasy coexistence with, and occasional occupation by, Russia, the government in Helsinki was determinedly neutral in the Cold War. But intellectually and politically, it was close to the West. On my arrival, I was hustled to the residence of Ambassador Mark Evans Austad, a well-tailored Republican businessman who had for some unaccountable reason been left in place when Jimmy Carter succeeded Gerald Ford in the White House.

While I shed my overcoat he told me that a group of Finnish officials would be arriving shortly for lunch, with my visit as an excuse to conduct some important business. As if by prearranged signal, the doorbell rang. The butler arrived, not to open the door, but to hand his boss a trayful of bloody marys, each sprouting a large celery stalk. The ambassador carried the tray to the door as the butler opened it. There stood half a dozen senior functionaries from the Finnish Foreign Ministry, all identically garbed in black suits, and all wearing a frozen expression that accurately matched the outdoor temperature.

As they entered, the ambassador handed each one an over-sized glass from his tray. The doorbell rang a second time, producing a similar batch of black-suited, frozen-faced Finns. As veterans of such occasions know, equipped with a second round of bloody marys and a fine luncheon wine, Finnish diplomats and bureaucrats are entirely capable of making the decibel level rise as toasts are exchanged, howls of laughter are heard, invitations extended and US-Finnish relations visibly improved. I sat at one of the small tables between the two Finns, who solved the Austad mystery when they told me their government had petitioned President Carter to keep the Republican ambassador on the job. The reason? "This wonder-worker has arranged the sale of more Finnish icebreakers for use in your Great Lakes than anyone else in Finland."

A day later the alcohol phenomenon in diplomacy expressed itself in a different way. The setting was a modernistic conference site in the birch forests some miles outside of Helsinki, where I was the American protagonist in a two-day foreign affairs seminar. The lead Finn was Max Jacobson, whom I knew as an outstanding ambassador at the United Nations who might have become Secretary-General if he had not been Jewish and subject to black-balling by the Arab states and their Soviet-bloc allies.

The first day's seminar proceeded in orderly but dull fashion. When it came time for the afternoon break, it seemed the plan was to explain to the American how to take a proper Finnish sauna. This really shook me. I informed them that we Americans had lots of saunas, and that I had almost been killed by one in Aspen, Colorado. After arriving from sea level to the mile-high conference site, I had been boiled to the shade of lobster and then made to leap into a pool only a few degrees above freezing. I told them my heart had probably stopped a for while, but I did recover.

My story produced uproarious laughter among the Finns who, like me, had stripped to the buff en route to the sauna room. I took their laughter to be ill-concealed contempt for hardiness-challenged

Americans. But I changed my mind when, after fifteen minutes during which an attractive female attendant ladled cold water onto the hot coals, they led me to an adjacent locker room where a large array of food and drink was laid out.

We sat down in our towels and started in on the beer, which soon abated my resentment. We then stepped into a warm pool, where my umbrage dissolved entirely. It was now obvious that their mirth was directed, not at me, but at the crazy Americans in a place called Aspen who engaged in self-flagellation and insisted on calling it Finnish. After another frolic in the virtual amniotic fluid and another beer, we dressed and returned to the meeting room, where the Finnish-American interaction acquired a decidedly more stimulating tone.

Sometimes, of course, the drinking is just for fun. A few years earlier in Istanbul, Turkey, after I had done my dog-and-pony show for the usual groups of officials, students, and newspersons, US Consul-General Jim Spain hosted a dinner for me. The Consulate-General was located on the north bank of the Bosporus, with stone steps leading down from the terrace into the water. It seemed that the dinner party would take place in Asia rather than Europe. That is to say, we would cross the Bosporus to the Asian side to be fed.

Turkish and American guests arrived, and we piled into a motor launch. Dodging the coal-burning ferries that ply back and forth along the Bosporus, we finally fetched up on the Asian shore. The restaurant was close by, and inside were long tables filled with happy Turkish diners. The table alongside ours featured a wedding party in full swing, including a pianist pounding away on an ancient upright piano.

Food and wine were brought, and our party became jolly indeed, confirming the hypothesis that international relations, in this case US-Turkish, were definitely enhanced by the grape. (Turkish Muslims are largely secular and, with exceptions, generally unfettered by the cultural strictures of their Islamic neighbors.) Suddenly a commotion broke out at the adjacent table, where it seemed the hired pianist had passed out. I must have boasted that one of my hobbies involved tinkling the keys, because the next thing I knew our host had offered my services to the wedding party. Thus, I wound up playing American pop standards for the happy local couple, their family and friends,

Europe to Asia: Crossing the Bosporus in Istanbul, Turkey.

while across the room American and Turkish officialdom and spouses climbed on top of their table to dance the night away. Who said diplomacy had to be grim?

The US envoy to Portugal was Richard Bloomfield (no relation), a lively guy whom I had known as one of the brightest Latin American experts in the State Department. On my first day he launched my visit with a generous — indeed, foolhardy — gesture at an embassy luncheon to which he had invited Portuguese officialdom. In his toast, he explained that he had tried unsuccessfully to find a blood relationship between us, but would vouch for me anyway. I had a momentary fantasy of generating a Lisbon newspaper headline reading "Bloomfield Denounces Portugal" but didn't follow through. I did, however, say the wrong thing about port wine, dismissing it as a boring sweet red digestive for old folks, while scoffing at the very notion of a good white port. My blunder momentarily disturbed US-

Portuguese relations, given the intense local pride, not to mention export income, surrounding port wine.

At the end of my Portuguese stay, Dick B. hosted a final supper party for me. The dinner, which again included Portuguese officials, was served in normal fashion in the dining room. But the last course was served at the top level of the embassy building, requiring the guests to climb a narrow stairway into a sort of attic with a door to the outside. Stepping through the door brought us onto an extraordinary glassed-in balcony cantilevered to overlook the Tagus—the river from which Henry the Navigator's caravels had departed on their 16th century voyages of discovery. On the table was spread an assortment of vintage *white* Portuguese port wines. The occasion was obviously meant to atone for my earlier gaffe, and appease the Embassy's charming but sensitive Portuguese contacts.

It did not take a protracted period of sampling to eat (or rather, drink) my earlier words of œnologic ignorance. I would not want to testify under oath to everything that happened while Portuguese honor was being restored. But I do recall that, quite late in the proceedings, my host and I agreed to surreptitiously swap jobs so he could magically become Professor Bloomfield and I Ambassador Bloomfield. Alas, it never happened.

1977: Non-Human Rights in Southeast Asia

US foreign policy has in recent years had an important human rights component reflecting domestic progress in that realm. This became extraordinarily salient under the Carter regime. The propagation of that policy around the world naturally targeted governments that repressed their people, resulting in a kind of dual diplomacy combining "normal" relations and what tyrants and autocrats took as attacks on their jugular.

When I served with the Carter National Security Council in 1979–80, the president's signature human rights policy was part of my overloaded portfolio. But my first exposure to his policy and its impact abroad came while I was still a professor. Out on the hustings as a US-sponsored cultural package, this time the locale was Southeast Asia, where I did my thing in Thailand, Malaysia, Singapore, and Indonesia.

It was three months after the new President had proclaimed the primacy of American human rights policy around the world. That was an implicit antidote to the Nixon-Kissinger *realpolitik* epitomized by the latter's remark, after dumping the Kurds in a deal with the Shah of Iran, that "intelligence operations are not missionary work."

The trouble was that the State Department had failed to explain to our ambassadors abroad just exactly how to implement the new policy, and in particular how to explain to the people in charge, Washington's stinging public critiques of human rights shortfalls in their countries. After Carter was defeated and I finally had the leisure to review all the classified human rights policy documents, I learned that it had taken one year for the initial pronouncements to be translated into specific policies, by which time much had, as usual, been overtaken by events.

In each Southeast Asian capital I visited, our ambassador was steaming over the awkward position into which the White House had put him. When I arrived in Singapore, the ambassador asked me if I knew just what Washington had in mind, and what he was supposed to do about it. When I pleaded ignorance, he said, "Well, you explain it to them." My chance to explain it to the Singaporean top disappeared when classmate Elliott Richardson simultaneously hit town as Carter's negotiator of the UN Law of the Sea Treaty. Elliott got not only the best guest house, but also a lock on Prime Minister Lee Kuan Yu.

Thus it was Deputy Prime Minister Goh Keng Swee to whom I paid my respects. Before I had a chance to tell him what a fine country he had, he launched into a spirited denunciation of Washington's bad-mouthing of his nation. "What," he demanded to know, "do you expect us to do with our communists, let them loose on the streets?" The American answer was, of course, "Yes, if they haven't committed any crimes." But all I could really say was that I was a private citizen and had no pipeline (yet) into the president's mind.

Indonesia's capital city Jakarta was an impoverished, over-crowded, lively, colorful place, with at least one low-tech device that delighted us, namely, a cork-like surface on our hotel tennis courts with lots of holes to absorb the daily afternoon rain showers. Another not so attractive low-tech device was the prison system, in which not only common criminals but also journalists, professors, and other intellectuals were frequently incarcerated by the repressive Suharto regime. As elsewhere in Southeast Asia, the political-military élites I was exposed to decried Jimmy Carter's human rights policy as naïve and hypocritical.

After finishing my assignment in Jakarta, a small plane took us to Jogjakarta, seat of the old Japanese empire. My seminar at the University took place in the shadow of an active volcano whose plumes were visible through the windows, making the heat overwhelming. When the seminar ended, I was invited by a carload of professors for a scenic ride around the city. When the car got up to speed, they delivered their message: "President Carter's human rights policy is the best thing that ever happened for us here. It means we're not alone but have powerful friends who believe in freedom and are prepared to say so. Tell your President to keep it up!" That high-speed human rights ride through the streets of Jogjakarta noticeably influenced my bureaucratic performance when, a couple of years later, I found myself on the White House staff dealing with the real thing.

The human rights story has a footnote. Two years later, just before I left Geneva to succeed Jessica Mathews as director of Global Issues at the National Security Council, I had a call from a Swiss academic colleague who asked if I would meet with the Iranian ambassador in Geneva before departing. US-Iranian relations were distinctly edgy following the eviction of the Shah and the installation of the theocratic Islamic regime of the Ayatollah Khomeini though the US Embassy had not yet been seized. More to the point, I was under wraps following the White House announcement of my appointment, and told to decline all but social invitations. My Swiss friend was insistent, saying it was vital that I make the meeting. With great reluctance, I finally agreed.

We met in the cafeteria of the lakeside Graduate Institute where I was teaching. The ambassador's message was stunning: "Please tell Washington to cancel its plan to send the man they have named as the new US ambassador to Iran." "Why?" "Because he comes from the CIA! How could they do something so stupid when what is needed is a calming effect on the rapidly-deteriorating relationship. Anyone with a commitment to democracy and human rights would be acceptable. But sending a CIA agent will only reinforce all the anti-American sentiment." He sounded frantic, and I reported the meeting at once, but when I started work in Washington, I had no time to follow the matter in detail. I did notice that, when the Iranian mob took over the American Embassy, we still had in place, not an ambassador, but a chargé named Bruce Laingen, who acquitted himself nobly.

1984: THE SERIOUS SIDE—LIFE UNDER APARTHEID

Before the late 1980s and the empowerment of the black majority, South Africa represented a particularly vile form of governance. That beautiful country was ruled by the Dutch-descended settlers, who had arrived there before the English. The ruling Afrikaans deprived the native African peoples of virtually all civil rights, and were only slightly more tolerant of the so-called "Coloreds" of mixed-race. All power remained in white hands until international opprobrium and perhaps a mounting demoralization on the part of the rulers brought to an end the enforced separation—Apartheid—of blacks from whites, even to the point of keeping the families of black city, farm, and factory workers exiled to distant "homelands" of highly inferior quality. The US had been ambivalent toward Apartheid all too frequently, but starting with President Carter, Washington had joined with American businesses and organizations, which condemned and boycotted the pariah regime.

When I finally was able to see this for myself, the end of the regime was six years away. (Three years earlier, the unreconstructed Afrikaaners running their Interior Ministry had stiffed not only me, but also their own Foreign Ministry by refusing me a visa after the State Department had arranged all the details of my tour with the Foreign Ministry. I learned later that my exclusion stemmed from the fact that I had recently worked for the South African racists' great enemy, that left-wing human rights panderer Jimmy Carter.)

This time, however, I was representing the board of trustees of the Boston-based World Peace Foundation at a conference of international relations institutes around the world convened by the gutsy South African Institute of International Affairs. Suppression of the huge non-white majority was still the name of the white government's horrendous game. I spotted a couple of places where the façade was crumbling. But the rest of what I saw didn't give me much optimism.

As a first-timer, I found Johannesburg cosmopolitan, Western, urban, upscale—a mile-high Toronto or Sydney crowded with high-rise apartment buildings. Its Saturday night scene could have been San Francisco, with gaily-lit streets filled with boutiques and non-puritanical amusements. More to the point, the crowds were white, black, "colored," and Asian. But on Sunday, with everything closed, the streets were empty of blacks, who were supposed to live elsewhere, and their families even further away in one of the arid, desolate tribal "homelands." The hotels and universities were said to be "open," and I did see an illegal black squatter's little nest perched behind a storefront. But black faces were few and far between.

The world-class restaurant in my hotel featured blacks in abundance, as waiters, busboys, even captains (but not maîtres d' or sommeliers). Their manner conveyed a subservience reminiscent of old-time European colonies. One black servant was publicly vilified by his white supervisor in a racially-superior tone of voice I hadn't heard since wartime India. But what also struck me among the blacks was a widespread kind of gentleness, without which a less forbearing people would surely have violently confronted their oppressors.

The setting of Cape Town, where our conference met, was one of breathtaking beauty, with mountainous walls of sheer granite framing blue water. Semitropical palms and flowering shrubs set off buildings, streets, mountain drives, and (mostly Anglo) suburban homes. On the fringe of the city lay a half-square mile of bulldozed red earth punctuated by one small mosque and two lonely churches. This was "District Six," whose "colored" residents had two decades ago been evicted and their homes bulldozed. It was still barren, thanks to the coloreds' quiet determination not to allow white gentrification to ruin their former homes.

The humiliating "petty apartheid" was being modestly reduced in Cape Town under an unusually permissive City Council. Gone were the signs segregating restrooms and other public facilities, and crowds mixed in the shops, eating places, and streets. The reason was clearly related to English settler influence, and also to the fact that Cape Town was the only South African city in which black workers were a minority. But the beaches—always the last to go (including in my home town of Boston)—were run by the provincial government and remained tightly segregated. While blacks could take part in con-

An apartheid wasteland: Crossroads, outside of Cape Town, South Africa.

ferences like ours, including the dinners and garden parties, they were all ambassadors or other notables from neighboring countries, and their personal tension was palpable.

Beyond the city, behind the University of Cape Town campus that was perched like a rambling palace along the dramatic escarpment of Table Mountain, beyond the port and the elegant suburbs, was Crossroads—a sprawling black shantytown whose residents were under decree to evacuate even farther from the city so that coloreds (who enjoyed official preference over blacks in the labor market) could be moved in to replace them.

Crossroads was an overwhelming experience. On a dusty back street, the dirty cinder block exterior of a tiny schoolhouse was graced with bright frescoes painted by white volunteer artists from the city. On the bare earth alongside the main highway, a lively bare-footed soccer game was underway. Everywhere people wandered like hungry cattle across sandy, treeless wastes.

Yes, small cracks were appearing in the façade of apartheid, and in a few years it would be an ugly memory. But before that happened, for one visitor it was the physical and human wasteland that was Cross-roads, with its tin and cardboard shanties and fields of blowing sand, that stayed in the mind's eye.

1993: Dancing with the Prime Minister

Norway, like some of its Scandinavian neighbors, is a constitutional monarchy, with a parliamentary system of representative democracy and plenty of democratic spirit. My experience suggests not only that country's active role as peacemaker and conciliator, but also the spirit of the Norwegian attitude toward its rulers.

What took me to Oslo this time was a meeting organized by Norwegian Foreign Minister Johan Jorgen Holst to support the work of an international public-private group called Commission on Global Governance, for which I was writing a paper. Holst, whom I had known for decades and who died tragically a year later, was a hero of the sadly aborted "Oslo Agreements" quietly negotiated in Norway between Israelis and Palestinians later the same year.

The meeting was at a resort hotel atop Holmenkollen Hill, site of Norway's historic Olympic ski jump, where one could look for miles down the Oslo fjords. Our earnest Norwegian hosts kept us talking in the splendid Viking-theme conference room from nine A.M. till six P.M. They were also hospitable. The first evening, Johan and his new young wife had a few of us to dinner. Four-year-old Edvard played around our feet during the cocktail hour, and I heard later how playing with the little guy had loosened up the stressed-out Israelis and Palestinian negotiators. Among the guests was a highly personable character universally known as "Sonny" Ramphal, who was then head of the (British) Commonwealth. Earlier he was Guyana's foreign minister, and he kindly assured me that his country had found useful the advice for which they paid me during their quarrel with Venezuela in 1973, although I happen to know that what really settled it was when the two foreign ministers got together for a drink.

The conference was the usual mixture of good and bad ideas, cynicism and idealism, egotism and modesty. One joy was getting to know the remarkable Sadako Ogata who, as UN High Commissioner for Refugees, was not only coping with twenty million refugees worldwide, but personally directing UN relief operations in war-torn Bosnia. A short, matronly, business-like Japanese woman, she was iron-willed in carrying out her mission, yet astonishingly modest and matter-of-fact about her accomplishments. She was the only panelist who was applauded.

Some other participants were equally unusual. Wu Jianmin, spokesman for the Peoples' Republic of China, was a conspicuous minority of one in his rhetoric about absolute sovereignty and non-interference in internal affairs (translation: "Keep your hands off Tibet"). In stark contrast was Jiri Dienstbier, who had until recently been Czech Republic President Vaclav Havel's well-regarded foreign minister (and former prison cell-mate). Dienstbier was paunchy, of medium height, snow-white moustache and hair, and penetrating blue eyes, along with an infectious laugh. When he told me he had read my books I blushed and said I had heard of him, too. But when I remarked that the faculty I had recently chaired at the Salzburg Seminar had included his country's finance minister and later president, Vaclav Klaus, he unloaded a ton of invectives about Klaus for allowing Czechoslovakia to break in two.

Former President Oscar Arias of Costa Rica had won the Nobel Peace Prize for resolving the Nicaraguan civil war. But at first I found him an enigma. Short, compact, and with a smooth-skinned round face, unblinking eyes and a helmet of coal-black hair, he came on as taciturn, even sphinx-like. After sitting next to him for a day and a half without hearing him say a word, I finally said everyone would be disappointed if he didn't speak. He did, and all of a sudden he was eloquent, moving, even inspiring in his moral corrective to our rather bloodless analytical dialogue on security, humanitarian intervention, and international peacekeeping.

Our reward at the end was to be bused down to the Oslo waterfront to board a modest-sized party boat on whose foredeck stood a little receiving line. When it was my turn, I shook hands with the Holsts and a long-time Norwegian acquaintance named Olaf Arne Brundtland. Next to him was his wife I had never met but long admired—our hostess Prime Minister Gro Harlem Brundtland.

We moved off into the harbor and cruised around the Oslo fjords into the wee hours. It was Mid-Summer's Eve—the longest day of the year, which meant it never got dark at night. It was a great national occasion when people gathered along the shoreline, lit bonfires, and partied. By eleven P.M.—the witching hour of the solstice—fires burned everywhere and people sparkled both on shore and on board our little craft.

President Arias, who had by now himself brightened considerably, joined me at a table on the open deck along with Sonny Ramphal, the Beijing automaton, and two attractive blondes from the staff. We were on our third glass of wine when Prime Minister Brundtland came and plunked herself down. We talked until the rock band on the fo'c's'le deck reached top volume, after which we shouted. A brisk breeze was now blowing, and the temperature dropped to around forty degrees Fahrenheit. Everyone but me seemed to have a sweater or parka. To warm up, I descended to the buffet and loaded up on the dazzling collation of gravelox, prawns, herring, lobster, sardines, and kippers—all cold.

When I regained the upper deck, Madam Prime Minister pulled me into a seat and this time the conversation got substantive: "Why is Secretary of State Warren Christopher so taciturn? House Chairman Lee Hamilton so edgy? President Clinton so worrying to well-wishers like herself?" I answered, "Because, as Christopher himself explains, he is 'Norwegian' (that really cracked her up); because Hamilton was sulking at not being Secretary of State; and because, because, because— but don't give up on Clinton, it's early, he's smart."

Sergei Rogov, the Russian negotiator with Ukraine on disposal of nukes, joined us in a spirited dialogue during which he comprehensively denounced President Gorbachev for having betrayed his two closest supporters (Shevardnadze and Yakovlev) and turned instead to the Russian Communist Party leader, who proceeded to organize an unsuccessful coup against him. Arne Olaf kept adding layers of clothes on his wife, who listened attentively while I froze. The Beijing propagandist joined us, cackling in an un-Marxist way at every capitalist joke. President Arias, by now grinning like a Cheshire cat, soon left us to do a slow dance with a pretty rapporteur.

Still trying to thaw out, I descended to the foredeck, where the three bearded, moonlighting dudes from the Ministry of Defense were really laying down sound. Johan Holst was doing a fast dance with his bride and four-year-old son, and soon Herself showed up. So it was that I found myself boogying the night away with the Prime Minister, trying hard not to upend us both every time the boat hit a wave.

By now the evening was magical as we slid through the fjords, bonfires on all sides, small boats everywhere, lights strung up the hillsides, people waving from shore, earsplitting music, and still more wine. Security? No choppers, Secret Service or Coast Guard, only one tiny two-man police boat bobbing along behind. When I asked my dancing partner about that, she told me that when she put the same question to their much-loved King his answer was, "Why should I when I have four million guards?" (i.e. the whole population of Norway). At some point I recall saying that in my country it isn't until the second year of an administration that new policies get firmed up, and the third year that they sort of work, followed by the fourth year when everything goes on hold for the election—but I don't remember her question. I got to bed at two A.M. and arose at five to catch my plane home, with sub-Arctic daylight at both ends.

10 LESSONS I
Can Foreign Policy Ever Be Rational?

So far this book has taken the scenic route through some places on the map of recent history where I was privileged to see—and sometimes be—the action. Now it's time to get airborne and look down at that landscape from a distance. The final chapter will bring this traveler face-to-face with the meaning of his voyage. But before tackling that, the reader deserves a better definition of a concept that seems to grip me—the need for more "rationality" in foreign policy. In other words, it's time to stop nagging people to make better use of history and logic, and to get specific.

But what if, after all my arm-waving on the subject, there *is* no realistic way that American foreign policy can be anything but improvised, unsystematic, and shaped by the unpredictable tides of global forces and the capricious currents of public opinion? As Harlan Cleveland has written, intuition and instinct need to play a major role in effective leadership. And so they should, if our highest values and hard-won experiences are to infuse an otherwise cold-blooded process. Or consider Graham Allison's famous three models of decision-making. The first is the abstract "rational actor model" where decisions are reached on a purely cost-benefit basis. But real life is found in his other models, where organizational loyalties and turf protection much better describe actual behavior in bureaucracies, both public and private. So the answer to the question posed in the title of this chapter is probably "No."

And yet . . . when it comes to how top officials analyze information and settle on policy, is it really good enough to stick one's finger in the wind, look into a mirror, and fly by the seat of one's pants? I am not just talking about choosing this tactic over that one. I am talking about high-level aversion to absorbing the lessons of the history. I am talking about failures in gathering and evaluating intelligence with honesty and open-mindedness. And I am talking about obstacles to planning ahead imaginatively.

The costs of these failures can be ruinous. The nation has suffered from flawed top-level decisions, concerning such vital matters as the war in Vietnam, plans for post-war Iraq, and self-defeating protectionist tariffs and subsidies. But these moves were nothing new. In the strife-torn world in which I came of age, America and the West failed to act on the logic of their vital interests in not confronting Nazi aggression until it was catastrophically too late.

During my State Department and White House service, I watched the government stumble from crisis to crisis, always belatedly, always behind the curve. That experience persuaded me that there simply had to be a better way of planning policies and anticipating events. As a government official, I knew that what systems analysts would call fully rational behavior was too much to ask for in the real world of policy and politics. So, as a scholar, I got interested in what management theorist Herbert Simon called "bounded rationality." The distant, but not wholly unrealistic goal, was to find better ways to make decisions about foreign policy and national/international security in an environment of limited knowledge and unavoidable constraints.

Someone once said that predicting the future is easy, what's hard is figuring out what's going on now. But that's only half true. Both policy analysts and practitioners may be steeped in knowledge about the past. But decisions about national security and foreign policy embody predictions, and to make forecasts is a little like the shadow-watchers in Plato's allegorical cave whose knowledge is not so much reality as it is perception combined with wishful thinking.

THE REAL VILLAIN: UNSPOKEN PREMISES

After the Bay of Pigs fiasco in 1961, President John F. Kennedy said two extraordinary things. One was that he would never again trust the experts. The other was that the policy was wrong because its underlying premises were faulty.

On trusting experts, JFK obviously meant depending on expert advice that is consciously or unconsciously biased. But he was only half right, since there are plenty of good experts. The chronic problem is the *lack* of expertise in the Oval Office where top-level decisions are finally made by a small handful of non-experts about issues like Vietnam or Iraq—highly portentous decisions that should depend on their validity of good knowledge of history, culture, and religion rather than, as President George W. Bush implied, a president's "instincts." Instincts reflect character and temperament, which are crucial, but so is attention to objective realities. A president and his closest advisers may or may not be aware of crucial background knowledge, or have strongly dismissed it as uninteresting, irrelevant, or damaging to a course they have set.

Kennedy's more serious charge targeted underlying assumptions. The premise he had in mind was that the 1961 Cubans were ready to revolt against Castro, akin to the 2003 premise that the Iraqis would greet our invading forces with flowers. Worst of all is the notorious logical fallacy of unarticulated major premises—the hidden assumptions that often lie behind foreign policy choices, skewing the professional analyses on which policy is based.

Again, misguided official beliefs about reality are nothing new, and earlier history is replete with examples. Sometimes the hidden premise is nothing short of racist. Before World War II, Americans disastrously assumed that the "racially inferior Japanese" would never dare attack us. In 1950 during the Korean War, General Douglas MacArthur assumed, on the basis of ego-driven certainty, that the Chinese would not attack if he drove up to their border along the Yalu River—this led to a US military disaster. In 1956, Britain, France, and US Secretary of State John Foster Dulles all incorrectly assumed that the shiftless Egyptians could never run the Suez Canal, so they rejected a peaceful solution and brought on a bloody war (the Egyptians proved perfectly capable of operating the Canal).

During the turbulent years on the campus, the radicalization of students and scholars led me to develop a little matrix, I correlated what Freud would call "manifest" positions or openly expressed attitudes with people's views about basic matters such as the use of force, the value of cooperation versus going it alone, and, most basically, a person's "latent" or unconscious view of human nature that in turn makes them optimistic or pessimistic.

I wound up with a 3-D spectrum ranging from hawk to dove, Hobbes to Locke, Calvinism to Unitarianism. My students, before being allowed to assert their own allegedly objective positions, had to try to identify their own biases, as well as the biases of the authorities they were citing. It was a painful but highly educational process. How much sodium pentothal, one wonders, would it take to run that kind of therapeutic analysis on presidents, secretaries of state and defense, national security advisers, and CIA directors?

THE LONG ROAD TO GREATER RATIONALITY

In my improved-but-short-of-ideal world, the policymaker's "pre-flight checklist" would look like this:

- Systematic rather than purely intuitive analysis, requiring a clear and coherent definition of: the problem, US interests, solution options, available resources, and the pros, cons, and likely consequences of each option. Don't think that's easy—it isn't.

- An honest look at the policy's often hidden underlying premises, and a gutsy post-mortem of approaches that haven't worked (an autopsy is practically never performed).

- Attention to history, so all incoming events aren't considered unique.

- Pre-testing policy by subjecting it to artificial stresses in a way that normal, polite conversation can't do (e.g., "gaming it out").

- Better assessment of the probable reactions of other countries and cultures than, as sometimes happens, looking into a mirror and saying "Ah, that's what they would do."

Let's be clear. I'm not saying that the foreign policy-making community isn't composed of people of high caliber. It is. And I'm not saying that the policy papers prepared for the Secretary of State and the President are not orderly and internally logical. They are. Or that the intelligence service doesn't ever get it right despite massive failures on Soviet strength, pre-9/11 terrorist threats, and Iraqi weapons of mass destruction. They often do. What I am saying is that institutions and their loyal members get committed to courses of action that may stop making sense, but are as hard to turn around as a 200,000-ton supertanker given the vested interests bureaucracies develop in guarding their turf from interlopers.

Another occasional enemy of rationality is the *committee process* that permeates the governmental system. Committees tend to fall victim to what Yale psychologist Irving Janis christened "Groupthink"— the pressures on people sitting around a table to achieve consensus while not directly challenging the boss's preferred policy. Such pressures for stability and continuity normally help keep the ship of state on a steady course. But they can also keep bureaucrats and diplomats from recommending anything beyond a minor change of course, which can be downright dysfunctional when the objective situation calls for a 45, 90, or even 180-degree turn.

The greatest obstacle to rational decision-making is of course the overwhelming force of presidential policy preferences. In the run-up to the invasion of Iraq in April 2003, the White House may have, as the president and vice president asserted, simply been seeking information when they constantly tasked the intelligence community with discovering whether there was a connection between 9/11 and Saddam Hussein, and if he had weapons of mass destruction. But the top-down pressure was there.

And "all politics is local" acquires special meaning when a president's political agenda often overrides one important foreign policy consideration after another. Whether it is the imposition of a dubious tariff on imported steel, or giant agricultural subsidies that undermine other US policies toward Third World development, or failure to supply adequate forces in Afghanistan and Iraq.

When the issue is something as politically painful as changing a failed policy, logic won't penetrate the process no matter how many committees meet on the subject (for example embargoes on Cuba that failed to remove its dictator for four decades, or the premature deployment of an untested missile defense system).

Worth mentioning is the fact that it is fallible humans, not computers, that populate the hierarchies. Former White House staffer

James Thomson wrote an article in *The Atlantic Monthly* about an occasion during the Vietnam War when President Lyndon Johnson sat his people around the table and polled them on a brainstorm of his. While waiting for his turn, Thomson composed in his mind a courageous speech in which he would point out the flaws in the presidential argument, the shaky premises on which it rested, and his own notion of the correct course for the nation. When it finally got to Jim Thomson, he heard himself saying, "That's a terrific idea, Mr. President, and I fully support it."

Systematic analytical methods and innovative computer uses are increasingly routine in industry and the military. As I learned when I attempted a twenty-year forecast for General Electric, which wanted to design new appliances that would sell later, one needs some realistic concept of the likely future political, economic, and social environments. In the military, force planning in terms of procurement, training, reserve requirements, and the like all have to be thought through well in advance of a decision to deploy. To land forces on a beachhead takes a lot of advance preparation. But in the political world, one can land overnight in the headlines without advance preparation of any kind whatsoever.

I'm not arguing that the political/diplomatic sector should slavishly mimic business or military. When the State Department tried to emulate the hot-shot systems analysis programs that Secretary of Defense Robert McNamara had introduced in the Pentagon during the Kennedy administration, it failed. One effort called "PARA" involved detailed country analyses as the basis for discussions with the State Department's top brass present, aimed at improving early warning of over-the-horizon problems. Not surprisingly, the bosses on the Seventh Floor had no time for leisurely in-depth discussions of places not on the current crisis agenda.

An even less promising import from the Pentagon called Net Assessment went a dubious step further in trying to quantify US relations with other countries. The results bore scant relation to reality, and reinforced the practitioners' allergy to newfangled devices that challenged experience-based intuition. Indeed, the bureaucratic sands are littered with schemes for formal modes of thinking in the foreign policy realm. Standard quantitative analytical techniques just don't seem to fit well in a field defined by small numbers (under 200 countries), group passions, and human foibles.

Unfortunately, the same allergy has kept State from using some more sensible tools of policy analysis such as our MIT history-based CASCON conflict analysis, an early warning system I have mentioned. Even the State Department's own think-tank—the Center for the Study of Foreign Affairs—was axed in the early 1990s by green eye-shade types as an easy target for budget savings.

Is There a Better Way?

For all these reasons, trying to bring more order to the disorderly world of foreign policy and international relations may be a waste of time. But a nagging voice tells me to reject the belief that all events are random, or that history has no patterns that can instruct us. I just don't believe that the customary decision-making methods represent the best we can do.

When, in the late 1950s, I moved from the crisis-ridden State Department to MIT, I was looking for clues from the thinking classes that might help my ex-fellow-bureaucrats get ahead of the curve. A recent innovation in political science had been the so-called "behavioral school," which I found valuable for understanding what was really going on under the official surface. I found less illumination in another fad that aimed at luring international relations scholars to mathematical approaches.

Another avenue did, however, appear to offer stronger magic: simulation of policy issues. With government support I experimented with role-playing simulation as an adjunct to policy research as well as teaching, a sideline that expanded to become the so-called RAND-MIT POLEX or political game. Additionally, my research team had a growing conviction that conflicts around the world share some elements in common, and that systematic analysis of factors in those conflicts might generate policy-relevant insights.

My conflict research evolved in a curious way. When I arrived at MIT, the CIA was the federal agency charged with funding basic foreign policy research on behalf of the "national security community." That arrangement became a casualty of Vietnam, and was probably not a great idea to start with. But in that era, CIA money was still acceptable on some campuses, and in various disguises helped students attend international meetings to debate their foreign peers. For me, it meant suddenly sitting on a substantial budget along with a free hand to rethink the question of how the United Nations served American national interests.

A decade later, social science got a bad name for helping Vietnam War planners (which I was not). Research grants from the State Department and the US Arms Control Agency became limited to "mission-oriented" studies, calling for answers to specified questions, rather than attempts to push the theoretical envelope. But when I first donned my academic hat, Washington was still sponsoring "basic" research. As in the hard sciences, that meant probes into fundamental political puzzles that might or might not produce an early payoff.

That nicely reinforced my new role as director of MIT's arms control project. For our first major study, we won a grant from the new US Arms Control and Disarmament Agency (USACDA) to look at Soviet interests (and disinterests) in arms control and disarmament. A second grant enabled us to examine "local conflicts"—the small wars around the globe that were causing a lot of grief, but were usually looked at as part of the superpower struggle between the USSR and the West.

The Harvard-MIT Joint Arms Control Seminar, which I co-chaired during those years with Harvard's brilliant and inventive Tom Schelling, at one time or another brought together many of the major strategists, arms controllers, and disarmers in academe and government here and abroad. But like virtually all conflict analysis at the time, it too focused on superpower relations and nuclear weaponry. Since everyone else was caught up in the big strategic picture, my research project had a clear run.

We assembled data from recent and current local conflicts, and tried to generalize about them. In the course of the research, Amelia C. Leiss and I developed a dynamic model of conflict we were persuaded could be applied to *all* conflict cases. That conviction was not easy to sell at first. The State Department sent three analysts to MIT for a week to learn what we were doing. Each was fascinated to find patterns in conflict situations arising in their own region of expertise. But institutional blinders caused their eyes to glaze over at data from other regions, however suggestive. The same happened when the UN also sent three experts to visit my office for the same purpose. Fortunately, the UN could be bullied more successfully than the State Department, and the UN Institute for Training and Research for a time adopted for its work the computerized conflict analysis system (CASCON) which Allen Moulton and I were building from our data.

The professionals are of course correct that no two political situations are *identical.* But they are wrong in refusing to notice that conflicts have some suggestive elements in common, and that they go through identifiable phases during which certain generic factors can be associated with movement toward or away from violence. As usual with myopia, doubters are deprived of potentially valuable insights and possible help in their quest for better early warning of developing conflicts.

The myth of absolute regional uniqueness when it comes to the anatomy of conflicts is made worse by the way the foreign policy machinery is organized. Throughout the 1990s, I moderated an MIT-financed monthly "Seminar on Foreign Policy and Global Issues" in the State Department's Foreign Service Institute (FSI). Sometimes my invited panelists were experts on such cross-cutting issues as democratization, global economics, the environment, or nuclear proliferation. But when the topic was that kind of "global issue," it couldn't be featured as such because State's diplomats-in-training were essentially organized by region. State of course deals with global issues in bureaus such as those covering international organizations, oceans, and science. Like the National Security Council, State has a senior official to head up some variation of "global issues" (my own role at the NSC). But for my FSI seminars, I had to smuggle cross-cutting global issues into programs that the culture insisted be presented to a class studying one particular region.

POLICY PLANNING: HOW RATIONAL?

Foreign policy planning doesn't mean drawing up blueprints or users' manuals to pull off the shelf when needed. It does mean thinking about the future, focusing on the larger purposes of foreign policy, and coming up with better ways to achieve those goals than just doing the same thing. That should require occasionally challenging the premises underlying currently-favored policies. Governments are not noted for challenges to the premises of official policy, or long-range thinking, or anything that looks or sounds "academic." Correcting for President Kennedy's lament that the Bay of Pigs fiasco happened because the premises of the scheme were never challenged is basically mission impossible. But it's still worth trying.

The State Department did something unprecedented in 1947 by creating a Policy Planning Staff to bring reflective thinking closer to unreflective action. It was to speculate on the future, think up alternatives to officially-accepted options, and come up with ideas which day-to-day operational people, whether on the country desks or in the big suites, never had time for.

It is still widely believed that the golden age of policy planning took place in Washington under the leadership of the first policy planning chief, the legendary George Kennan. Many governments have set up policy planning staffs on his model. In principle, the model was a sound one: it made sense to have a select group charged to think outside the box. After all, if IBM (after fighting the idea) had not done just that, the PC would have been delayed for years, and it took a generation for the Pentagon to actually deploy the "smart" weaponry it now uses (although some more World War II-type forces might have made Iraq a safer place).

When, some years ago, I interviewed the planning staffs in fifteen foreign governments, I found two interesting things. The first threw a special light on the built-in obstacles to serious forward planning. The common definition of a realistic time-frame for policy planning turned out to be "six months to a year"—hardly different from that of a thoughtful desk officer.

My second finding was that most planning staffs were faithfully emulating what they believed to be the Kennan model. But they did not appear to have read Kennan's memoirs all the way to the end, where he concluded that policy planning under his leadership was a failure. That seemed to me overly self-critical, given the key role his planning staff (reportedly over Kennan's objections) played in aspects of post-World War II European recovery. Then I realized that the key to this apparent paradox was that when the planning staff reached its apogee, it was not acting as a planning staff but rather as a mission-oriented task force charged with developing a specific policy program.

A task force assigned to craft a needful policy program is a good way to overcome bureaucratic inertia. But it really is not the ideal model of policy planning. That model calls for abstracting the planners from the policy stream so they can bring their critical faculties to bear on future policy. Instead of being turned into action officers, they should act as what some government agencies call a "murder board," or a "Team B," charged with critiquing proposals generated by the action people and, if necessary, challenging their underlying assumptions.

An argument can certainly be made that thinking should not be allocated to only one part of an organization. But some distinctions are valid. A good way to distinguish between operations and speculative, possibly unorthodox thinking, is to consider *first, second, third, and fourth-order* issues. Most internal policy debates focus on third-order issues. ("How can we pressure Saudi Arabia toward reform?") A second-order question ("How long can we regard Saudi Arabia as an ally?") cuts deeper, challenging ingrained positions, Congressional sensitivities, budget allocations and careers, and is not to be tossed lightly into other peoples' in-baskets. And a first-order issue ("Do we really have vital American national interests in the Gulf?") goes to the roots of national strategies and values, and should be the occasion for a national debate. (Fourth-order issues — "Do US personnel in our Middle East missions really need space heaters for their offices?" — is what the lesser bureaucrats do.)

In my ideal world, the division of labor leaves policy planners with first and second-order issues to wrestle with on behalf of the top command. The catch is that in the bureaucratic world, if they are to be considered useful and relevant they often have to focus on third-order questions. The consequence is that, to be deemed "useful," policy planners often wind up doing things that look like operations. As the planner in the State Department bureau responsible for United Nations policy, I was deemed most useful when I joined the crisis managers in drafting cables on the current Middle East crisis. I don't think I was being cynical when I defined policy planning as "what a policy planner happens to be doing at any given moment" (neither did a recent head of British foreign office planning, who said this definition got it right).

What about independence of judgment? Isn't that just what is needed when a reality check indicates dumping a failed policy, or throwing a very different light on a familiar diplomatic landscape? But again, the paradox is that planners and intelligence analysts are most valued by their clients when they deviate only marginally from current thinking. To stray too far from the official line draws the fatal charge of being "unrealistic." So the planner is trapped between the objective need for independent, challenging thinking, and the self-protective requirement to be deemed "useful" by busy day-to-day practitioners focused on short-term deadlines.

The news is not all bad. Some planning products have had a highly beneficial effect on policy. All the past American planning chiefs I have interviewed cited concrete triumphs as evidence that they had profoundly influenced policy (conversely, the majority of staffers who worked for them told me they had felt blocked by the built-in dilemmas of their trade). One of the ablest of the planning chiefs, Winston Lord, argued persuasively that he was able to advance fresh ideas by writing speeches for the secretary of state. A major speech can certainly be a stimulus to policy change. But it was perhaps more typical when, less than two months into the George W. Bush administration, it was announced that the newly-appointed director of policy planning would also be the US point man for Northern Ireland peace.

A NEAR MISS

It should be clear that the main obstacle to improve thinking and planning in American foreign and security policy is structural and inherent in the nature of the beast. The State Department is an operational agency whose officers focus on current relations with foreign countries and international organizations. It is different from a factory, whose workers down on the floor make things, while the brass upstairs have to be future-oriented if they are to market the product. In the White House-State Department-Pentagon policymaking system, the people upstairs do basically the same things as the grunts on the factory floor, only at higher levels. The only way I know to build better thinking and planning into that system is through institutional change. Cyrus Vance as Secretary of State tried to do that, but the effort aborted.

The backdrop for that effort was something called the "Murphy Commission." In the mid-1970s, Washington was seized by one of its periodic urges to rethink the way the government is organized to conduct foreign policy. The Murphy Commission consisted of distinguished personages, half appointed by the President, the other half by the congressional leadership. This meant that, in order to arrive at a consensus, the commission would probably avoid anything in the way of real change.

This didn't stop its executive director, my former State Department boss Francis O. Wilcox, from pushing the limits. Armed with a substantial budget, he commissioned an array of heavy thinkers to heavily rethink. I was delighted to be asked to take another crack at the conundrum of how to increase the system's capacity for policy planning while not alienating the policymakers.

Eight possible arrangements came to mind, which I tested against four criteria: freedom to deal with a wide range of issues, a future-oriented time-frame, independence of judgment, and a clear linkage to authority so good ideas would get a hearing and hopefully be implemented. With the customary unrealism of the academic, my optimum solution was a revolutionary blending of executive and legislator brainpower as the only real way to get a coherent *national* perspective on the nation's problems. My scheme was not only politically impractical, but probably unconstitutional as well. I therefore opted for my second highest-scoring plan, namely a dumbbell-shaped private-public arrangement linking official policy planning with inputs from qualified outsiders. I envisaged regularly-scheduled brainstorming sessions to help stir up the in-house mud with external thinking on alternatives to current and future policy.

In the end, the Murphy Commission watered down anything that looked controversial, including my recommendation. I got a second chance, however, when Cyrus Vance became secretary of state in 1977. I visited him soon thereafter, and took the occasion to lobby for my second-best scheme. To my delight, the scheme was approved, the internal process began, and it looked as though something might happen. Alas, in the end there was neither the money, time, nor energy to push it to completion.

REMEMBERING THE FUTURE

So far I have focused on the past, looking at tools like systematic uses of history to provide better guidance to the present. How about the future? The forecasting method used by most people, apart from hunches based at best on experience, at worst on wishful thinking, is to project today's reality into the future and assume more of the same—the highly popular and bureaucratically safe technique of straight-line extrapolation. It may be no worse than any other method. But the actual record of such "conservative" forecasting is not all that impressive.

In the fall of 1979, evidence started to accumulate in Washington that the internal situation in Afghanistan, then a Soviet ally, was deteriorating to the point that Moscow would have to either invade, or give up its favored political position there. Intelligence reaching the White House showed a steady military buildup in the Trans-Caspian Military District, culminating in the sighting of special communications vans previously used only in actual field combat operations.

But the post-1945 USSR had never used its forces outside its borders except in its Eastern European empire, and the net intelligence judgment, evidently short of historical knowledge of 19th century Russian incursions into Afghanistan, said the Soviets probably wouldn't invade. They did. So a couple of years later, when the intelligence community, once burned, saw an escalating political crisis in Poland, it predicted that Russia probably *would* invade. It did not. Before 9/11 they failed to connect the dots. Before Iraq they connected too many.

Is there any better way, other than consulting the entrails of a chicken? Maybe there is, even if the future is basically unknowable. For me anyway, the forecasting method that seems most productive is, like all others, subjective, but can sometimes generate promising results. I refer to future-oriented "Scenarios"—plausible depictions of alternative futures from which one can pick, choose, and presumably learn. And, by the way, ideally, a good scenario will be tested with a well-designed political game that brings it to life in ways not open to either a genius locked in a closet, or a committee striving for consensus.

One reason I like multiple scenarios is to give people choices that avoid the classic staff recommendation that says, in effect, "Mr. President, you have three options: all-out war, surrender, or what I'm about to propose." Each scenario must use the same key factors so you have a set of parallel pictures drawn from the same basic palette, but painted in different ways to portray variations on the future scene.

Scenarios can range from "more of the same" to radical change. "Best-case" analysis is notorious for falsely reassuring the boss, and "worst-case" for falsely scaring Congress into bolstering appropriations. It is hazardous to propose extreme deviations from policy. Yet a censored menu of futures is likely to miss its target, while a bold spectrum has at least a chance to capture the elusive reality-to-come, even if the extremes sound inconceivable or naïve. General Shinseki was prescient when he estimated to Congress that several hundred thousand troops were needed to do the job in Iraq—but that was an unacceptable worst-case estimate for which he was, of course, allowed to retire.

An exercise I did some years ago asked how Europe might look seven to ten years into the future. I was not in the forecasting business, so I cast about for promising techniques. I didn't find any, so I simply tried to identify the key factors likely to be relevant in the decade ahead, such as Soviet actions, US policy, and Western European cohesion. I then wrote five scenarios that allocated those variables in different ways.

Looking back, a surprising amount of reality emerged, not from the "realistic" scenario, but from my radical No. 5 with its assumption of a greatly diminished Russia whose *embourgeoisement* effectively drained communism of its moxie. It "unrealistically" assumed withdrawal of Soviet forces from Germany, a less coherent NATO, and an isolationist-trending America. Everyone, including myself, considered those outcomes to be off the wall. In the 21st century, they look a good deal more plausible.

Another example: In the mid-1970's, the US was deeply committed to supporting the Shah's regime in Iran. The administration sent to the Senate Foreign Relations Committee for approval a multibillion dollar package of arms sales to Iran and Saudi Arabia. The State and Defense Department submissions consisted of boilerplate restating official confidence in the stability, friendliness, and durability of both regimes. A sorely frustrated Committee decided in September, 1976, to hold a full-scale public hearing to consider the matter. As a professor, I had recently returned from a State Department-sponsored speaking tour of the Middle East including Saudi Arabia and Iran, and was invited to be one of two witnesses, with the request to be candid.

In the course of my testimony, I tried to do that with the help of some illustrative scenarios. The first couple of scenarios projected current trends in non-controversial terms. But to loosen up thinking, I added a couple of alternative futures including a worst case that embodied unspoken fears and taboos. It suggested the possibility of "radical changes" in one or both states—a heresy that ran contrary to ingrained assumptions. It suggested that in Iran, "forces are in motion that significantly increase the chances of profound internal change." It noted that where "traditional societies are hurled, without preparation, into a Western version of rapid development, they become profoundly unstable and even revolutionary." Iran, a socially-stratified, autocratic society, could fit that model, particularly since it was sending abroad thousands of its students, risking an explosive outcome I dubbed "catastrophic modernization." What would be the effect of such an explosion on relations with the US? It was possible that a post-revolutionary Iran might be friendly to the US. But "one might equally predict a period . . . of radicalization" causing Iran "to turn on the United States as a symbol of 'imperialism'."

In sketching that highly unpopular scenario, I was certainly not making a prediction, but rather trying to depict one possible outcome that had nagged at me since visiting the Shah's Teheran. Unfortunately, within two years it started to come true.

11 LESSONS II
My Moderate Utopia

WHAT HAVE I LEARNED?

Here is where I try to figure out what I believe about America and its place in the world. Two apologies. The first is for being politically independent, and thus the despair of partisan family and friends. I can even live with the collected essays of George Orwell entitled *My Country Right or Left.* So don't look for fiery partisan rhetoric.

The second apology is for seeing most foreign policy choices in gray tones rather than in stark black and white. I admit to secretly envying people who, through ignorance or single-mindedness, derive moral satisfaction from oversimplifying the complicated. I sympathize with the president who reportedly yearned for a one-armed economist so he didn't have to keep hearing "on the one hand, but on the other hand." But alas, one major learning experience has been the degree of ambiguity in complex policy issues.

Indeed, much evidence confirms the observation of a sage New Zealand diplomat that most big decisions are a matter of a 51–49 percent tilt to one side or the other of a close argument. This kind of waffling can be intellectually crippling, but it can also be highly educational. If "Death to the Infidel" is the motto at the loony end of the political spectrum, my own position is defined by the splendid motto quoted earlier in the book: "Faith can move mountains, but it's doubt that gets you an education." President John F. Kennedy liked to quote a saying that "civilization is a race between education and catastrophe,"

186

and he was right. Education can save the world—*if* there are also jobs for its human products.

In the dangerous planet we inhabit it is not just desirable, but imperative to try much harder to overcome the ignorance and prejudice that infect major sectors of human society. I don't care how beautiful the dream of Paradise is in the head of the zealot for whom the unbeliever has no moral legitimacy and is consigned to the eternal flames, possibly with the fanatic's help. Today the enemy of civilization is that religious zealot, of whatever creed, who claims a total monopoly on the Truth. If I ever become a protest marcher, I plan to carry a placard that reads, "Spare us from the men of principle."

THE SPLIT-LEVEL REALITY

Some Americans who have a voice in policy debates believe things that make it difficult to develop a rational foreign policy. The competing mindsets fall into two broad categories: "strategist" and "humanist." I happen to share some of their core beliefs including the strategist's realistic grasp of power relationships and the humanist's abiding concern for human welfare. But at the far reaches of each camp lurks a distorted view of reality.

For simplicity, let me caricature the extremes. For the hard-core strategists, dominant realities are conflict, the role of force, and a focus on national security that trumps everything. They see nature as a jungle where, like 17th-century theorist Thomas Hobbes, the overriding requirement is for order, backed by superior force to fend off "a war of all against all." From them the Preamble to the US Constitution both begins and ends with the sole injunction to "provide for the common defense."

Despite the bitter lessons of post-invasion of Iraq, the hardcore strategist prefers US military power to be used only to fight and win wars, and only now grudgingly acknowledges the relevance to national security of post-war nation-building and peacekeeping. This myopia doubtlessly accounted for the scandalous failure of the Pentagon and White House to provide competently for the massive and complex post-conflict requirements.

Extreme strategists show contempt for dreamy idealists who "don't understand reality," and decry as quixotic and even dangerous

the latter's predilection for broad interpretations of the national interest. I can't document this, but I would place a bet that those at the
far fringe of hawkdom feel in their gut a deep pessimism about human
nature, leading to deep suspicion of any real or imagined constraints
on the country's total freedom of action. They frequently have to eat
their words.

Simplicity is also useful in caricaturing the hard-core planetary
reformers. For them, the Preamble to the Constitution begins and
ends with "promote the general welfare." Their agenda is dominated
by concern for economic, social, and ecological fairness through re-
distributive justice, strengthened national and global governance,
and protection of natural resources. Their intellectual sources are the
18th- and 19th- century preachers of the infinite perfectibility of man
and the inevitability of progress, along the lines expounded, respec-
tively, by French mathematician Marquis de Condorcet and English
philosopher Herbert Spencer.

Hard-core humanists are incorrigibly optimistic about human
nature, and reject as immoral both military alliances and the underlying concept of balance of power in the world's strategic geometry.
In the undefined peace they seek, military force is anathema except
for rare humanitarian purposes. They are uncomfortable with anything beyond peaceful means to oppose aggression and tyranny, particularly if the United States offers to lead the charge.

Their core belief is that all conflicts can and should be resolved
through the UN, even the ones that obviously can't.

Both sides claim a moral purpose that is valid if one accepts their
definition of morality. But they pose a rotten choice for those seeking
usable answers. Having existed in both their worlds, I have concluded
that life can be best understood, not by looking at it through either of
their lenses, but only with what might be called "binocular vision." I
propose to give both sides a pair of binoculars for Christmas.

That sounds glib. Does someone using binoculars really have anything more useful to offer? The rest of this chapter tries to answer that
question. Let me start with a bit of autobiography that may account for
a brain whose right hemisphere is idealist, and left hemisphere realist.

I was raised in New England by a pair of genuine idealists. One
was an opera singer and lifelong pacifist. The other wound up doing

such unidealistic things as advising three mediocre Republican presidents. When they began their careers as social workers in Boston early in the 20th century, they were besotted with the spirit of 19th-century New England Transcendentalism, complete with belief in the aforementioned perfectibility of man (and woman, for which both campaigned) and inevitability of progress. These they passed onto their offspring.

It was inevitable that my own juvenile imprinting would undergo a major mid-course correction when I found myself on an aircraft carrier in a war in which the bad guys were out to kill us. Four years in the wartime navy, plus eleven in the State Department, and later service in the National Security Council, involved growing encounters with a different reality. Transformation into a practicing political scientist completed the process, yielding an improbable mix of Unitarian-type optimism and a Calvinist-type view of history-as-tragedy. My chosen label for this hybrid product is "Idealistic Realist" (or vice versa). Which leaves me with a bunch of dilemmas that true realists and true idealists somehow manage to avoid.

Trapped in Dilemmas

In my church we sing with enthusiasm about one world of universal brotherhood and sisterhood, free of conflict, and ruled by Tennyson's "Parliament of Man." Of course we live in "one world," in the sense that people everywhere share a common desire to live in peace and be left alone by their rulers, not to mention the homogenizing effect of universal threats and a globalized economy. But translating that vision into operational reality has been frustrating ever since Thucydidies observed that people like the Athenians were periodically "born into the world to take no peace and give no peace to others."

Reality is certainly not found in the lunatic fear of an all-powerful "One World" in the minds of extra-chromosome types in camouflage suits who scan the skies for black UN helicopters. But neither is it found in proposals for world government that, apart from their political implausibility, ignore the risk of world tyranny or global civil war with no recourse to any higher authority.

What is left to aspire to? Let me propose as a goal for American foreign policy the creation of *a substantially improved system for cooperative action by states in a world of infinite diversity, dangerous threats, and extraordinary opportunities.*

This rests on two big realities. The first is *diversity*. As Harlan Cleveland writes, it is a world with no one in charge. It is a world with a Babel of tongues, a kaleidoscope of tribes, a panorama of cultures. The second reality is that we live in a world of *states*. Few serious students of politics would disagree that, despite porous national borders and the relentless erosion of national sovereignty by globalized trade, finance, information, and weaponry, the 400-year old national state system, however weakened, is likely to survive as the most practical scheme yet devised for incorporating clusters of cultures and values, and for operating a manageable human community.

The challenge, then, is to greatly improve *the system of cooperative action* by independent states—surely a daunting task in our diverse and state-based world. Yet I believe it to be not only a worthy aspiration, but highly rational if the future is to be less chaotic and conflict-prone. Let's deal first with why what I wish for may *not* be entirely reasonable.

I want the US to work cooperatively on a broad range of issues with other countries, a stance which the evidence persuades me is, more often than not, in the US national interest. But alas, sometimes the interests of others (e.g., France in the Iraq War) are even more unreasonable than ours. Like presidential candidate George W. Bush in 2000, I want the US to be more humble in taking into account the opinion of others—to wear its power lightly. As President, Mr. Bush went to the other extreme, assuming that (with the help of God) he had the right answer to everything.

In defending his "my-way-or-the-highway" brand of diplomacy, President Bush argued that the US doesn't need anyone's "permission" to defend itself. No sensible person would deny that proposition (and neither does the UN Charter's "right of self-defense" provision). In the case of Iraq, survival was not at stake and much agony might have been averted if diplomacy had been allowed to run its course, including UN weapons inspections that we now know were effective. But when national security is genuinely at risk, with an attack imminent, of course it would be irresponsible to subject the fate of 290 million Americans to the judgments of a majority of states some smaller than my hometown, not to mention avowed enemies.

I want the US to act like the charter member of the "international community" it has been in the past, and I want it to make a serious commitment to strengthening, not weakening, that community. Before the 2000 election President Bush's future Secretary of State Condoleezza Rice dismissed the idea of international community as a phantom. But the Bush White House learned the hard way that even a militarily powerless "virtual community" like the UN is real enough when the US seeks the moral authority and political legitimacy it needs to secure support, as happened when the post-invasion of Iraq became chaotic. But I have to admit that the international community is by no means as real as the familiar communities we live in, and is certainly no democracy in any but a rhetorical sense.

What else? I want international law to flourish, with the US once again the pacesetter, and I want America to be faithful to its own rhetoric by working to improve flawed international treaties instead of trashing them as George W. Bush did. But I am willing to acknowledge at least a bit of merit in the fear that, given America's global presence and the natural resentment of the "hyperpower," the International Criminal Court (incidentally, not created by the UN but by a grouping of states) might at least in theory act prejudicially against Americans. Finally, I want the world's leading consumer and major polluter—the US—to be at the forefront rather than the tail end of global environmental efforts. But let's admit that originally the Kyoto Protocol unwisely excluded the poor countries, some of which, like China (already with seventy-five of the world's ninety-two most air-polluted cities) and India, will soon be the biggest polluters of all.

In balancing wish with reality, I admit to putting my thumb on the scale in favor of wish. Clearly, the obstacles to my own "neo-internationalist" agenda are very real. The UN is weak and riven with dissension, and unenforceable treaties do not protect us from determined lawbreakers. All this and more is true. But the biggest reality of all for US foreign policy is the demonstrated fallacy that enormous military and economic power makes it possible to run the world, particularly if there is no stomach among Americans for playing empire.

The US can't be any smaller, less rich, or less powerful than it is. There may be times when the peril is so great America must act first and then explain. But as a general rule, it seems to me the US national interest will be best served with a policy, freed of arrogance and bluster, which uses diplomatic, economic, and psychological power to rebuild a robust and effective international system of cooperation in sectors we and most others care about deeply such as security, human rights, and the economy. This means *working from inside the system with those willing to help fix its flaws.*

In short, I want America to push with vigor in my proposed direction, the immortal words of Admiral David Farragut at the Battle of Mobile Bay ("Damn the torpedoes, full speed ahead!") on its national lips. But in terms of leadership style, which can be decisive in setting this nation's external image, I would act on the equally immortal advice of General Andrew Jackson at the Battle of New Orleans to "elevate them guns a little lower."

Four Big Changes

A perfect world would feature universal love and understanding, a fair deal for all humankind (including both sexes), and no conflict. Sobered by encounters with the world out there, my own utopia doesn't much resemble the transfigured human condition described by full-bore utopians like Thomas More, Robert Owen, or Karl Marx (and certainly not the nasty paradise crafted by psychologist B.F. Skinner). Mine is a Moderate Utopia—an MU for short.

The bedrock aspirations for my MU are: first, minimizing violence and war through a far more effective system for peaceful change and conflict-prevention. Second, collective security against aggression and terrorism, and elimination of genocidal weaponry. Third, consistent support for a universal claim to individual freedom, equal justice, and equal opportunity. And fourth, far more purposeful and better-funded international action to resolve common social, economic, and environmental problems.

Four changes in both attitude and strategy would flesh out these aspirations. First, as I have reiterated, only a decent education can widen the path toward that which is most urgently required for a more peaceful and just global society, namely *tolerance of those who are "different."* The word "education" comes from the Latin and means "to lead out" (implying "from the darkness"). In my MU every effort is made to get real schoolrooms established in the Middle East and other places where education has been nonexistent or a transmission belt for religious zealotry.

But that's not enough. This time, the would-be reformers should write on the blackboard 100 times that the *madrassas* which teach fanaticism and hatred succeed because they also feed and clothe poor little boys. This is the same hidden reality that makes part-time terrorist organizations like Hamas succeed: they also provide the local social services, which their corrupt and incompetent governments fail to. The first recommended change is a focused strategy of all-out education help.

Another avenue for education in the broadest sense is through global electronic networks that can liberate people of all ages by expanding their knowledge of the wider world. The Internet is already helping to drag many Chinese and Iranians out of officially decreed ignorance. In my MU, the same thing happens in the Middle East, Africa, and other regions where conflict is fueled by fanaticism and lack of knowledge.

We don't need another campaign in which outsiders say "do it my way and be saved." We need to support those inside who want to work for a social and economic environment that says to both sexes "be all that you can" and *also* makes sure there are jobs if the young take the trouble to get educated.

The second change is the *spread of political democracy*. That means not just elections, although they are a start. The bedrock of participatory democracy is a political system where bargained *compromise* rather than guns and bombs is the accepted way to get things done among factions, majorities and minorities, and assorted religious groups. Democracy is not just a structure but a *process,* which over time develops a vigorous civil society, an effective rule of law applying equally to the top dogs, equal rights for women, a safety net for those at the bottom, freeing up of entrepreneurial energies, and emancipation from the straitjacket of political or religious control. Democracy had better also mean honest government, or people strangled by official corruption will begin to yearn for return to the superficially well-ordered tyranny.

And not so incidentally, the evidence suggests that democracy usually also means fewer wars, both civil and interstate.

The third change is a *reformed global economic system* that rewards investment and entrepreneurship, but has new rules ensuring greater fairness in the distribution of benefits. Globalization and free trade policies have greatly benefited the rich and some of the poor. But others have suffered, both from the incompetence and venality of their own rulers, and from the hypocrisy of America, Europe, and Japan. Their huge domestic subsidies have barred food, cotton, and textiles from poor countries, while leaning on the poor countries to open up to Western manufactures and services in the name of free/ fair trade. What a marvelous way to create new centers of rage. In my MU, globalization is still a good thing for most, but acquires a more rational visage.

The bookshelves are filled with reports in which good people from many countries argue for greater equity in the human condition, with little impact on policy. But just maybe the new preoccupation with terrorism will supply the needed incentive for vulnerable rich countries to get serious about economic and social development of the global poor as a practical strategy for creating a safer world for people to live in. An effective program requires leadership capable of imagining and launching an all-out assault on the towering social and economic deficits in the stagnant, conflict-breeding quarters of the globe, something akin to President Truman's Point Four program, which transformed development for poor countries—and was seen by the American people and Congress as serving the wider national interest.

The fourth change is a *drastic restructuring of the international security system.* That system was designed to cope retroactively with the imploding world of the 1930s and 40s. In my MU, the institutions of 1945 we live with today will be transformed to fit the realities of the 21st century, as detailed shortly.

GOOD NEWS, BAD NEWS

In our world, the organized international system is based on independent states that insist on their sovereign status no matter how eroded their power by economic and financial globalization, proliferating unconventional weapons, and the Internet. That reality puts strict limits on what the United Nations can actually do. And there are other limits. The UN budgets would not buy one B-2 bomber. And even if everyone cooperated and programs were generously funded, no organization with 191 CEO's can ever be really efficient, particularly considering that the UN Secretariat's requirement of geographic representation means it really can't be a meritocracy.

The General Assembly particularly combines good and bad news. That all-member body is notorious for meaningless resolutions, perpetuation of unneeded or outmoded sub-bodies that are really job programs, and destruction of many a noble tree to print vast piles of paper few actually read. Reforms were earlier advanced for weighted voting to account for population and economic disparities, and associate membership for tiny atolls posing as states. They all failed in the way most entitlements, once given, tend to become irreversible.

But the core purpose of a universal organization is neither administrative efficiency nor untrammeled executive action. Yes, action is essential to deal with urgent security matters, and I will be focusing on that. But an equally valid purpose is to supply a unique forum for every country in the world to express its views, exchange ideas with others, and occasionally form a consensus that, at its best, creates norms for the organization and its members to act upon. These norms have included universal human rights principles, rules for demilitarization of outer space and prevention of nuclear weapons proliferation, and many other useful syntheses of broadly agreed human and global needs. The General Assembly (GA) can only recommend. And like any representative body, it has both costs and benefits.

In the light of the well-known weaknesses of the UN as a political body, the surprising thing is the number of national objectives that for practical reasons are actually dealt with collectively. This is most visible in economic, social, technical, and financial sectors where coordinated action in the UN system of agencies has proven indispensable even for the wealthiest and most powerful.

People are generally familiar with the World Bank and International Monetary Fund. But glib critics of "tying America's hands" rarely seem to notice the role of UN agencies: in preventing the spread of epidemics and confronting global health scourges like SARS, AIDS, and malaria (which kills far more people than AIDS); standardizing world-wide air traffic through common safety procedures and language (English), without which every international flight would become a lethal crapshoot; fighting the global drug trade; coping with financial crises and humanitarian disasters; monitoring elections in countries moving toward democracy; and bringing social, economic, and political development to the poor.

I will be coming back later to the scary topic of proliferating weapons of mass destruction including nuclear, biological, and chemical. Here let me only mention that Washington never gave the UN credit for the effective work of its International Atomic Energy Agency in tamping down Saddam Hussein's nuclear ambitions before the 2003 Iraq War. The Bush administration found it useful to bad-mouth the UN weapons inspection process, which we now know was effective in detecting and destroying and monitoring the dictator's biological and chemical weapons capability. And though the UN's economic sanctions on Iraq were badly flawed, they had in fact succeeded in closing down imports and construction of mass destruction weaponry as well as long-range missiles, before the US launched its attack based on the contrary assumption.

These functions of the UN and its Specialized Agencies make the UN system particularly valuable for poorer and weaker nations. They also deal with problems the rich countries want handled but cannot manage alone. But the fact remains that *the UN is judged by the major powers and their publics first of all by its performance or non-performance on issues of war and peace.*

REFORMING THE UN SECURITY SYSTEM

The UN Security Council is where things are supposed to get done rather than just talked about. In other words, its job is to take *action*, ranging from mediation of disputes through peacekeeping, all the way to carrying out Security Council decisions on using force.

If the UN Security Council is to survive as a multilateral security organization in the post-9/11 environment of existential threat, sudden violence against civilian populations, and growing availability of deadly weaponry, something better is needed than the old patterns. It's true that the UN is no stronger or more effective than its member states allow it to be, and it's also true that diplomats, like other people, don't appreciate being treated with contempt, as the Soviets did for years and, alas, some American leaders did more recently. But fatigue or lack of imagination seem to me a poor argument for simply allowing the world's only security body, like its parent League of Nations, to simply die a slow death. Given the deep divisions in the contemporary world, there may be no reform or rearrangement that will ensure more unanimity among the major nations who inevitably must lead the way. But considering the alternatives as well as the high stakes, it seems to me worth a try.

What, then, might be done to improve the organization's capacity to respond forcefully in the face of armed aggression, warfare between countries, terrorist threat, or domestic genocide and "ethnic cleansing?" How do you get action by countries capable of action and at the same time give them the legitimacy the UN can bestow?

The news about the UN Security Council is not all bad. The Council has had many successes we almost never hear about in averting conflict through diplomacy. UN peacekeeping has had some rocky times, including scandals in the Congo. But along with regional bodies like the African Union it remains the only internationally acceptable means to deter, moderate, or monitor local conflicts that roil the neighborhood. A high-powered expert panel produced a report in late 2004 containing some admirable recommendations for tackling this daunting challenge. My own approach goes further. But I would happily settle for either.

But the problems at the core of the UN security function are formidable. The ideal of *universal* collective security to enforce the community's will against egregious violations of international peace and security worked in 1991 in ejecting the invading Iraqis from Kuwait. But the half-century Cold War testified to UN impotence to affect a superpower standoff. And where there is no consensus among the Council's members, universal collective security as originally conceived is no more feasible today than it was in 1945. Iraq illustrated the Council's impotence in the face of a great power, this time the US, which insisted on making its own rules for when force should be used.

Paradoxically, the Iraq War highlighted a countervailing reality about the Security Council, namely the curious strength of what might be termed its "virtual power." The US and its partners went to war on the assumptions, both questionable, that the threat was imminent, and that UN inspections were a failure. Lacking broad international support and encountering unanticipated setbacks, the US and UK subsequently had to do an about-face in 2003 and return to the Council for political and moral support. The actual power and cohesiveness of the fractious Security Council was no greater than before. What the Council seemed to possess was a kind of power I called "virtual" — ephemeral and earlier dismissed by the Bush team, but somehow able to bestow or withhold essential legitimacy, even for the sole global superpower.

Yet another paradox is that if the Council bestows legitimacy, *what about the legitimacy of the increasingly unrepresentative Council itself?* It is obvious that the Council must be enlarged if it is to reflect the contemporary world rather than that of the five World War II victors. But to do so poses an excruciating conundrum. Enlargement would probably make Germany, Japan, India, and Brazil permanent members, and permanent members have a veto over enforcement and other significant actions.

The veto was abused for years by the USSR, and used half a hundred times by the US to defend Israel on Middle East issues. But the veto was the precondition for them to join the UN, and can't be totally abolished if they and the other permanent members—China, Britain, and France—are to remain in the UN. The pair of alternatives proposed by the UN panel referred to earlier would leave the veto power in the hands of the original five permanent members. That may work, although new permanent members are likely to chafe at second-class status, and having nine or more permanent members using the veto as currently defined would make the Security Council even more prone to paralysis.

The only way I can see to resolve the dilemma is *to accept that the veto cannot be done away with on core issues such as the use of force, and to expand the list of Council actions short of the use of force that can be passed without a "great power" veto.*

So-called procedural issues, as well as some peacemaking decisions, can now be passed by majority vote. But there are plenty of important decisions short of enforcement action that could be decided by votes ranging from two-thirds to four-fifths majorities, depending on their significance. The list runs from war-deterring actions such as monitoring along a border (as in Macedonia), to robust war-limiting and war-terminating peacekeeping missions (as in the Congo), to post-hostilities policing (as in Bosnia).

The list of non-vetoable-but-hard-to-pass topics would also include potentially embarrassing, but by no means apocalyptic issues of the kind that permanent members in fact vetoed in recent years. Examples: disapproval of undesirable behavior by a member state; renewal of already-approved peacekeeping missions; dispatch of observers to report on breaches of ceasefires; charges of violation of diplomatic immunity; and complaints that a member state wants to have discussed.

Military enforcement would still be subject to veto, but reducing the list of vetoable subjects will still be a hard sell. But adding new categories of required majorities could break the logjam and enable Council membership to be expanded without the threat of greater paralysis.

A second issue deserves attention. The notion of *coalitions of the willing* has come to represent a presumed alternative for getting action when the Security Council doesn't provide the necessary means. This notion has had a curious life story, starting with sudden popularity in 1991 when Bush *père* organized a UN-mandated coalition of forty countries to drive Saddam Hussein's invading army out of Kuwait. The phrase "coalitions of the willing" fell approvingly on many a statesman's lips.

The idea became controversial when it was used as code for the US-dominated grouping of mostly small "coalition" forces that invaded Iraq in 2003. The initial US-British et al. invasion and conquest of Iraq, launched while UN debate was unfinished and the UN inspectors' job incomplete, left a legacy of resentment and mistrust even among those who welcomed the liberation of the Iraqi people from tyranny, and its neighbors from aggression. In the newer usage, the coalition notion has come to mean an "enforcement" operation outside the UN and without an approving Security Council vote. There is no problem with that if a state is under *imminent threat of attack* and must defend itself without any diplomatic delays. But we know now that was not the case in 2003.

I feel a certain responsibility to try to clarify what was originally conceived as a nifty device to fill the political space between two fantasies—that of a UN-run world, and that of unhampered national freedom to police the world alone. When, in 1971, the *New York Times* carried my suggestion for a "coalition of the law-abiding," and soon thereafter Harlan Cleveland and I coined the phrase "coalition of the willing," we had in mind a *useful add-on to the UN process, not a competitor, always with the exception provided for in Article 51 of the UN Charter of "the inherent right of self-defense."*

Our kind of UN-sanctioned coalition of the willing was intended to expand the ability of the system to confront challenges to international peace and security that the larger community wants to see done, but the UN either can't or won't handle itself. For example the UN-authorized US-led coalition reversed Iraq's 1990 seizure of Kuwait. As early as 1950, the UN's so-called police action in Korea was in fact a coalition of the willing in the sense that sixteen countries under US as the "executive agent" acted on a UN mandate to beat back aggression. The original proposal for coalitions of the willing did not have in mind an optional military action in defiance of all but four members of the Security Council with no imminent threat—as in 2003. Our idea of coalitions envisaged a posse of state volunteers, but a posse authorized by the Council except in the rare case when a threat *is* genuinely "imminent," which it was not in Iraq.

The toughest question remains that of the conditions under which it *would* be politically and morally legitimate for an ad hoc coalition of the willing to initiate preventive enforcement action *without prior UN sanction.* The answer is that it would require the most extraordinary circumstances, like a documented threat of imminent use of weapons of mass destruction by a state or terrorist organization such as Al Qaeda, or one of history's mercifully rare cases of threat emanating from a Hitler or other would-be conqueror with unlimited and non-negotiable aims. Under almost all other circumstances, the route to enforcement action with wide backing and popular support remains a UN stamp of approval for such actions the wider community endorses, but can't carry out itself.

Such ad hockery is not mentioned in the UN Charter. Under the Charter, collective security to deal with threats to the peace was supposed to be managed by the five great powers. The Cold War killed that, and the realities of power still make it a non-starter. But if the UN Constitution is a living instrument that adapts to changing reality, so is the Charter. That document said nothing about peace-keeping. It was a UN-Canadian middle-of-the-night invention in October, 1956, when Egypt was attacked by Britain, France, and Israel.

Another useful innovation was the UN-authorized "multina-tional force," devised in Lebanon in 1982, applied in the 1990's in the Balkans (supplemented by NATO in Kosovo), and in East Timor under an Australian lead. The "International Security Assistance Force" for Afghanistan was a mix of the two, featuring a Security Council man-date and one country's leadership (subsequently handed over to NATO). The same kind of mix with UN sponsorship has tamped down con-flict in West Africa, and in 2004 became the belated format for the overwhelmingly US-dominated force in conquered Iraq.

SOME OTHER POLICY PRESCRIPTIONS: A WISH LIST

OUTLAWED WEAPONRY

Biological and chemical weapons are banned by international agree-ments. (President Nixon unilaterally shut down the US biological weapons program, saying that possession encouraged others to threaten us.) Enforcing these agreements is extremely difficult, but detection technology is improving. In my MU, rather than dismissing such treaties as weak or inconvenient, the US works to make as ef-fective as possible existing chemical and biological weapons conven-tions, including abandoning the unrealistic notion that others should be subjected to intrusive inspection, but not, of course, the US.

If we want to be accurate, nuclear weapons are the only true weapons of *mass* destruction, and US policy correctly seeks to curb pro-liferation (although the G. W. Bush administration may have invited others to ignore its anti-proliferation drive by announcing development of new types of nuclear weaponry and stressing their presumed usefulness).

I would love to live in a world without nuclear weaponry, and presidents, military and civilian leaders, and strategic analysts have long concluded that a nuclear arsenal is unusable except to deter others. An impressive array of former generals and admirals have recommended a policy of what they call "abolition" of all nuclear weapons. Unfortunately, short of universal brain surgery some kind of deterrent nuclear force will be necessary so long as the know-how exists. But my more rational world envisages a fundamental change in US strategy aimed at breaking apparent reliance on thousands of unusable, mutually genocidal devices.

In my MU, the US changes its policy from opposition to acceptance of "no-first-use" of nuclear weapons. Saying we might use nuclear weapons first neither persuades nor deters, since not only is it unbelievable, but it does nothing to affect non-state terrorists who, unlike states, are the only potential users who do not fear certain retaliation by the mightiest military force in the world. Numbers are not the real problem. But further cuts in stockpiles sends a positive signal to others. I envisage the US announcing that it plans to eventually cut its strategic nuclear stockpile to something like 400 concealed and deliverable strategic warheads, while gradually destroying its unusable "small" tactical nuclear weapons along with stockpiles of fissionable material.

Is that unilateral disarmament? Not if a secure deterrent force is maintained. In fact it should lead to a safer world, with US security enhanced rather than diminished, for five reasons. First, keep in mind the axiom that *it isn't certainty but uncertainty that deters*. A small number is as likely to deter as a large number, as was vividly demonstrated when Bush II switched from confrontation to diplomacy when confronted with a probable handful of North Korean weapons.

Second, history shows that sensible unilateral moves are usually responded to positively. The US would use its clout to lead other nuclear and would-be nuclear powers in a more rational direction.

Third, intensive diplomatic pressure would be exerted on acknowledged nuclear weapons powers—Russia, China, France, India, Pakistan, and the UK—to follow suit. To Isreal, unacknowledged as a nuclear power, the US would offer formal guarantees against military aggression in exchange for eliminating its nuclear stockpiles. The US would continue to apply a full court press including both carrots and sticks on North Korea to do what South Africa, Argentina, South Korea, Taiwan, and Brazil did earlier, namely scrap their embryonic nuclear weapons programs. Nuclear wannabee Iran would be given attractive incentives to shut down its program or have it shut down.

Fourth, the International Atomic Agency's inspection powers would be made far more airtight, the Nuclear Non-Proliferation Treaty would be forcefully reaffirmed, and the Comprehensive Nuclear Test Ban Treaty, trashed by the Bush II administration, would be ratified.

Fifth, and most important, no one will successfully blackmail a US that retains not only deliverable nuclear power adequate to annihilate, but also a high-tech conventional military capability a dozen times greater than all its competitors.

If leadership means anything, such a constructive lead by the world's foremost power to break the deadly nuclear stalemate has at least a chance to engage everyone else for whom a manageable nuclear arsenal is costly as well as inherently dangerous. Moral authority may not be measurable. But in an initiative aimed at making the world a genuinely safer place, along with improving US security, it would be better employed than flaunting a huge but unusable nuclear arsenal.

TERRORISM

What about non-state terrorists with no return address? Intensive global police work is underway to roll up the Al Qaeda and other networks. Terrorism is a tactic pursued by zealots, and far more can be done to marginalize and isolate the fanatics who preach death to the infidel. Unrelieved despair is a breeding ground for terrorists in places like Palestine, Saudi Arabia, and Chechnya. A persuasive case exists for improving the economic lot of the people in terrorist-breeding places. But improving living conditions will not by itself alter the lethal agenda of the transnational Islamist zealots. A purposeful counter-strategy aimed at "draining the swamp" in which terrorism breeds should focus on specific problems of unemployment, warped education, corrupt government, and socio-economic stagnation that combine to create an environment of hopelessness.

That is the tactical reason for substantially upgrading the funding of economic, social, and political development programs in poor countries. There is also a larger strategic reason for more focused support of local advocates for better education, honest government, human rights, and generally better lives. It is the best strategy for the rich man who finds that he has built his mansion in the slums.

Religious fundamentalism is, by definition, bigotry. (It's no accident that the word "bigot" derives from "by God.") The enemies of civilization include not only hopped-up Islamists, but all religious zealots who believe their particular Messiah will whisk them to Paradise while everyone else burns in the flames. The bloodiest mix is when religion becomes fused with nationalism and ethnic hatred.

I have always believed that if a clash of civilizations is taking place, it is not between the West and the Islamic world. Rather it is between those within each culture who believe in peaceful coexistence versus death to the unbeliever. If history teaches any lesson, it is that peace, whether domestic or international, is a function of *mutual toleration.* Political democracy—the type of governance most likely to foster internal and international peace—is premised on a minimal tolerance, underlying a political culture of compromise that allows civic life to be peaceful rather than violent.

Historian Arnold Toynbee theorized that a new "universal religion" usually follows a historic "Time of Troubles." In my MU, the new "universal religion" is a spreading philosophy of mutual tolerance—not just lip-service tolerance, but Industrial Strength Tolerance marching behind the banner of "Live and Let Live."

THE CONFLICT AGENDA

Preventing conflicts rather than having to deal with them when they turn bloody is the Holy Grail of diplomacy. There is in fact a lot of preventive diplomacy that succeeds but generally goes unsung. In my modestly improved world, many more of the festering territorial, border, and other disputes that might lead to war are submitted to the International Court of Justice.

The World Court, flawed as it is, is probably as impartial as any international body can be. But despite being a principal architect of the Court, the US has accompanied high-flown rhetoric about the rule of law with decades of gross under-utilization of the World Court. Others have followed our lead. America can profitably rediscover its own aspirations by retaking the lead in submitting to the Court or the World Trade Organization (or to long ignored compulsory arbitration) quarrels that don't affect vital national security interests, while encouraging everyone to do the same. This is not "getting a permission slip" from foreigners, as some demagoguery in high places would have it. It is getting more benefits from the rule of law we preach.

Timely conflict anticipation is a hard sell. Officials coping with crises don't focus on things that haven't yet happened. But a new investment in conflict prevention is not starry idealism. A cost-benefit analysis of historic conflicts shows that the price in blood and money is far less if dealt with at an early stage than after mayhem occurs. The still unresolved war between North and South Korea, and two chronic conflicts that have bedeviled the past half-century—Israelis versus Palestinians, and India versus Pakistan over Kashmir—all now feature nuclear weapons in the arsenal of at least one side. A little morality play starring India and Pakistan suggests the danger:

History's bloodiest war stemmed from miscalculation. An incident led to an outrage, an outrage led to war, and war led to nuclear-tipped missiles arcing in both directions toward mutual holocaust. In living color, a stunned world saw mushroom clouds rising in Karachi, Pakistan, and Madras, India; craters where cities once stood; multitudes of innocents blinded; sweeping panoramas of a moonlike landscape, followed by climate change in the Northern Hemisphere; a global food crisis; ultraviolet radiation; and existential despair.

Analysts later speculated that, while neither side planned to use their nuclear weapons, there had probably been a computer failure in New Delhi. But . . . in the end . . . the very concept of blame seems irrelevant. . . . The demonic horror . . . brought home to everyone the universality, not of brotherhood, but of the vulnerability of man. . . . It was neither idealism nor love of mankind that brought peace but the reality therapy of [nuclear] war. . . . Wisdom came not through treaty but through tragedy. . . . The cost was high but, in the end, reality was the only effective teacher.

What was left of India hastily agreed to a plebiscite in Kashmir— as mandated by the UN half a century earlier. All the other nuclear-weapons nations, having looked into the abyss, finally acknowledged that to use their weaponry would threaten civilization itself—and got rid of it.

The above comes from the winning essay in a 1985 *Christian Science Monitor* essay contest on "How Peace Came to the World." I would rather have peace produced by a more intensive conflict resolution and proliferation-prevention strategy than in the apocalyptic fashion described imaginatively by former Colorado Governor Richard Lamm in his prize-winning essay.

FIXING PEACEKEEPING

If conflicts are to be managed once they break out, the UN must be a good deal more capable of patrolling killing fields, fighting back the murderers, and protecting the people it was sent to help. To do the job properly, its weaknesses need to be fixed so the world never again witnesses the shameful spectacle of retreat in the face of thuggery in Somalia and Haiti, or of standing aside while over half a million Rwandans or thousands of Sudanese in Darfur province are slaughtered or thousands of Bosnians in Srebrenica, whom the UN has guaranteed to protect, are massacred.

Blame for these tragic failures is widely shared. When in 1993, eighteen US servicemen serving alongside the UN's humanitarian force in Somalia were killed and dragged through the streets of Mogadishu, that particular mission had been directed by the US, not the UN, although Washington seemed to let the UN take the mounting political heat. The US, along with feckless European leaders also let the slaughter and ethnic cleansing go unopposed in the Balkans for all too long before finally acting.

The UN's capabilities were improved when multinational forces authorized by the UN in East Timor and Afghanistan were empowered to use force, not just in self-defense, but if necessary to carry out their mission. But one of the chronic problems of UN peacekeeping is the lack of training of some of the military units offered by smaller countries. Some have proposed a standing force, which the Security Council could launch without delay when urgently needed for peacekeeping. It is an article of faith among conservatives that such a project is unthinkable, despite the fact that their hero Ronald Reagan once enthusiastically propounded it. ("We must work toward a standing UN force — an army of conscience — that is fully prepared to carry out [protection of] human sanctuaries through force if necessary.")

A "standing UN force" conjures up an army of stateless mercenaries marching around UN Plaza in New York under the command of an all-powerful UN bureaucracy. Realistically, few UN member states are likely to go this route and a standing UN force is not going to happen any time soon. But that obscures the urgent need, agreed to but never implemented, for an effective, well-defended, and trained *stand-by* force for rapid reaction to international criminality or chaos. A recent UN report, the so-called Brahimi Report, recommended useful reforms in UN peacekeeping, which could provide a good basis for action, if the will existed for action.

For all the hand wringing on the subject, little has actually been done to improve the quality and ready availability of non-great-power UN peacekeeping forces, despite the many studies and reports recommending reforms to the member states. I can't suppress the temptation to wheel out something that nicely illustrates the glacial pace of progress on this front. Here is what sounds like a new proposal to strengthen UN peacekeeping:

I propose the creation of a modest standby force trained and equipped to be available in a condition of readiness and availability when needed. Its primary roles would be observation, patrol, and civil-pacifying functions. At the same time the force should be equipped to defend itself and to hold off equivalent-sized armed units until it could be reinforced.

The proposal envisages battalion-sized units rotated by governments to a training center for six months of specialized training. They would be returned home and held in ready reserve for immediate deployment on call of the UN Security Council. Over five years a 25,000-strong force would be created.

That sounds pretty reasonable, and responsive to the epidemic of ethnic conflict and small wars, doesn't it? I'd better confess that it comes, complete with detailed plans for organization, curriculum and financing, from a book of mine written in 1964.

WHAT'S THE PROPER US ROLE?
Inherent UN weaknesses aside, one obstacle to a steady US policy is chronic misinformation. Not all Americans realize that US forces are deployed in virtually none of the UN's 54 peacekeeping missions. Nevertheless, a small number of US casualties in Somalia, plus serious flaws in other "Cases From Hell" in the 1990s, created an allergy

in Washington to multilateral intervention. During the Clinton years, liberals lost their nerve in the face of UN fiascos and right-wing venom, while unilateralists dismissed the multilateral approach as soft-headed. Both liberals and conservatives sobered up somewhat as peacekeeping made a better showing in places like East Timor and parts of Africa.

The issue for Americans is not direct US involvement. When it comes to putting boots on the ground in chaotic places, Americans are usually attracted, not without reason, to the 4th Cardinal Rule of Diplomacy: "Never get between a dog and a lamppost." Not all conflict situations merit direct US involvement, and UN peacekeeping does not normally need the heavy superpower footprint. What it needs is money and logistical support, with others providing the lightly-armed manpower. The US in fact did this in recent years in such places as Liberia, Haiti, and Sudan.

Even more needed is a more realistic grasp of the national interest in peace and stability in regions where the US has major interests and assets (i.e. in creating a more peaceful neighborhood in which to live). As a practical matter, if Washington isn't going to answer when 911 is dialed, someone else had better separate combatants, police "failed states" that lack a government, and protect innocent civilians from genocide or starvation. The last nine US presidents, starting with Eisenhower in the Congo, have responded to pressure to intervene in local conflicts by saying "get someone else to do it." The "someone else" has been, for better or worse, the United Nations and one of its related regional organizations like the African Union in Sudan. That's going to continue to be true, hopefully resting on improved foundations.

WHAT ABOUT SOVEREIGNTY?

American nationalists fret about "surrendering sovereignty" through treaties and cooperative mechanisms such as the UN. But however militarily and economically powerful a country like the US, it should be evident that achieving broad US goals requires showing a "decent respect" for the opinions of others. Achieving US goals also sometimes requires that sovereignty be, not surrendered, but *pooled* with that of others, as already happens on many fronts cited earlier such as in health, safety, and other functional sectors.

Iraq showed skeptics that the same is as true for major military ventures as for curbing epidemics. Consulting and cooperating on such matters does not constitute a favor we confer on undeserving foreigners. It is a necessity that serves the national interest, as brilliantly recognized by the generation of equally patriotic Americans who helped design the present international system.

Support for the UN idea does not have to mean blind support for the 1945 model. It means devising better ways to bring up to date the principles and purposes set forth in the Preamble to the UN Charter, which make as good sense today as they did then. Reforming the UN has never been easy. But it is instructive to recall that, in that extraordinarily creative five years of institution-building from 1945 to 1950, the US painstakingly consulted, negotiated, and collaborated with its battered allies to build a new international system that has endured for more than a half-century.

THE WIDER NATIONAL INTEREST

Even the modest reforms suggested above will generate opposition from those who fear that giving up untrammeled freedom to act is "contrary to US national interests," regardless of demonstrated benefits. There is nothing new about this argument. For centuries, US foreign policy debates featured nationalists whose narrow version of "national interest" was their mantra and touchstone, opposed by internationalists who rejected the national interest test as too narrow and selfish.

National interest is not easy to define. Yet it is a concept all governments find useful for grounding their national strategies. A new stress on US national interests was created by 9/11. Indeed, for many countries the battle against terrorists calls for a sharpened focus on homeland security. George W. Bush was convincing in defining his primary task as protecting the American people. But for the rest of the foreign policy agenda, history is persuasive that US interests are better served by the premise that what's good for neighbors, allies, and trading partners is probably also good for America.

This premise is intensely practical, but an important part of it is also psychic. A good example is the feeling of most Americans that actions are more legitimate when supported by the international community, ephemeral as that community may be. Consider the reasons modern America has gone to war twice in Europe, twice in the Gulf, as well as once in Northeast Asia, Southeast Asia, and the Balkans. In most cases, rhetoric aside, a principle larger than US security or advantage was also at stake, whether defeating fascism, opposing aggression and genocide, or demonstrating determination to root out terrorists and deter potential nuclear proliferators. In each case, the US acted in its "national interest," with demonstrable benefits to the US. But a broader definition of national interest lay behind virtually all those major engagements.

All governments consult their national interests before making crucial decisions. But no other country agonizes over this abstraction quite so dramatically. An argument has raged for two centuries in America over narrow ("realistic") versus broad ("idealistic") concepts of national interest. Alexander Hamilton laid out the realist argument when he said "an individual may . . . indulge the emotions of generosity and benevolence . . . even at the expense of his own interest. But a government can rarely, if at all, be justified in pursuing a similar course." His boss George Washington warned that "No nation is to be trusted further than it is bound by its interests." Twentieth century diplomat-scholar George Kennan argued that, while the highest moral act of the individual is what he called self-abnegation, it is not open to leaders to sacrifice the interests of their country for an abstract principle.

There was also hyperbole among the idealists. In his second inaugural address, Thomas Jefferson proclaimed "We are firmly convinced, and we act on that conviction, that . . . our interests soundly calculated will ever be found inseparable from our moral duties. . . . I know of only one code of morality, whether singly or collectively." The "universal interests" argument resumed in 1917 when President Woodrow Wilson proclaimed that "the United States has gone to Mexico to serve mankind."

If that was a bit thick, considering that American troops had just bombarded Vera Cruz, it was downright offensive when he told his colleagues at the 1919 Paris peace conference, "You can see that the representatives of the United States are . . . never put to the embarrassment of choosing a way of expediency, because they have laid down for them the unalterable lines of principle."

During the Vietnam War, Undersecretary of State George Ball charged that the Europeans "have little experience in the exercise of responsibility divorced from narrow and specific national interests." Running for president in 2000, George W. Bush warned against arrogance, but sometimes carried the self-admiring posture to the point of infuriating traditional allies and making some US actions unnecessarily friendless and costly. Yet when, in his second inaugural in 2005, he asserted that "America's vital interests and our deepest beliefs are now one," he was indulging in a form of hyperbole that had resonated through two centuries of American history.

There are limits to what the US can do, and American proposals for reforming the world and its machinery will sit poorly with people who are already angry that the US is the new "hyperpower." But to the extent their prejudice was reinforced by what can only be called imperial swagger, I am convinced that a more muted American voice, along with a more cooperative approach to common problems, can make possible a renewed leadership role for the US based on the common objectives of a friendlier and less threatening world out there.

AMERICA AS ROLE MODEL

There is a deep-seated region of the American psyche that yearns to turn away from the sordid outside world in order to perfect American society and serve as a model for others to emulate. It's a form of isolationism, but one with a more admirable posture than that of ostrich with its head in the sand. The notion of America as a role model derives from an even more long-standing belief that this country *is* different from ordinary, garden-variety countries and has a God-granted license to be judged uniquely virtuous. The historian's label for this is "American Exceptionalism."

Flip a dollar bill to the reverse side with its Great American Seal, and check out the dual mottos: *annuit cœptis*—it (referring to the Eye of Providence) has favored our undertaking, and *novus ordo seclorum*— a new order of the ages. So far as I know, the only other national currency featuring such universalistic, messianic slogans was issued by the revolutionary Bolshevik regime in 1917. Both the Founding Fathers in Philadelphia, and Lenin's utopian zealots in St. Petersburg believed deep down that their mission was to renovate not only their new country, but the whole world.

Woodrow Wilson said of America's destiny that "It has come about by no plan of our conceiving, but by the hand of God." Indeed, the belief that this country is unlike any other always had a religious basis. Early Americans, declaring America to be "God's American Israel," described it as "the new Jerusalem." A favorite metaphor, much overworked by subsequent politicians, was John Winthrop's image of "a city on a hill." Puritan Jonathan Edwards saw it as the "glorious renovator of the world," and revolutionary agitator Tom Paine wrote that "we have it within our power to begin the world all over again." As its first president noted, America "seems peculiarly designated by Providence for the display of human greatness and felicity."

A persistent theme has been America's destiny as a moral and political beacon to light the way for others. For Henry Clay, the American contribution was to "keep the lamp burning brightly on this western shore, as a light to all nations." In the 1820s, when Greece rebelled against its Ottoman rulers, orator Edward Everett could say that "When the old world afforded no longer any hope, it pleased Heaven to open this last refuge of humanity . . . [America] is the last solemn experiment of humanity."

In 1821, as later isolationists were pleased to discover, President John Quincy Adams proclaimed that America "goes not abroad in search of monsters to destroy. She is the well-wisher to the freedom and independence of all. She is the champion and vindicator only of her own." But Abraham Lincoln continued the older missionary refrain when he said, "The Declaration of Independence [gave] liberty, not alone to the people of this country, but hope to the world for all future time," while preacher Ralph Waldo Emerson described this country as "a beacon lighting for all the world."

As the US became more of an economic and military player, its missionary role acquired a more gritty kind of visage. Senator Albert F. Beveridge, intoxicated with the new mix of religion and power, told the Senate nearly a century ago that "[God] has given us the spirit of progress to overwhelm the forces of reaction throughout the earth.

He has made us adept in government that we may administer government among savage and senile peoples. Were it not for such a force as this the world would relapse into barbarism and night. And of all our race He has marked the American people as His chosen nation to finally lead in the regeneration of the world."

In the same spirit President McKinley explained his annexation of the Philippines: "There was nothing left for us to do but take them all, and educate the Philippinos and uplift them and Christianize them." This rather squirrely version of sacred mission echoed in 1940 when Senator Kenneth Wherry proclaimed that "with God's help, we will lift Shanghai up and up, ever up, until it is just like Kansas City," and then when John Foster Dulles intoned that "the inevitability of change should be greeted as an opportunity to make the world one that measures up more closely to Christian ideals."

This isn't just ancient history. To Ronald Reagan, God "has always in the divine scheme of things kept an eye on and guided [America] as a promised land," and George W. Bush proclaimed that "Our nation is chosen by God and commissioned by history to be a model to the world." As Henry Kissinger summed it up "America constituted a universal cause."

There is plenty in this moralistic American tone to annoy our friends and enrage our enemies. Self-righteousness is not pretty, and comes close to hypocrisy if the preacher is also out to make a buck, in the spirit of Senator Beveridge's concluding words about the holy American mission, which "holds for us all the profit, all the glory, all the happiness possible to men." Democracy is what America does best. But like all missionary work, it can also do damage. The late strategist Herman Kahn quipped on returning from war-torn Vietnam, "We'll make democrats of them even if we have to kill them all."

Let me make my own view clear. It will annoy the chronic America-basher, but the fact remains that with exceptions such as the recent period, many around the globe *have* in fact regarded America as the ideal model for what their society might look like if freed of tyranny, oppression, and lack of opportunity. When the bloody 20th century first unfolded President Theodore Roosevelt was boastful but prescient in declaring that "we here in America hold in our hands the hope of the world and the fate of the coming years." Woodrow Wilson's wish to "make the world safe for democracy" may have been unrealistic, but it was not hypocritical, any more than John F. Kennedy's assertion a few decades later that "We are the watchmen on the walls of freedom, not by choice but by destiny" or "America's ultimate goal of ending tyranny in the world" proclaimed by George W. Bush in his second inaugural.

Resentment of the powerful is to be expected. Some criticism of American policies and attitudes heard around the planet are rooted in envy, and some in the US global economic reach and military omnipresence. Some near-pornographic "cultural" exports that flood foreign streets and homes outrage other peoples' religions and traditional values. Some high-level swagger, bluster, and apparent scorn for the rest of the world and its institutions gave this country the disadvantages of empire, but none of whatever benefits there may be.

The fact remains that America *is* different, not because of innate moral superiority, but because of more practical virtues. Take the spirit of entrepreneurship and the energy that enables this country with 5% of the world's population to create a third of its economic output. Consider too that every family in this country including Native Americans (but not slaves) had a forebear who had the get-up-and-go to pack up and leave in search of a better life. One has only to go where people marinate in their history, like the Balkans and Middle East, to appreciate a place where, as historian Barbara Tuchman once sardonically but candidly put it, you can't change your grandparents but you can forget them. (When I recently quoted this to an audience in Romania I was cheered by the young, but shouted at angrily by the old.)

History shows few if any nations, in particular major powers, as altruistic. But the United States *has* often acted in an unselfish fashion unfamiliar to history. Europeans who are old enough know that American power helped greatly to save their lives and their economies. (Winston Churchill called America's World War II Lend-Lease Act "the most unsordid act in history.") Many foreign constitutions and political systems are modeled on those of the US. Millions abroad have a love affair with American styles, movies, TV shows, fast food, social mobility, and economic opportunity. This country has taken in, as no one else has, the tired, the poor, and the huddled masses of the world. And venomous critics of American policy can sometimes be found standing in line at US consulates for the chance to move here or get an American education.

It is tempting to call today's United States an "empire," and few love an emperor. But in all fairness, name one other empire in history with less desire to annex other people's territory. Name one which has expended more blood and treasure to protect freedom and security for other nations in jeopardy, without asking more than the right to invest capital, hire cheap labor, extract oil, recycle TV sitcoms, and sell information services and soft drinks. Winston Churchill was, as usual, right in his reported dictum that America can be counted on to do the right thing — after trying everything else.

IDEALS, CONSISTENCY, AND HYPOCRISY

When World War I ended, President Woodrow Wilson wanted the world to "know that [America] puts human rights above all other rights." Half a century later this became operationalized as policy when President Jimmy Carter made the mistake of saying in his inaugural address that "our commitment to human rights must be *absolute*" (emphasis mine). His administration denounced abuses in the USSR, Cambodia, Paraguay, and Uganda. But it wasn't long before he told the Shah of Iran how much he admired His Majesty's commitment to democracy, commended Portuguese dictator Antonio Salazar, uttered words of praise to Philippine dictator Ferdinand Marcos, and kept quiet about abuses in South Korea, Saudi Arabia, Yugoslavia, and China. There were reasons for all of this, and Carter's record since his presidency compares favorably with virtually all his fellow ex-presidents.

The fact is that the global interests and responsibilities of the United States translate into some policies that inevitably are based less on ideals and principles than on *realpolitik* and — to switch from German to French — on *raison d'état*. (Isn't it curious that we frequently use foreign words to describe morally dubious policies!) This reality sometimes makes the highly vocal US commitment to human rights and democracy look hypocritical, and somewhat less extravagant rhetoric might help create a more balanced picture.

In times of war, security concerns invariably trump peacetime ideals. During the Cold War, from Stalin's resumption of hostility toward the West in 1946 to the late 1980s when Moscow abandoned its global crusade and empire, US policy displayed the equivalent of wartime pragmatism. There were many occasions during the Cold War when US leaders acted on FDR's famous World War II justification for backing an unlovely partner. ("He may be an SOB, but he's our SOB.") The result was that, while condemning abuses in the Communist empire, Uncle Sam famously climbed into bed with a whole raft of dictators, thieves, and even mass murderers. Remember Zaire's Mobutu? Taiwan's Chiang Kai-Shek? Cuba's Batista? Nicaragua's Somoza? Iraq's Saddam Hussein before he tried to gobble up Kuwait?

Sometimes that pragmatism was justified on strategic grounds. But at other times it was based on moral obtuseness or bureaucratic laziness. The 1990s represented a brief "peacetime" hiatus. But after the murderous 9/11 assault the US shifted back to wartime pragmatism, once again embracing dubious client states in Central Asia and the Middle East as partners in the fight against terrorism as hosts of needed bases for search and rescue missions, and protectors of oil reserves crucial to the world economy.

In the world of hard foreign policy choices, I guess that sometimes you have to rise above principle, sacrifice moral consistency, and work with regimes in power. But it's time to substitute a limp handshake for the embrace of tyrants who offer short-term stability but often longer-term ruination for themselves and those who support them. Where immoderation, dictatorship, or official thievery prevails, it's time to stop falling in love with the charming élites, and range America's power decisively alongside the elements of moderation and honesty who will in the long run serve American interests and those of their people far better.

Love-hate relationships may be the best a hyperpower can hope for. But their sharpest edges can be smoothed when American attitudes and policies more conspicuously reflect what Abraham Lincoln called the "better angels of our nature." Like it or not, the US will still have to take the lead in confronting major security challenges. But unless the leader persuades others to follow, the leader may become everyone's adversary, which is not what most Americans have in mind. Others will follow only if the US shows, in the words of the Declaration of Independence, "a decent Respect to the Opinions of Mankind."

THE BOTTOM LINE

Political scientists continue to wrestle with an abstract clash between realism and idealism, but that turns out to be a false polarity, existing in pure form only in the minds of theorists. Idealism without realism is ineffective sentimentalism, realism without idealism is cynical, brutal, and equally ineffective. The trick is to wrap one's arms around complex reality where raw power is real, but must always be tempered with moral authority and political imagination.

It is tempting to conclude, with 19th-century worry-wart Matthew Arnold, that we are "wandering between two worlds, one dead, the other powerless to be born." The future is unknowable and we live on a hinge of history, reminiscent of the era described by Lord Melbourne when "all the sensible people are wrong and all the damn fools are right."

There is plenty of danger abroad in our times. Fanatics in the Islamic world with a nihilistic ideology have launched a global assault on Western civilization, and their murderous plotters pose unpredictable dangers to people everywhere, particularly the United States. The Arab world has yet to be reconciled with the descendants of the Crusaders, while its corrupt leadership stifles progress, perpetuates poverty, ignorance, and unemployment, and supplies fuel for radical movements and terrorism.

But let's not lose sight of the fact that the world outside the always-neuralgic Middle East still matters enormously. The two other major nuclear powers—sort-of-democratic Russia and sort-of-Communist China—face uncertain futures. More countries are making it, but the gap between rich and truly poor continues to grow. Western Europe is still America's primary source of culture and law, but it has recently acted as its primary source of criticism. The Iraq War and the unresolved Palestinian cause combined to transform the early post-9/11 support for America into subsequent resentment and alienation. If we lived by the headlines there would be little ground for optimism.

Yet fewer people are actually being killed in warfare between countries than any time in modern history. Democratic practices are gradually spreading. Some minorities in fact coexist peacefully with a majority culture. In many currently conflicted multi-ethnic societies, people rubbed along peacefully before neighbor was incited by demagogues to turn on neighbor.

Despite the headlines, some global hot spots are cooling down. Forces for moderation exist, if sometimes invisibly, within nations, and inside religious and ethnic groups, and I have to believe that in the long run history is on their side. That is not because progress is necessarily inevitable and mankind infinitely perfectible. It is because unprecedented channels of information are cracking open closed societies to the point that no repressive regime will be able to block for very long awareness of norms of civil and social rights to which many aspire.

The world's dangers have to be confronted, in particular by the only country fated, for better or worse, to take the lead. But in the longer run, the best antidote to the dark forces will be the growing awareness of people everywhere that they too have "inalienable" rights. They will be far more likely to prosper when women are treated as equals, when education can have real consequences for them, and when they have a voice in their governance. As these things come to pass, helped by strong yet compassionate leadership, there may yet be a chance for the world to change for the better.

INDEX

Aaron, David, 46
Abbas, Mahmoud, 128
Acheson, Dean, 29, 32, 52, 151
al-Assad, Hafez, 127, 137
Albright, Madeleine, 45, 55
Allen, Richard, 55
Allison, Graham, 170
Allon, Yigal, 42, 43
al-Sowayal, Ibrahim, 131
Anderson, Dillon, 52
Arafat, Yasser, 128, 137
Arbatov, Georgi, 83, 84, 96, 98, 99,
    102, 104, 114
Arias, Oscar, 167, 168
Austad, Mark, 156, 157
Austin, Warren, 127
Baez, Joan, 47, 48
Baker, James, 55
Ball, George, 211
Beam, Jacob, 101, 102
Bebler, Alex, 144
Berger, Samuel, 55
Bloomfield, Lincoln Jr., 96, 98, 101
Bloomfield, Richard, 159, 160
Blumenthal, C. Michael, 104, 111
Bohlen, Charles, 39
Brezhnev, Leonid, 105, 112, 115
Brooke, Edward, 17
Brundtland, Olaf Arne, 167
Brundtland, Gro Harlem, 167
Brzezinski, Zbigniew, 43–58, 112
Buchan, Alistair, 41, 142

Bunche, Ralph, 20
Bundy, McGeorge, 53, 58
Bundy, William, 71, 72
Burchinal, David, 145, 146
Burr, Aaron, 52
Bush, George W., 25, 128, 172, 181,
    190, 191, 201, 209, 211, 213, 214
Bush, George H. W., 16, 22, 55, 104
Byrnes, James, 52
Carlucci, Frank, 55
Carter, President Jimmy, xii, 16, 20,
    43, 48, 49, 50, 104, 109, 111, 114,
    127, 156, 157, 160–63, 215
Carter, Rosalyn, 46–48
CASCON, 2, 65, 176, 178
Castro, Fidel, 172
Chace, James, 32
Cheney, Richard, 56, 57
Christopher, Warren, 47, 55, 168
Clark, Dick, 46
Clark, William, 55
Cleveland, Harlan, 3, 82, 170, 190, 200
Clinton, William, 45, 48, 55, 58, 104,
    127, 168
Conant, James B., 6
Cooke, Cardinal, 19, 20
Cordovez, Diego, 152
Craven, John, 90, 91
Cutler, Robert, 52
Dallin, Alexander, 84
Davies, John Paton, 31, 32
de Palma, Samuel, 17

219

Denktash, Rauf, 151
Deutsch, Karl, 145
Dienstbier, Jiri, 167
Dulles, John Foster, xii, 6, 15, 16, 26–39, 52, 172, 213
Dulles, Avery, 28
Eagleburger, Lawrence, 55
Eden, Anthony, 39
Eisenhower, Dwight D., 14, 15, 26, 27, 38, 52, 128, 141
Ellis, Joseph, 24
Ellsberg, Daniel, 71, 72
Falin, Valentin, 115
Fieser, Louis B., 6
Ford, Gerald, 54, 104, 109, 111, 156
Fulbright, William J., 18
Gabriel, Charles, 89
Garrison, Mark, 116
Gati, Toby, 104, 114, 120
Gavin, James, 82
Gerson, Louis, 32
Gilpatric, Roswell, 63
Goh Keng Swee, 161
Goodpaster, Andrew, 85
Gorbachev, Mikhail, 114, 117, 119, 120, 168
Gray, Gordon, 52
Griffith, William, 67
Gromyko, Andrei, 22, 83, 99
Gromyko, Anatoly, 83, 84, 99
Hadley, Stephen, 57
Hafez al-Assad, 127, 137
Haig, Alexander Jr., 55
Halberstam, David, 71
Hamilton, Lee, 168
Healey, Dennis, 42
Henderson, Loy, 127
Herter, Christian, 15, 52, 77
Hickenlooper, Bourke, 22
Hickerson, John, 14
Hill, Fred, 78
Hilton, Francesca, 139
Hiss, Alger, 28, 29, 32

Holborn, Fred, 30
Holst, Johan Jorgen, 166, 168
Honeyman, Nan Wood, 8
Hoopes, Townsend, 33
Hoyt, E. Palmer, 8
Hussein, Saddam, 121, 122, 132, 199
Ibn Saud, 129, 130
Idi Amin, 139
Issraelyn, Victor, 98
Jacobson, Max, 157
Janis, Irving, 174
Johnson, Lyndon B., 24, 53, 62–64, 71, 128
Johnson, Harold K., 88
Kahn, Herman, 75, 213
Keith, Kenton, 137
Kennan, George, 179, 210
Kennedy, John F., 6, 15, 24, 30, 43–44, 51, 53, 62, 71, 171, 172, 179, 186, 214
Key, David McKay, 34
Khalid Anani, 132
Khalid ibn Abdul Aziz, 130–33
Khrushchev, Nikita, 97
Killian, James, 60
Kissinger, Henry A., 19, 21, 40–42, 50, 53, 54, 58, 96, 101, 125, 127, 128, 152–54, 161, 213
Klaus, Vaclav, 167
Kleiman, Robert, 106
Kohler, Foy, 89
Kokoshin, Andrei, 97, 102
Kosygin, Alexei, 139
Kozyrev, Andrei, 117
Kyprianou, Spyros, 150
Laingen, Bruce, 163
Laird, Melvin, 90
Lake, Anthony, 45, 55
Lamm, Richard, 206
Leiss, Amelia, 2, 177
Lincoln, George A., 90
Linkletter, Art, 18
Lodge, George, 82

Lodge, Henry Cabot Jr., 15–18, 21–23
Lord, Winston, 181
Loy, Frank, 46
MacArthur, Douglas, 10, 172
Makarios, Archbishop, 150, 151
Mandel, Robert, 81
Marshall, George, 11, 52, 53
Mathews, Jessica, 162
Matlock, Jack, 111
McCarthy, Joseph, xii, 6, 30, 37
McCloy, John, 142, 143
McDonnell, James, 110
McFarlane, Robert, 55
McGrory, Mary, 47
McHenry, Donald, 49
McLeod, Robert Walter Scott, 32
McNamara, Robert, 53, 175
Millikan, Max, 67, 75, 77
Millis, Walter, 34
Mondale, Walter, 46
Moulton, Allen, 3, 65, 178
Murphy, Robert, 36, 37
Murphy, Richard, 137–39
Muskie, Edmund, 54
Nasser, Abdul Gamal, 38
Nichols, Calvin, 13
Nitze, Paul, 53
Nixon, Richard, 16, 17–24, 41, 44, 53, 54, 62, 64, 96, 104, 109, 128, 131, 161, 201
North, Oliver, 57
Ogata, Sadako, 166
Orek, Osman, 87, 151
Ormandy, Eugene, 18
Ovinnikov, Richard, 19
Owen, Henry, 46, 48, 77, 99
Palmieri, Victor, 46
Peale, Norman Vincent, 19, 21
Perkins, Milo, 7
Petrovsky, Vladimir, 117
Poindexter, John, 55
Ponomarev, Boris, 110, 111
Popper, David, 150

Powell, Colin, 55, 56, 57
Primakov, Yevgeny, 105, 109, 115, 120
Pye, Lucian, 69
Quant, William, 43
Rabasa, Emilio, 153
Ramphal, Shridath, 166, 168
Rashid al Rashid, 136
Reagan, Ronald, 24, 47, 55, 58, 95, 113, 114, 213
Reeves, Raymond, 88
Rice, Condoleezza, 57, 191
Richardson, Elliot, 47–49, 146, 161
Ridgway, Matthew, 63
Rockefeller, Nelson, 40, 41
Rogers, William P., 53, 54, 90
Rogov, Sergei, 168
Roosa, Robert, 108
Roosevelt, Eleanor, 14, 15, 29, 30
Roosevelt, Franklin, 8, 24, 52, 130, 216
Rostow, Walt, 53, 58, 77, 85, 86
Rumsfeld, Donald, 56, 57
Rumyantsov, Aleksei, 100
Rusk, Dean, 14, 29, 30, 53, 126
Sadat, Anwar, 128
Sakharov, Andrei, 102
Schaffner, Franklin, 11–13
Schelling, Thomas, 1, 65, 75, 78, 177
Scowcroft, Brent, 54, 55, 104, 114, 116
Scranton, William, 104, 114
Selin, Ivan, 114–16
Sharon, Ariel, 128
Sheen, Fulton, 28
Shevardnadze, Edward, 168
Shields, Mark, 47
Shinseki, Eric, 184
Shulman, Marshall, 84, 104
Shultz, George P., 55, 78
Simon, Herbert, 171
Sonnenfeldt, Helmut, 104, 114
Souers, Sidney, 52
Spain, James, 158
Sprague, Charles, 9
Stassen, Harold, 52

Stephanopoulos, George, 58
Stettinius, Edward, 52
Stevenson, Adlai, 156
Temple, Shirley Black, 18, 20
Thomson, James, 175
Truman, Harry, 16, 31, 52, 126, 194
Tuchman, Barbara, 214
U Thant, 17–21
Vance, Cyrus, 44, 45, 54, 55, 104, 120, 182
Vincent, John Carter, 31, 32
Watson, Thomas, 115, 116

Welles, Sumner, 52
Wilcox, Francis, 18, 38, 182
Williams, G. Mennen, 85
Wilson, Woodrow, 210, 212, 213
Wriston, Henry, 142
Wu, Jianmin, 167
Wyzanski, Charles, 60
Yakovlev, Alexander, 168
Yeltsin, Boris, 105, 119
Yost, Charles, 17, 19, 20, 63, 104
Young, Andrew, 49
Zhurkin, Vitaly, 84, 97–99, 102–4, 117